SACRED STEEL

Music in American Life

A list of books in the series appears at the end of this book.

SACRED STEEL

INSIDE AN AFRICAN AMERICAN STEEL GUITAR TRADITION

Robert L. Stone

UNIVERSITY OF ILLINOIS PRESS

Urbana, Chicago, and Springfield

1   2   3   4   5   C   P   5   4   3   2   1

∞ This book is printed on acid-free paper.

Publication of this book was supported by
a grant from the L. J. and Mary C. Skaggs
Folklore Fund.

Library of Congress Cataloging-in-Publication Data
Stone, Robert L., 1944–
Sacred steel : inside an African American steel guitar
tradition / Robert L. Stone.
p.   cm. — (Music in American life)
Includes bibliographical references and index.
ISBN 978-0-252-03554-8 (cloth : alk. paper) —
ISBN 978-0-252-07743-2 (pbk. : alk. paper)
1. Church music—African American churches.
2. Hawaiian guitar music—History and criticism.
3. African American guitarists.
4. African American church musicians.
I. Title.
ML3556.S876   2010
787.87'171994008996073—dc22   2010024455

To my loving wife, Judy

Contents

Photographs begin after pages 76 and 148.

Preface

The hair stands up on my arms and the back of my neck as I listen to my field recording of Aubrey Ghent soulfully finessing an unaccompanied hymn on his battered lap-steel guitar. The year was 1992. Today, eighteen years after hearing "sacred steel" for the first time, I find the power of this rich and complex music has only increased as I have immersed myself more deeply into it.

From first hearing, I recognized that the steel guitar music of the Keith Dominion church was some of the most expressive music ever played on the instrument. A few months later I would experience, through the powerful playing of Sonny Treadway, an equally compelling, but distinctly different, sample of the steel guitar music of the Jewell Dominion church. When my colleagues and musician friends heard some of my early field recordings they reacted similarly: they just could not get over how passionate—and how distinctly African American—this music was. From the beginning, we realized that once the public had a taste of this music the floodgates would open; listeners would demand to hear more of the compelling music and musicians would be invited to perform publicly. Commercial recordings would surely follow and some of the musicians might become stars. Musicians' lives would be changed. All this did indeed happen.

The music of the Keith and Jewell Dominions stands solidly on its strength of musical expression alone. But more than that, this music is part of a *tradition,* a tradition that for six decades was virtually unknown outside the family of churches from which the music springs. The music flourished and evolved unnoticed right under the collective noses (and ears) of aficionados and scholars of American roots music, gospel devotees, and guitar fans. Rock star and guitar icon Eric Clapton perceived the tradition-bearers as a sort of secret society before learning more about the tradition through his association with Robert Randolph.

Since 1997, when the first sacred steel recordings were produced and distributed internationally by Arhoolie Records, public presentation and consumption of the music has continued to increase. Today, Keith Dominion *wunderkind* Robert Randolph has a rock-star-magnitude recording contract with Warner Bros. He has been nominated for three Grammys and has appeared on numerous large-audience television programs including *The Tonight Show, Late Night with Conan O'Brien, Austin City Limits, Live with Regis and Kelly,* and shows on VH1.

But there is much more to this music than what one hears on recordings or sees on stage. The steel guitar music of the Keith and Jewell Dominions is functional music that is an integral part of fiery and demonstrative Holiness-Pentecostal worship services. To understand the music and to have a reasonable frame of reference from which to listen, one needs to understand something of the nature of the beliefs, manner of worship, power structure, and aesthetics of the church, and the cultural milieu in which the music exists and the musicians interact and operate.

One of the challenges in writing a single volume about this music is the breadth and depth of the tradition. There are some two hundred churches located in two dozen states—from Florida to California, from Detroit to Alabama—and probably an equal number of steel guitarists who serve in them. Furthermore, the steel guitar traditions of the Keith and Jewell Dominion churches are distinctly different, even though there has been considerable cross-pollination between the two. Florida alone, with more than forty Keith and Jewell Dominion churches, is more than I can begin to cover in depth. After eighteen years of documenting the music, I continue to encounter, at every turn, capable steel guitarists—mature musicians as well as youngsters—who were previously unknown to me.

At first I planned to not include the Jewell Dominion in this book, as my experience in documenting its steel guitar tradition was minimal. But I soon realized that approach was not feasible because the two traditions were too closely related; many of the musicians have been members of both dominions or have played for worship services in both. My solution was to devote a sizeable chapter to the Jewell Dominion. In the other chapters I use the Keith Dominion tradition as the default viewpoint, inserting information from the Jewell Dominion as needed.

Similarly, I chose to present with some depth only a few steel guitarists who were, in my opinion, important in shaping the music, rather than undertake a more superficial treatment of a greater number of musicians. Some musicians, because of their belief in the sanctity of the music, have chosen not to be presented here (among the most notable being Ronnie Mozee, the steel guitarist who plays for Jewell Dominion national meetings).

The book begins with my discovery of the music, the series of events that launched a journey of continuing exploration and documentation. I then trace the history of the church and how the steel guitarists operate within the context of church meetings. At this stage an important theme is introduced: the negotiations of power and musical aesthetics between the musicians and clergy. These negotiations probably began when the earliest steel guitarists plugged in their amplifiers and commenced to play in the 1930s, and continue to the present day, perhaps more heated than ever.

Experience has taught me that the overwhelming majority of people—including music scholars, whom I thought would know better—have misconceptions about the steel guitar. I have devoted a brief chapter to explain the instrument, trace its fascinating history, and present some definitions in an effort to clarify some of the confusion.

This African American tradition is solidly connected to the Hawaiian music fad that began in the mainland United States early in the twentieth century and continued into the early 1960s. In fact, many among the congregations still refer to the instrument as the "Hawaiian guitar," or simply, "the Hawaiian." Troman Eason, who studied with a Hawaiian musician, and his younger brother, Willie, were among the first Keith Dominion steel guitarists to spread their musical influence over a wide geographic area.

Much of this book takes the form of oral history told in first-person narratives. I firmly believe that is the best way for the tradition-bearers to communicate their stories, not only of their musical lives, but of the cultural milieu in which they live, or lived. In my opinion, Willie Eason's stories alone are worth the price of admission.

The pedal-steel guitar has become preferred over the older lap-steel guitar among Keith Dominion musicians in recent decades. Chuck Campbell of Rochester, New York, was very influential in bringing the pedal-steel into national prominence and Glenn Lee played a similar role in Florida. Both men also introduced many new musical ideas that have had lasting impact in shaping the soundscape of the Keith Dominion. Today, Robert Randolph's pyrotechnic playing on his thirteen-string pedal-steel further reinforces the desirability of the instrument among younger musicians.

Recent years have brought changes in the national leadership of both dominions. In the Jewell Dominion the change marked the end of seven decades of dominance by members of the Jewell family, but without apparent impact on the church's steel guitar tradition. The change in Keith Dominion leadership resulted in a conservative administration that has profoundly impacted the steel guitar tradition by forbidding the musicians to play outside of the church and declaring some veteran steel guitarists ineligible to play for national-level meetings.

As the steel guitarists move further into the twenty-first century, the musicians are faced with deciding whether to continue membership in the Keith Dominion and adhere to a strict doctrine of playing only for church services or to perform before an admiring public and risk expulsion from the church. Robert Randolph's great success in the secular music industry continues to inspire untold numbers of aspiring young people, both within the Keith Dominion and from other churches, to take up the instrument. Writing in 2010, it is difficult to state how this music will continue to be shaped, who will play it, and in what contexts it will be played. The presentation of the Keith and Jewell Dominion steel guitar traditions to the public has, however, had undeniable impact on American vernacular music. It seems certain that such impact will continue for some years to come.

Being a white man documenting an African American sacred music tradition presents its own set of challenges. Access to church records was not available to me, and some people mistrusted me and were not willing to divulge much—an attitude easily understood, given the history of race relations in this country.

Difficult moments notwithstanding, this work has been most rewarding. I have made many friends—some of whom are now deceased—and have learned to appreciate aspects of African American culture of which I was previously unaware, or aware of only superficially. More importantly, I have witnessed the sense of pride people experience when their traditional culture is documented in the respectful manner it deserves.

To my knowledge, I am the first person to attempt to thoroughly document the steel guitar tradition of the Keith Dominion. It is a great thrill, an honor, and a tremendous responsibility to be in that position. I have strived to proceed with care, understanding, and professionalism in telling the story of this passionate music and the people who play it.

Acknowledgments

First, I thank the musicians, clergy, and congregations for opening their churches, homes, and hearts to me so I could attempt to document their fascinating and compelling musical tradition. Keith Dominion Bishops James C. Elliott and Charles E. Campbell were especially supportive, as were Jewell Dominion Bishops Naomi Manning, Eunice Treadway, and Calvin Worthem. Bishop Worthem and Rosette Coney were particularly helpful in assisting me in collecting archival photographs.

Among the musicians and congregations, several became close friends who gave freely of their time and facilitated my work. I give heartfelt thanks to the Campbells, the Easons—especially Jeannette—the Nelson family, the Lee family, Calvin and Grace Cooke, the Beards, Ron Hall, and Elton Noble.

The first field recording project was made possible by a grant from the National Endowment for the Arts, Folk and Traditional Arts Program and the support of the Florida Department of State. I am deeply grateful to Chris Strachwitz and Tom Diamant of Arhoolie Records for their vision, enthusiasm, and support in working with me and others to produce a series of CD albums of the music, and through the Arhoolie Foundation, the *Sacred Steel* documentary video.

A host of fellow steel guitar enthusiasts whom I met through Bob Lee's Steel Guitar Forum (www.steelguitarforum.com) lent valuable assistance. John Marsden provided several citations of the Kahauolopua brothers from early Oahu magazines; Michael Lee Allen freely shared his extensive knowledge and documentation; Les Cook provided information on Jack Penewell; Max Laine emailed from Finland scans of 1940s magazines; Dirk Vogel helped me locate Oahu magazines; *Vintage Guitar* magazine contributor Michael Wright also helped with early Hawaiian guitar history and documentation; and Andy Volk lent his support in many ways.

Robert Laughton, Doug Seroff, and Chris Strachwitz freely offered their discographical expertise, as did Opal Louis Nations, who also provided biographical information on the Jewell Gospel Singers and archival photos. Thanks to Suzanne Flandreau, research librarian and archivist at the Center for Black Music Research, for always helping when I called. I am grateful to Pat Morse for transcribing the "House of God March" and to Jim Sain for digitizing the transcript. I sincerely appreciate the accurate interview transcripts by Caroline Welch.

I may have never learned of the Keith and Jewell Dominion steel guitarists had it not been for my good friend Michael Stapleton, who also volunteered his assistance on several of the earliest field documentation trips. I am forever grateful to Ian McLatchie for his expert editing of the manuscript and thoughtful suggestions for improvements, to Craig Morrison for his most helpful comments, and to Louis Simon for his excellent copy edits.

Above all others stands my wife Judy. Without her love, support, and encouragement I could have never completed this project.

1 Discovery

"Hey Bob, listen to this!" It was my close friend and bandmate Mike Stapleton calling from the Banjo Shop in Hollywood, Florida, just south of Ft. Lauderdale. Compressed and distorted by the low fidelity of telephone transmission, what I heard sounded like amplified blues harmonica—but not quite. It was the soulful and compelling voice of African American gospel music played on the electric lap-steel guitar, the first of several samples of the music I would hear via Mike's telephone calls from his store over the next several weeks. On more than one occasion he left a musical message, sans any spoken explanation, on my telephone answering machine.

It was the summer of 1992, and I had been working for less than two years as a folk arts coordinator at the Bureau of Florida Folklife Programs in the tiny town of White Springs (population 800), on the banks of the Suwannee River, about thirty miles south of the Georgia border. I commuted daily from Gainesville, sixty miles to the south. In 1986, when I was living in suburban southwest Miami-Dade County, Mike and I had formed Gumbo Limbo, a band that played Cajun dance music. After I moved to Gainesville in 1989, we managed to keep the band going despite hundreds of miles between members. Mike and I spoke frequently on the telephone for both personal and business reasons.

The Banjo Shop was a gem of a music store that drew vernacular string musicians from all over the southern half of the state. Aware that I was always looking for leads for traditional artists, Mike was in the habit of giving me contact information for musicians who patronized the Banjo Shop. And there were plenty; musicians from a rich diversity of cultures visited the store. There was a champion Yugoslavian fiddler, Bolivian *charango* players, a Tongan who played the ukulele and steel guitar, Mexican *mariachi* artists, Puerto Rican *cuatro* players, legions of old-time and bluegrass pickers and fiddlers (for years the Banjo Shop had the longest running weekly bluegrass jam listed in *Bluegrass Unlimited* magazine), and black gospel musicians.

Mike co-owned the business with two brothers, Dave and Paul Stype. Paul played the Dobro and dabbled in electric lap-steel guitar. The Banjo Shop's large inventory of new, used, and vintage string instruments always included a selection of lap- and pedal-steel guitars—instruments rarely stocked by most music stores. The store also sold Peavey amplifiers, the brand preferred by many steel guitarists. Among the patrons were black men interested in the electric lap-steel guitars. When they tried out the instruments, Mike immediately took notice of the music they played. It had nothing of the sweet, twangy quality of the country music with which steel guitar is commonly associated. Instead, this steel guitar music spoke in a rich, rhythmic, African American voice that shouted Pentecostal praises to the Lord, moaned soulfully, and soared like Aretha Franklin singing a hymn for a steamy Sunday service.

Mike cannot recall who the first African American steel guitarist to try out instruments at the Banjo Shop was, but my early contact lists show Gussie Stokes, Kalvin "Champ" Kimmerlin, and Lee Pough to be among the first to visit the store and play the steel guitar. Although all three gave Mike their contact information, which he forwarded to me, they all told him they were lesser players and that Aubrey Ghent and Glenn Lee were the best in southern Florida, the ones we *really* needed to hear. Before too long Glenn Lee was in the Banjo Shop seeking a remedy for a Peavey amplifier he had damaged while playing at maximum volume for a lengthy church meeting. About the same time Mike obtained Aubrey Ghent's telephone number. These two contacts set in motion a journey that continues to bring new discoveries in a musical subgenre heretofore virtually unknown outside the churches where the music is made—even to specialists in African American gospel music.

On November 7, 1992, I made my first trip to southern Florida to document Aubrey Ghent and Glenn Lee. Mike accompanied me to Ghent's home in the early afternoon, but could not stay for the evening session with Glenn Lee. Ghent was living in a modest concrete block dwelling at 2715 Avenue D in Fort Pierce in the heart of one of the town's African American neighborhoods, a home he shared with another single man. Fort Pierce has a large African American population, approximately equal to its white non-Hispanic population, and Avenue D is one of the main thoroughfares in the city's African American community. The east end is mostly bars, barbeque joints, barbershops, and beauty parlors. As one travels west, residences and churches become the dominant structures.

Ghent reiterated that he was part of a tradition of African American gospel steel guitar music that spanned three generations and included dozens—perhaps hundreds—of steel guitarists who played in churches from Miami to Detroit, but was little known beyond the House of God, Keith Dominion church to which he and his extended family belonged. He explained that his father, Henry Nelson, was a master steel guitarist who had been playing for half a century and his uncle, Willie Eason, who had retired to St. Petersburg, had been playing and singing since the 1930s. He spoke graphically about the significance of steel guitarists in the House of God.

> We've got to the point where in all our worship services we can have a keyboard or organ—Hammond organ, Korg—the guitars, drums, and so forth. We use the whole works. But if the steel player's not there, the folk will say it just wasn't right. They expect that steel. And when a steel player walks in the door, everybody goes, "Wow!" The steel player is really a big, big key musician in House of God churches. Everywhere you go they will tell you that in the House of God church. If you're a steel player, you're somebody. I mean, in most churches you say, "Where's the organist?" In the House of God it's, "Where's the steel player?"[1]

He also stated that many people in the church called the instrument the "Hawaiian guitar," a term that had given way to "steel guitar" in the mainland United States by the 1950s.

We were flabbergasted when Ghent told us there were about fifty House of God churches in Florida and, because the steel guitar was at the top of the musical instrument hierarchy, there were almost an equal number of House of God steel guitarists in the state. But the biggest shock came when he began to play.

Ghent drew up a metal and vinyl straight-back dining room chair and sat behind a steel guitar he had borrowed from fellow House of God steel guitarist Lee Pough. The instrument was rough and funky looking; someone had taken half of a double-neck eight-string Fender Stringmaster, painted it red, fitted it with three rusted homemade chrome legs, and strung it with six strings. It might not have been pretty, but it had the distinctive Fender sound that I would later learn was the preferred choice of House of God musicians and congregations. Mike observed that Ghent's metal fingerpicks had seen so much use that the tips had paper-thin, jagged edges. Playing without any accompaniment whatsoever, Ghent began to play some of the most beautiful, soulful music we had ever heard. The first tune was "It Is No Secret," a popular hymn written by white country singer Stuart Hamblen in the 1950s.

We were immediately struck by the sensitivity with which Ghent rendered the melody and his ability to improvise freely and tastefully. His control of pitch was simply amazing; he could play notes with dead-on intonation past the end of the fretboard, or subtly bend pitches to create mood and tension. His vibrato was lush and voice-like; some time later he told me that he tries to make his instrument sound like a female opera singer. He was a master of the melisma—the technique of making several notes from one syllable of text—and employed it as deftly as the best black gospel vocalists. His music was refreshing, compelling, and distinctly African American. It was like nothing we—or virtually anyone from outside the sphere of the House of God—had ever heard before. We knew we were on to something huge, but we had no idea of what a rich musical world we were entering into. What Ghent presented that day was a mere first glimpse of a deep and varied musical tradition integral to a vibrant system of belief, ritual, and worship.

As we continued the interview, Ghent rendered two more pieces, each uniquely moving and eloquent: a swinging up-tempo spiritual, which he did not name, and Thomas A. Dorsey's "Take My Hand Precious Lord." His rendition of the Dorsey classic included a segment for which he employed a wah pedal. Before he played it he spoke of the late Bishop Lorenzo Harrison of the Jewell Dominion, who was known for his use of a very large wah pedal, with a sort of tremolo effect built into it. Harrison's name and the significance of the pedal meant nothing to us at the time, but I would later learn that the Jewell Dominion steel guitar tradition was every bit as rich as that of the House of God, Keith Dominion, which Ghent represented. When I mentioned that I was going to attend the Florida East Coast Dioceses State Assembly at Ely High School auditorium in Pompano Beach that night to document Glenn Lee's playing, Ghent told me to be prepared for a high-energy service. When he said he hoped it would not be too much for me, his words struck me as odd. How could a church service be "too much?"

When I entered the auditorium at Ely High it was like walking into a Pentecostal hurricane. The State Assembly was already in full swing and the band was roaring. Only the vocals were controlled by the house PA, so the instrumentalists all had their beefy amplifiers turned to maximum volume. Even so, at times the congregants nearly drowned out the loud instruments with their rhythmic clapping. People danced ecstatically in the aisles and up in the front of the auditorium, near the band. Some spoke in tongues. Female ushers, dressed in white and looking very much like nurses, protected those who had lost physical control from careening into others, or from collapsing.

Then there was the racial aspect. Although I was born in New Rochelle, New York, and had attended integrated public schools there through the second grade, I had been raised in the segregated South. We moved to Miami in 1952, when I was eight, and eventually settled in Cutler Ridge, in southwestern Dade (now Miami-Dade) County. I graduated from South Dade High School in Homestead, located in an agricultural area known as the "Nation's Winter Vegetable Basket" and the "Tomato Capital of the World," and many of the blacks living in the area were agricultural workers. The school football team was the "Rebels" and the school band was outfitted in uniforms with a Confederate motif. At football games the audience rose to its feet as the Rebel band played "Dixie" and "The Star-Spangled Banner" during the opening ceremonies. Now, here I was, the only white person among about four hundred blacks rejoicing, clapping, dancing, and speaking in tongues. The manner in which the House of God congregations worshipped and praised God could not have been more different from the Christian Science services I had attended until I was about fifteen.

Glenn Lee, just twenty-four at the time and sporting a high, wavy pompadour, led the band from behind his crimson Emmons double-neck pedal steel. Unlike his sedate country-western counterparts, he swayed, rocked, and often gave flourishes with his picking hand—a gesture, I would later discover, that could be traced to Willie Eason's charismatic performances in the 1930s. He played through the biggest wah pedal I had ever seen; it looked like something that belonged in the cab of a dump truck rather than connected to a musical instrument. (It was the very pedal that Ghent had mentioned Lorenzo Harrison having played. Lee had inherited it from his uncle Lorenzo.) The rhythm section pumped out throbbing, funky grooves for Glenn's swooping, soaring, pedal-steel leads. His older brother, Alvin, walked his fingers up and down the mammoth fretboard of his six-string electric bass; Kenneth Ellis played chords and shuffles on his Les Paul guitar; and Benjamin Beckford aggressively pounded the drums and gave the crash cymbals a workout. Glenn Lee had a lot more variety in his playing than Ghent did. For the up-tempo praise and shout music, his approach was similar to Ghent's, but hymns and other slower-tempo pieces were another story. For these numbers he frequently worked the instrument's foot-pedals and knee-levers to bend notes, which resulted in passages that echoed the familiar twang of Nashville country music.

Recording music in the field is always challenging, and this trip was especially so. I was equipped with a new-fangled portable digital audio tape (DAT) recorder and a pair of condenser microphones. Like most people accustomed to recording analog tape and new to DAT recorders, I overloaded the tape several times on my first few recordings at the session with Ghent earlier that day. I had learned not to do that by the time of the assembly in Pompano Beach, but the music and congregation were so loud I could not monitor the recording in the headphones. Despite the challenges, I captured enough of Ghent's and Lee's playing to convey the compelling and refreshingly different sound of House of God steel guitar.

I returned to Gainesville and edited my rough recordings to make a tape of the best music of useable quality. I thought the music was terrific, and when I played it for my colleagues and musician friends the response was unanimous: this was some of the most expressive and compelling guitar music they had ever heard. And it worked so well in the context of African American Holiness-Pentecostal worship. The steel guitar could shout, cry, soar, or moan like a great gospel singer. Unrestricted by fixed frets, capable musicians like Ghent and Lee could closely imitate the subtleties in pitch and vibrato of a human voice. It could be played rhythmically and it was loud.

I wrote a grant application for the Florida Folklife Program to the Folk and Traditional Arts Program at the National Endowment for the Arts requesting $6,800 to partially fund a survey of the music in Florida and the production of six hundred copies of an audiocassette tape/booklet album. The Florida Folklife Program was awarded the grant, and by December 1995, released *Sacred Steel: Traditional Sacred African-American Steel Guitar Music in Florida*. The booklet and cassette were housed in a vinyl album, close to the same size as those used today for DVDs. The thirty-two-page booklet included historic and contemporary photos, presented brief biographical essays about the artists, traced the development of the musical tradition, and described how the steel guitarists functioned in the context of worship services.

The Florida Folklife Program's *Sacred Steel* audiocassette/booklet album caused an immediate wave of interest among scholars, critics, journalists, and fans of American roots music. And the name of the album caught on. Almost from the very beginning, the term "sacred steel" was used by many to denote the music, which was hailed as a whole new musical subgenre. I knew that this was important music that, with proper distribution, could find a wide audience. Marketing has never been a strong suit at the Florida Folklife Program, and in the recorded music business the old axiom "distribution is everything" certainly applies. Also, about the time the cassette album was completed the Florida Folklife Program had been downsized and moved about one hundred miles west from White Springs to Tallahassee, a change that, at least in the short term, made distribution even more difficult. For personal reasons, I elected not to transfer to Tallahassee. (Since 1997, I have worked from my Gainesville home office as the full-time statewide outreach coordinator for the Florida Folklife Program, a position funded primarily by a grant from the National Endowment for the Arts' Folk and Traditional Arts program.)

Eager for the rest of the world to have a chance to hear the passionate and compelling music, I sent a copy of the album and letter of introduction to the two organizations I thought might be interested in licensing it for distribution: Arhoolie Records of El Cerrito, California, and Smithsonian Folkways. Within a few days Arhoolie president Chris Strachwitz phoned me at home during the Christmas–New Year holidays to say that he was inquiring about the album of "incredible" African American steel guitar music.

I was quite familiar with Strachwitz's work and Arhoolie's extensive and unique catalog of North American regional and traditional vernacular music, and was flattered by his enthusiasm for the *Sacred Steel* album. We talked for a while about my fieldwork and the Keith and Jewell Dominion steel guitar traditions, and I told him who to contact to get started on the licensing process. After working out the details, Arhoolie Records signed a licensing agreement with the Florida Department of State. Strachwitz borrowed the original ADAT multi-track and DAT stereo tapes, remixed and edited the album, and released it under the same title, with slightly different content, as Arhoolie CD 450 on January 21, 1997. The success of this first Arhoolie release and the international interest it generated led to several more Arhoolie albums, recordings on other labels, and a documentary video produced by the Arhoolie Foundation. But there is much more to this music and the context in which it is played than is apparent in the recordings and video.

In the pages that follow, I explore the history and development of this fascinating musical tradition, present some of its most significant tradition-bearers, illuminate the contexts in which the steel guitarists operate, and examine some of the conflicts and struggles that the musicians and clergy negotiate.

The musicians, ministers, and other folks presented in this book are remarkable people who have many compelling stories to share. I let them tell their stories in their own words as much as possible, as they can tell them much better than I could ever hope to. But before they speak it is worthwhile to consider the history of the church, some of the beliefs, and the manner of worship from which this most expressive music springs.

The Churches

Beliefs, Social Milieu, and the Development
of the Steel Guitar Traditions

The music that has become known as sacred steel cannot be fully appreciated or understood without having some knowledge of the history, beliefs, and practices of the Keith and Jewell Dominions. Both are Holiness-Pentecostal churches, and as such, place importance on dramatic religious conversion and living life according to a rather strict doctrine of Holiness. Religious services are very demonstrative. Music—both instrumental and vocal—plays a central role in worship and the steel guitar is the dominant musical instrument. The nature of worship services is reflected in what the steel guitarists play and how they play it. Those who experience the music only through listening to recordings or seeing artists perform at public venues will have a limited, and probably somewhat skewed, perception of the art form. For example, a listener unfamiliar with this manner of worship may perceive the music as repetitive and excessively loud and dramatic—that is, "over the top." But characteristics such as repetition and wild, intensely dramatic passages serve important functions in worship services and other church meetings. Some may regard the music as just another form of rock or blues party music, but there is much more to it when considered in the context of the church. The music provided by Keith and Jewell Dominion steel guitarists is an integral part of church ritual, and everything they play—from delicately rendered music for prayer and meditation to driving praise music—serves to heighten the worship experience.

The church later known as the House of God was founded in 1903 by "Mother" Mary Lena Tate (née Street).[1] She was born in 1871, to Belfield and Nancy Street of rural Dickson, Tennessee. Her father and older brothers worked as farm laborers. In 1889, she married David Lewis. Mary and David Lewis lived in Dickson and had two sons, Walter Curtis and Felix Early. Mary and David Lewis were devout Methodists, a denomination prevalent in the area at the time.[2] Around the turn of the twentieth century, Mary L. Lewis received a "call" into the ministry and embarked on a life of evangelizing, first in Tennessee, then in Kentucky and Illinois. At first she preached in the streets or wherever she could draw an audience. Eventually she and her followers, known as the "Do Rights," purchased property and established regular meeting times for worship services.[3] She and her second husband, evangelist Elijah Estes, established the church in Alabama in 1905 as part of the Holiness Movement. It was not until 1908 that it became a Holiness-Pentecostal church. In that year, Mary Street Estes was stricken with an unidentified illness that rendered her bedridden and unable to walk. Apparently near death, she had a profound experience, receiving "the baptism of the Holy Ghost and fire."[4] She reportedly sprang from her bed, shouted with joy, and was healed. Following this experience, she added the Pentecostal concept of baptism of the Holy Ghost with the evidence of speaking in tongues to her beliefs and teachings.

In 1908, the church held its first General Assembly in Greenville, Alabama, and shortly after filed for incorporation. To file for incorporation, a church name was selected based on I Timothy 3:15 ("But if I tarry long, that thou mayest know how thou oughtest to behave thyself in the house of God, which is the church of the living God, the pillar and ground of the truth"). Mary Street Estes attempted to file for incorporation using the name "The House of God, Which is the Church of the living God, the Pillar and Ground of the Truth," but when the attorney insisted that the name was too long she agreed to shorten it to "The Church of the Living God, the Pillar and Ground of the Truth." Although the phrase "House of God" was not included in the church's name on the incorporation charter, Mary Estes and her followers continued to refer to the church by the longer name, or for brevity, just "The House of God," after incorporation.[5]

In 1914, Mary Estes married her third and final husband, Elder Robert Tate, and became known as "Mother" Tate, an honorific title that remains in use to this day. Sometime early in her evangelizing she had begun to use Magdalena, rather than her given name, Lena, as her middle name.

The church's rules, practices, prohibitions, beliefs, and organizational structure are delineated in the Decree Book, of which the "first and revised" version was published in 1923. Activities and substances specifically prohibited by the 1923 edition of the Decree Book, and still in effect today, include: wine, grape juice, unfermented wine, whiskey and beers; opium, morphine, cocaine, and other harmful drugs; gambling, checkers, cards, and dominoes; the reading of novels; wicked dancing instituted by the devil; shows, parks, movies, baseball games, and horse races; the singing of reels, ragtime songs, jazzy songs, and all jazz and wicked songs; and wicked festivals and all places of amusement for sinners.[6] The driving, rock-like praise music heard in the churches today has evolved in a milieu that eschews aspects of popular culture and secular life that most people from outside the sphere of the church would consider harmless.

From its original locations in Alabama and Georgia, the church grew as Mother Tate and her son, Bishop Felix E. Lewis, evangelized and established congregations in several northern Florida cities, including Ocala, Jacksonville, Gainesville, and Crystal River. Leaders who emerged from the Florida diocese included Elders W. L. Nelson, Julius R. Lockley, and Bruce L. McLeod. W. L. Nelson's son, Henry, would become one of the most influential steel guitarists in the church. J. R. Lockley would later lead the traveling troupe of musicians and ministers known as the Gospel Feast Party, which introduced pioneering steel guitarists Troman and Willie Eason to congregations throughout the eastern United States. Lockley would also be in charge of the musicians at future General Assemblies in Nashville, Tennessee. The church expanded northward, and within a few years, was established in twenty states and Washington, D.C.

Mother Tate died in Philadelphia, Pennsylvania, on December 28, 1930, after contracting frostbite and gangrene in one of her feet. Her passing precipitated a heated power struggle fueled partially by the value of the organization's substantial real estate holdings. After about a year of meetings, the church was divided into three factions: the Keith, Lewis, and McLeod Dominions.[7] The leaders of the respective dominions, Bishops Mary F. L. Keith, Felix E. Lewis, and Bruce L. McLeod, were all related to Mother Tate: Lewis was her youngest son, Keith was her daughter-in-law, and McLeod was her step-son-in-law. Under the new organization Lewis, Keith, and McLeod were all designated as chief overseers. The House of God was still one church and each chief overseer was given authority over sixteen, or one third, of the forty-eight states. When Bishop McLeod died, his wife, Bishop Mattie Lue McLeod, was selected as his successor. When she married Deacon William B. Jewell, she became Bishop Mattie L. Jewell and her faction became the Jewell Dominion.

Dissension continued to grow, and in 1939 the church was officially divided into three separate organizations, each with its own name and charter. Bishop Lewis kept the original name of the church, "The Church of the Living God, the Pillar and Ground of the Truth." Bishop Jewell added a phrase to form "The Church of the Living God, the Pillar and Ground of the Truth, *Which He Has Purchased with His Own Blood*" (italics added).

Bishop Keith chose "The House of God, Which is the Church of the Living God, the Pillar and Ground of the Truth, Without Controversy, Inc., Keith Dominion." The division of the church into three dominions would have a decisive influence on the future role of the steel guitar in church services. The Keith and Jewell Dominions both developed strong steel guitar musical traditions that are closely related, yet distinctly different. This book attempts to illuminate the forces that have shaped, and continue to shape, the distinctive character of Keith and Jewell Dominion steel guitar music. There are some steel guitarists in the Lewis Dominion, but because the instrument never achieved prominence in that church, Lewis Dominion steel guitar music and musicians are not discussed here.

Clergy and congregants often refer to the churches as the House of God, Keith Dominion and the Church of the Living God, Jewell Dominion. For the sake of brevity I use Keith Dominion and Jewell Dominion throughout this book. "House of God" is found in a few interview quotations, and refers to the Keith Dominion.

Bishop Keith was born Mary Frankie Giles in 1888, in Lumpkin, Georgia. The Giles family was converted when Mother Tate came to Georgia to evangelize in 1911. Mary Giles married Mother Tate's eldest son, Bishop Walter C. Lewis, and they had six children. Mary Lewis was called to the ministry and, in time, appointed to the rank of elder by Mother Tate. In 1921, her husband died from pneumonia. Keith Dominion oral tradition holds that she then made a vow to God that if He would help her raise and educate her children, she would commit herself to the education of every person she encountered. In 1927, she married Deacon Lonnie Keith. She founded the House of God Home for Children in East Chattanooga, and the Keith Bible Institute (KBI) in nearby Ooltewah, Tennessee, which offered an elementary school education and a variety of religious courses. She provided many young people from impoverished families with clothing, meals, and housing in the KBI dormitories. After graduating from sixth grade at KBI, these children attended public school, finishing at Booker T. Washington High School in Chattanooga. At KBI there were also classes for young adult ministers. Through a collaboration with the Moody Bible Institute, many received degrees in divinity and theology.

Bishop Keith helped many members attend college, especially Tennessee State University, a historically black college that borders Heiman Street, across from the Keith Dominion's present headquarters sanctuary at 2717 Heiman in Nashville. The overwhelming majority of bishops and other high-ranking persons in the church today are among the dozens of individuals who benefited directly from her efforts. Bishop Keith was also firm in her conviction that women should be included in leadership positions within the church, a fact that is reflected by the significant numbers of women in the clergy today.[8]

As the Keith Dominion grew in membership and geographic range, the role of the annual General Assembly in maintaining organizational stability and unity, as well as shaping the steel guitar tradition, became increasingly significant. The General Assembly is the largest annual meeting in both dominions. The presence and prominence of the steel guitar at the General Assemblies provides a good indication of the status of the instrument in Keith and Jewell Dominion church meetings from a national perspective. The music played at the General Assembly has a profound effect on steel guitarists throughout both dominions. There, aspiring musicians absorb the music of nationally prominent steel guitarists, take note of their instruments and equipment setups, and return home with new elements to introduce into the music they play at local churches.

For years, the General Assembly was conducted under a large tent, remembered as large enough to cover about three to five hundred congregants, erected on the headquarters' property on Heiman Street. Because the property belonged to the original church and the three dominions claimed equal rights to it, the General Assemblies for the three dominions were held simultaneously, or more accurately, in shifts. Sharing one tent for worship services provided ample opportunities for the musicians of the three dominions to observe one another and to share musical ideas. Despite the ongoing rivalry of the dominions, musicians displayed a spirit of collaboration, and many had close friends and relatives among members of the other factions.

As tensions among the leaders of the dominions escalated in the 1930s and '40s, the headquarters property was sold to the city of Nashville and the Keith and Jewell Dominions built separate, but adjacent, permanent headquarters buildings on Heiman Street. The Keith Dominion's first permanent sanctuary, located at 2005 Heiman Street, was dedicated in 1948. The separate buildings largely solved the problem of friction during worship services. However, the buildings were close enough so young steel guitarists from the Keith Dominion could easily walk over to the Jewell Dominion services to hear steel guitar innovator Lorenzo Harrison and his band. The informal musical exchange in Nashville lasted until 1962, when the Jewell Dominion relocated its headquarters to Indianapolis, Indiana.[9]

Making a "joyful noise" (Psalms 100:1) is an essential element of Pentecostal worship. Before the advent of electric guitars, the congregations of
the Keith and Jewell Dominion churches played a variety of acoustic string
instruments including guitars, banjos, and pianos, as well as an array of
percussion instruments. If they could afford them they used manufactured
instruments such as bass drums, hand cymbals, and tambourines. Many
of the congregants improvised percussion by rubbing a washboard with a
bent wire coat hanger, beating on a cowbell, or simply beating or scraping
whatever objects were at hand that served the purpose. Observations can
be made from the photo of the congregation of the Corinth, Mississippi,
Jewell Dominion church circa the early 1930s, included in this book. In
the first seated row are two resonator guitars, a flat-top wooden guitar
(on the extreme right), a ukulele banjo, and between the banjoist and the
resonator guitar on the left, a man holding what appears to be some sort
of improvised percussion instrument. Acoustic guitars were sometimes
played using "bottleneck" or "slide" technique. But the loud clapping,
strong singing, and sound of various percussion instruments employed
by even the smallest of congregations easily buried the relatively weak
sound of the loudest acoustic guitars. Larger congregations could easily
overcome the sound of a piano or organ, both of which are considerably
louder than acoustic guitars.

The first electric steel guitars became commercially available in 1932, but
only thirteen instruments were sold in that year.[10] The instrument caught
on, however, and within a few years electric steel guitars were selling
briskly. The availability of electrically amplified steel guitars enabled the
voice of the instrument to be heard above the sound of the congregations.
The early amplifiers were not very loud, but in time, powerfully amplified
electric (steel) guitars would change the music of the Keith and Jewell
Dominions, much as they changed popular secular music.

The music played and sung at the assemblies during the 1930s and '40s
was more melodic than that heard today. There was apparently a greater
emphasis on hymns and spirituals during those decades. Although the
electric steel guitar was among the band instruments played, it was not
the dominant instrument it is today. Up-tempo music for the "praise" or
"shout" portions of worship services was played and sung in the old-
time, vocal-driven jubilee style of the period; voices dominated, not instruments. Guitar and voice amplification developed slowly. Steel guitars
played through the low-powered amplifiers of the 1930s and early 1940s

were generally not much louder than a piano, and large, powerful amplifiers did not begin to appear until the mid- to late-1940s.

When Bishop Keith became chief overseer of the House of God in 1939, she and her staff worked to expand the church. Bishop J. R. Lockley was an important figure during this period of evangelism and expansion. His troupe of musicians and preachers called the Gospel Feast Party traveled throughout the eastern United States, from New York to Miami, inspiring congregations and onlookers as they played lively music, sang, preached, and danced. A talented singer with a strong tenor voice, Lockley was in charge of the music at the Keith Dominion General Assembly for years. He often began the daily worship services at the General Assembly by leading a series of spirituals and gospel songs. His repertoire included "Life Is Like a Mountain Railroad," "When the Roll Is Called Up Yonder," "Telephone to Glory," "When I See the Blood," "In the Garden," and "I'll Fly Away." "He was quite a songster," recalled Bishop Charles E. Campbell. "Everyone looked forward to that."[11]

Bishop Lockley's son, J.R. Jr. (usually referred to simply as "J.R.") is remembered as one of the most important musicians to play at the General Assembly from the 1930s through the early 1950s. He excelled on the vibraphone and also played the double bass and lap-steel guitar. "The steel guitar, I say, was not the leading instrument during this time because the steel players were not that skillful," explained Bishop Campbell. "I would say J.R., I believe, was head and shoulders, as far as playing music, above all the rest. . . . That [vibraphone] was a big thing—Bishop Lockley would stop singing and he would play it."[12] Bishop Lockley kept a tight rein on the musicians. "If you did anything that was out of line, failed, or turned your guitar up, you were out of there! That was it. No back talk or nothing. You were out of there."[13]

Among those who remember the pre–World War II General Assemblies, the consensus seems to be that Troman Eason was the first to play the electric steel guitar at the Keith Dominion General Assembly in Nashville sometime around 1938, perhaps as early as 1936. According to his oldest surviving daughter, Ella Mae Berry, he was proficient enough to teach steel guitar by at least 1937. Troman's brother, Willie, sixteen years his junior, was one of the earliest to play steel guitar at the General Assembly, although it is unclear when he made his first appearance. Perhaps his debut came in 1939, after traveling south with Bishop Lockley's Gospel Feast Party band in the winter of 1938–39. But Lockley was upset with Willie

Eason after he left the Gospel Feast Party to play on his own sometime in the spring of 1939, and his disapproval may have delayed Willie's General Assembly debut for a year or two.

Troman and Willie's brother, Henry, also played steel at the General Assembly, probably in the 1940s. Henry Eason's steel guitar music is remembered as a mix of the styles played by his brothers (their music is thoroughly discussed in later chapters) and he was not as important in shaping the Keith Dominion steel guitar tradition as were Troman and Willie. Troman Eason apparently dropped out of the church a few years before his death in 1939. Just how often Willie and Henry Eason played at the General Assembly in the 1940s is not clear, but those who recall the music played at the General Assemblies during that era invariably mention both.

Henry Harrison, brother of Jewell Dominion steel guitar legend Lorenzo Harrison and later the Keith Dominion bishop with whom young Calvin Cooke would travel, also played at some Keith Dominion General Assemblies during the 1940s (his son, H. L. Jr., also played steel guitar at the General Assembly a few years later). Two female steel guitarists played in the mid- and late-1940s: Elder O. L. Pasco and Elder B. B. Barber, both now deceased.[14] Some interview subjects recalled that during the 1940s and early 1950s there were years when there may have been very little, if any, steel guitar music played at the Keith Dominion General Assembly, as the instrument was not yet firmly established. Willie Eason may have been excluded, or voluntarily stayed away from, the General Assembly during this period because he played independently at non–Keith Dominion events, busked on the streets, made commercial gospel recordings, and produced gospel concerts, all of which were activities frowned upon or banned by the church.

Upon her death in 1962, Bishop Keith was succeeded by James W. Jenkins, one of the many whom she had assisted in attaining an education. Ordained a minister at age thirteen, he rose rapidly in the ranks of the clergy and received a Doctor of Divinity Degree from Trinity Hall College and Seminary. Jenkins was highly skilled in financial matters. He developed a comprehensive budget system, carefully managed the organization's cash flow, obtained tax exempt status from the federal government, and embarked on a massive building and renovation program. He acquired considerable real estate on Heiman Street, a Nashville neighborhood that suffered from some degree of crime and physical decay. Existing buildings were demolished or renovated and new buildings were erected. In all, some 45 churches were remodeled and more than 125 new churches were erected under his direction. Today, Keith Dominion property in Nashville along several blocks of Heiman Street, including the three-thousand-seat Headquarters Sanctuary, which was erected without a mortgage, gives testimony to his financial acumen and the success of his administration. Bishop Jenkins died in 1990.

Bishop Jenkins's successor, Bishop James Colvin Elliott, of Sarasota, Florida, served as chief overseer during a period of unprecedented technological change. As mass media and the internet became pervasive in American life, isolation from the secular world as advocated and practiced by Mother Tate, Bishop Keith, and to a lesser extent, Bishop Jenkins, was no longer a realistic concept. For the most part, Bishop Elliott maintained a progressive attitude towards technology, media, and integration of the membership into the "Information Age." He supported the Florida Folklife Program's project to survey and document the church's steel guitar music and produce the *Sacred Steel* cassette/booklet album and the Arhoolie Foundation's *Sacred Steel* documentary video.[15] His two sons became church musicians: James (known to most by his middle name, Denard), is a steel guitarist, and Terrence, a bassist. Having a son who was a steel guitarist was likely a factor that influenced Bishop Elliott to keep the instrument at the top of the Keith Dominion's musical instrument hierarchy.

However, Bishop Elliott was somewhat ambivalent about the attention Keith Dominion steel guitarists and other musicians received. He never openly chastised or sanctioned the musicians who played outside the Keith Dominion, and at several large gatherings he declared over the public address system that he was proud of all the Keith Dominion musicians. But he was quick to make it clear that he and the clergy, not the musicians, were in control. He declined offers from Arhoolie Records to sell at church events CDs that presented Keith Dominion artists. Even promotion and sales of audio recordings produced by the church itself was minimized. The revenue the church might have acquired from sales of such recordings was apparently insignificant in comparison to the statement made by not selling the albums: the musicians are subservient to the church and clergy. At the same time, to commemorate the church's Millennium Celebration at the turn of the twenty-first century, Bishop Elliott authorized a team of Keith Dominion members to produce the first professional-quality recording of church musicians and choirs made by the church. Several videos, which documented church history and special events, were also produced during Bishop Elliott's administration.

The situation in the Jewell Dominion regarding the steel guitar was

quite different from that of the Keith Dominion. Lorenzo Harrison became
Bishop Jewell's official steel guitarist and *the* lead musician at the Jewell
Dominion General Assembly soon after he married Bishop Jewell's adopted
granddaughter, Nettie Mae, in September 1942. While a variety of steel
guitarists were cycling through the Keith Dominion General Assembly and
the instrument was slowly being worked into a position of importance
in that church during the 1940s and 1950s, Lorenzo Harrison had firmly
established the instrument in the Jewell Dominion on a national level by
probably 1943 or 1944. Young Harrison's skills as a steel guitarist and his
ability to help congregations become infused with the Holy Spirit through
his music improved quickly as he traveled with Bishop Jewell to play for
large meetings throughout the geographic range of the Jewell Dominion.
Within a very short time he firmly established the steel guitar as the dominant instrument in the Jewell Dominion and his manner of playing it as
the dominant sound.

After the first Keith Dominion headquarters sanctuary building was
erected in 1948, the big tent was still used as a sort of auxiliary space
for various daytime meetings for many years, apparently into the 1960s.
Rhythm guitarist Harvey Jones (1922–) is one of the oldest church musicians with a good memory for events of the 1940s and 1950s. He traveled
with Lorenzo Harrison and drummer Corroneva Burns to play for Jewell
Dominion worship services, revivals, and assemblies from 1942 through
1957, and was Bishop Jewell's chauffeur for most of that period. Jones
recalled playing under the big tent erected each year for the General Assemblies. By the mid-1940s, amplifiers had become loud enough to be
heard for some distance. "When they started playing," Jones remembered,
"we drew people from south Nashville, from two, three miles away. People
come in there, because we had the sound goin' all over that city."[16]

In the secular world, the 1950s and 1960s marked the emergence of
youth culture, rock and roll, and increasingly more powerful electric guitar
amplifiers. While Keith and Jewell Dominion congregants lived within the
sphere of "the church" they were not entirely isolated from the influences of
secular society, which church members commonly refer to as "the world."
Electric guitarists in general are interested in the latest technological developments, and Keith and Jewell Dominion steel guitarists are no exception.
During the 1950s and 1960s the music at the General Assembly led by
steel guitarists became louder and much of it began to sound like blues
and rock and roll.

Keith Dominion member Henry Nelson, with his one-chord "drive" approach to praise music, was one of the first of the young steel guitarists to play loudly and wildly. According to his older sister, Mary Linzy of Ocala, Florida, he began to play at the General Assembly after he graduated high school in 1950.[17] Nelson continued to play at the General Assembly through probably 1958, although it is not certain that he played every year or how much he played at any General Assembly during that period. Regardless of the exact years Henry Nelson played at the General Assembly, it was his fiery music of the 1950s that did much to solidify the important position of the instrument in Keith Dominion worship services. Sometimes he engaged in heated negotiations of aesthetics and power with members of the clergy and congregations. He also traveled throughout Florida, South Carolina, and parts of Tennessee to play at state assemblies and regular worship services at churches within the dioceses of his father, Bishop W. L. Nelson. Because the total number of congregants in these dioceses may have been about 40 percent of the national Keith Dominion membership, playing for these church meetings added substantially to the degree of his musical influence.[18]

Henry Nelson began a hiatus from the Keith Dominion in 1959, the same year that fifteen-year-old Calvin Cooke of Detroit played his first General Assembly. Cooke clearly recalls that Nelson was "nowhere in sight" in 1959, when he played at the General Assembly for the first time.[19] By 1961, Cooke's music had shifted from a more-or-less melodic approach to music that was more driving and freely improvised. Although some of the more conservative members reacted negatively to Cooke's new music, calling it blues and rock and roll, many congregants—especially the younger folks—loved it. Most importantly, Bishop Keith endorsed it. Furthermore, because Cooke had been playing at assemblies, revivals, and other large church meetings for Bishops Keith and Henry Harrison throughout the geographic range of the Keith Dominion, the flamboyant young steel guitarist had gained a national following.

Cooke's presence at the General Assembly helped pave the way for other musicians from the Motor City, including Maurice "Ted" Beard Jr., Ronnie Hall, and Charles Flenory. Both Beard and Hall shared common musical influences with Cooke: they grew up in families that belonged to the Jewell Dominion and were exposed to the music of Lorenzo Harrison as youngsters, and as teens they were influenced by the music of Felton Williams. Guitar amplifiers were quite powerful by the early 1960s, and young Keith Dominion steel guitarists often engaged in a sort of sonic war. "Felton and Beard battled with their amplifiers," Ronnie Hall recalled of the Detroit music scene. "Whoever had the strongest amplifier won."[20] Nowadays, a large selection of powerful amplifiers is available to steel guitarists and first-rate equipment is within the economic grasp of most church musicians. In the earlier years, that was not the case, and those steel guitarists who could afford the most powerful amplifiers had a distinct advantage when playing at large church meetings such as the General Assembly.

Ronnie Hall clearly remembers his first experience playing the steel guitar at the General Assembly. Unwittingly, he found himself in the center of a conflict rooted in family turmoil. Bishop W. L. Nelson was upset with his son, Henry, who left Florida under difficult circumstances, remarried, and joined the Church of God in Christ (a very large Pentecostal church not connected with the Keith and Jewell Dominions) in New York, where his father-in-law served as pastor. The bishop took out his anger on the budding young steel guitarist from Detroit. Ronnie Hall's vivid recollection of the incident speaks to the tenuous position of the steel guitar in the Keith Dominion at that time:

> On the Keith Dominion side, the steel guitar was not the prevailing instrument. It wasn't. It really didn't evolve until right around the last part of '59 to '63. Because in '63, I was the one that came down and played under the tent and they tried to outlaw me from playing.
>
> There was a big controversy about that. At that time, Ted [Beard] had come out of the army. He was there with his family, but he wasn't there to play. He was there to accompany his father, who was getting up in years, to establish as a bishop. Well, in 1963, after I graduated from [high] school, we went to the General Assembly and I carried this monstrosity of a guitar that I made, and we played under the tent. And once we cranked that thing up, man, people—they used to have what they call "committee meetings" during the day—and when that thing would sound off, all of the sudden the committee meetings would break up. People would find reasons to leave the meetings and come back out to the tent. Well, we'd be out there and the dust would be rising [from congregants dancing]. They'd be out there just shoutin', you know. The music, you could hear it for two miles. So, during the day, the heat of the day, they would be out there and we were playing and they were really having a good time.
>
> So, somebody asked us, "Why don't you guys come and play at the temple at night? 'Cause it's kind of boring in there?" And I said, "Okay," so we hooked it up. We hooked it up to play—that was my cousin, [rhythm guitarist] Charles Rue, and myself. We ran into some of the most terrible opposition. They said, "Oh no. You can't bring that stuff in here. We're not going to have that."[21]

The source of the opposition to Hall's music was Bishop W. L. Nelson. "He raised the roof," recalled Hall. "He didn't want us in the temple with that stuff." Disappointed and frustrated, Hall presented his case to the chief overseer: "Fortunately for me I had a friendship with Bishop J. W. Jenkins at that time, who was their chief overseer. And he was staying in the dormitory next to the temple, or the assembly hall. And I went over and knocked on the door and poured out the story. I said, 'You know bishop, this is really crazy. We came down here to be a blessing to the church and the people seemed to enjoy it. And this is the dream of a lifetime, to play in the General Assembly. What's the story here? I just don't think it's right.'"[22]

Much to Hall's delight, Bishop Jenkins told Bishop Nelson to let Hall and Rue play for the evening service. Hall continued:

And so Jenkins told him, says, "No, let the young men play. If we find that it's more disruptive than it is an aid to the service, we'll let Lockley's bunch and the rest of them have it." And I said, "Okay." And so we went and we only had one or two that didn't like the idea, but the majority of the people, they "caught fire."

[That was] right around '63. Just came out of high school. And I remember 'cause the strongest part of the memory of it was I had built my own guitar. The young people gathered around and said, "What is that? I mean, I've heard of this but never seen one like this." Especially the guys from Florida, they were crazy about it.[23]

The appointment of Ted Beard (ca. 1968) as Coordinator of Music for the General Assembly was a milestone event that signaled for once and for all the dominance of the steel guitar among the instruments played in the Keith Dominion.[24] When he appointed Beard, Chief Overseer Jenkins instituted two requirements for *all* musicians to be eligible for consideration to play at the General Assembly. First, each musician's "Report" must be at least 96 percent paid. The Report comprises a list of twenty-five specific tithes, offerings, donations, contributions, and assessments, each counting 4 percent. Second, each musician must obtain a written statement from his pastor, presiding elder, state bishop, and the chief overseer that indicates he is in good standing. That is, he or she has been attending services regularly, is not rebelling against the church, not creating bad publicity for the church, and has not been arrested or engaged in other behavior deemed inappropriate for a member of the Keith Dominion.[25]

Sometime in the early 1970s, Henry Nelson began to play again at Keith Dominion meetings. Just exactly how he balanced his participation in Keith Dominion events with activities in the Church of God in Christ is not clear, but apparently he was involved in both churches simultaneously for a period. Chuck Campbell (1957–), son of Bishop Charles E. Campbell, former state bishop of New York, remembered his first encounter with Henry Nelson. "In August of 1972, I have my first Henry Nelson sighting in the New Jersey State Assembly in Orange. This is a part of my territories where I played. I come in expecting to play on a Saturday night and Bishop 'Big Bill' Nelson is in the house from Florida with his son, Henry Nelson. The guy picks one note, the church, including many from downstate New York, fall out! Sounds like noise to me, but the people act as if Jesus has returned. This is the start of a new era, although I don't know it."[26]

In 1973, Henry Nelson returned to play at the General Assembly. Because he had left the Keith Dominion to join the Church of God in Christ, he could not begin to meet the strict criteria for eligibility to play at the General Assembly. But Bishop Jenkins told Beard to let Nelson play. After all, he was the son of Bishop W. L. Nelson, the man who had established dozens of churches in Florida and South Carolina, and had died just six months earlier. Henry Nelson was enthusiastically welcomed back into the fold by the congregations and clergy—especially those from Florida and South Carolina, if not by all the musicians.

About the time of Henry Nelson's return to the Keith Dominion General Assembly, some musicians had begun to experiment with the pedal-steel guitar, a modern variation of the steel guitar that offers expanded harmonic potential (the pedal-steel guitar is discussed more thoroughly in chapter 4). In 1974, Chuck Campbell, the revolutionary teenaged pedal-steel guitarist from upstate New York, would become a member of the select few to play steel guitar at the General Assembly. Campbell related the events that led to his entry into the inner circle:

> The 1974 General Assembly found a lot of lobbying going on for me to play. Ted had gotten a Sho-Bud pedal-steel that year too. Ted said I wasn't ready to play and refused to find a spot. My father got a petition with different bishops' signatures stating I could play on their day. Calvin also wanted to give me one of his days to play; this was asking for daytime only [not prime evening time]. Ted said he didn't see it happening. It so happened that while getting his Sho-Bud set up by the store, coming down the stairs he hit his head on a low hang that you needed to duck to miss, putting a cut that needed stitches. He finally gave in and gave me a Monday morning while he went to a doctor's appointment. I played with Darryl Brundidge on guitar; Ted's sister, Alfreda Beard, on one-string bass [imitating electric bass on the lowest string of an electric guitar]; Phil Campbell played drums.

We were a hit, as many players proclaimed I was the first to get it right with the pedal-steel. All the players with me had little or no General Assembly experience, but we were definitely blessed. The Taylor boys said, "I told you they've been scared of you since '69." Ronnie Hall said, "That's what I had in mind for pedals." And Charles [Flenory] and Calvin declared they knew I would do it.[27]

After the 1974 General Assembly, Campbell continued to develop his pedal-steel guitar technique and help others set up their pedal-steels. Early in 1975 he experienced religious conversion, which had a major effect on his playing.

> I finally was converted and received the Holy Spirit in January of 1975 at a revival in which more than seventy-five people were converted. My life was heading in the wrong direction, as I had started experimenting with alcohol and drugs; my first encounter with alcohol and drugs was at church conventions and assemblies from my peers. My grades in school were failing and my mentors told me if I wanted to be the best, get the Holy Ghost. Wow, what a difference! I turned around three school quarters of failing grades, getting accepted to Tennessee State University. I also learned to play "in the Spirit," which to this day is invaluable. Gaining an understanding of playing from a spiritual level helped me begin to feel the power of the great church steel players. Henry Nelson was the best I've witnessed. Being able to voice the songs, which take on such a personal meaning to converts, meant so much more to me. Playing great licks just for the sake of licks was no longer the objective.[28]

Missing the 1975 General Assembly gave Campbell fresh perspectives on the senior steel guitarists: "I missed the 1975 General Assembly preparing for graduation and college entry. I heard the tapes from that year; Calvin and Ted broke out their pedal-steels. Ted played only a few E9th a-b pedal moves and has never been the Ted we idolized [when he played] the double eight-string Fender [lap-steel].[29] Calvin sounded like himself but actually used the pedals for 'whammy bar' leads. Ted sounded good, but there was an intangible swagger lost. Henry Nelson, being the only General Assembly regular using a lap, became the main force [for lap-steel guitar] for years to come. Henry also began his campaign of 'pedal-steel makes you concentrate on the instrument and not the Spirit.'"[30]

Chuck Campbell returned to play at the 1976 General Assembly, where he joined the inner circle composed of three senior steel guitarists: Henry Nelson, Calvin Cooke, and Ted Beard. The four dominated the steel guitar music at the General Assembly for the next seventeen years. From time to time they would let other steel guitarists make a cameo appearance, usually on a weeknight, when the congregation was smaller, but otherwise the four held court through the 1993 General Assembly. In the spring of 1994, Nelson had the first of a series of strokes that curtailed his playing. The remaining triumvirate—all pedal-steel guitarists—continued to dominate the General Assembly until steel guitar positions began to open up in the late 1990s. During the three decades of the 1970s through the 1990s, several backup musicians rotated through the band that played at the General Assembly. In addition to Ronnie Hall, another rhythm guitarist who often played at the Generally Assembly was Larry Taylor of Miami, Florida. Chuck remembers Taylor as one of the best Keith Dominion guitar players of all time, a statement of some gravity when one considers that many believe Chuck's brother, Phil, is the best guitarist in the Keith Dominion today. Kenny Ellis (Bishop Elliott's son-in-law), of Sarasota, also became one of the rhythm guitarists to play regularly at the General Assembly.

Henry Nelson's final General Assembly appearance in 1993 marked the end of an era. The lap-steel guitar was no longer played at the General Assembly by a venerated master and the instrument had lost a major, influential advocate. Musicians continued to play the lap-steel guitar throughout the Keith Dominion and the instrument is still in widespread use today. With the General Assembly triumvirate of Cooke, Beard, and Campbell all playing pedal-steels, however, it was clear that the pedal-steel guitar would become the preferred instrument among the most highly esteemed musicians. But it would take a while for the newfangled instrument to truly come into its own.

Although Cooke and Beard both played pedal-steels, the manner in which they played and the way they configured the pedals and knee-levers of their instruments did not make extensive use of the expanded harmonic and melodic possibilities that these devices afford. Consequently, their use of the pedal-steel guitar did not have a significant effect on the music they played, except for a change in timbre (tone). The most popular lap-steels among Keith Dominion musicians were Fenders: the Stringmasters with two eight-string necks and the similar single-neck version, the Deluxe 8. Both of these Fender models are renowned for their rich, fat tone. Beard and Cooke played Fender lap-steels for two decades, and Nelson played a Fender Deluxe 8, which he fitted with six, rather than eight, strings. The characteristic sound of the Fender Deluxe and Stringmaster models became part of the Keith Dominion tradition, and they are sought out today, more than three decades after production ceased in 1980, by many church musicians.[31] The mechanism, chassis construction, and pickups of pedal-steel guitars all contribute to a timbre that many—but by no means all—steel guitarists believe is not as full as that of a lap-steel. The timbre of lap- and pedal-steels is a subject of much debate among musicians and instrument makers; however, even those who argue that a pedal-steel can sound just as rich as a lap-steel generally agree that the two instruments' sound different. When Beard and Cooke switched from lap- to pedal-steel guitars the timbre of their music changed.

While Beard and Cooke chose to use the pitch-changing potential of their pedal-steel guitars in a limited manner, Chuck Campbell was determined to apply the full potential of the instrument to music played in the Keith Dominion. He had a solid understanding of chord construction and became skilled at adjusting the various components of the pitch-changing mechanism of pedal-steel guitars to perform optimally. He experimented extensively with tunings, pedal changes, and electronic effects. Chuck Campbell would continue to shape the Keith Dominion musical tradition at the national level with his pedal-steel innovations. Similarly, Glenn Lee, a talented young multi-instrumentalist from Perrine, Florida, would inspire dozens of young Keith Dominion musicians in his home state to play the pedal-steel guitar.

Today, there are significant differences between the music of the Keith and Jewell Dominions. Most result from conventionalization of Jewell Dominion music by Lorenzo Harrison and his sidemen, especially the earliest: rhythm guitarist Harvey Jones and drummer Corroneva Burns. The moderate, loping tempos, reserved drumming, and finger-picked rhythm guitar of the classic Jewell Dominion ensemble results in music that, while fully effective in serving to help the congregation to become filled with the Holy Ghost, is generally not as frenetic as the music played in the Keith Dominion.

On the average, Keith Dominion music is usually—but not always—louder than that heard in the Jewell Dominion. If for no other reason than to be heard over the drummer, who is much louder than his Jewell Dominion counterpart, it would be necessary for a Keith Dominion steel guitarist and the rest of the ensemble to play more loudly. But is seems that the Keith Dominion steel guitarists deliberately play much louder than necessary just to be heard over the drummer. In the vast majority of churches, only the minister or vocalist is heard through the loudspeakers of the public address system. The loudness levels of the instrumentalists (except the drummer) are controlled by the setting of each musician's amplifier, a situation that left unchecked often results in loudness levels continually creeping upward. Therefore, an important element of being a top Keith Dominion steel guitarist, on the local, regional, or national level, is having a powerful amplifier. Often there is some degree of power struggle between the minister and the musicians to maintain a certain volume, but if a steel guitarist is really determined to play with increasing loudness, he can be difficult to control, especially during heated praise music when there is no vocalist.

Differences in loudness are apparent not only between the two dominions, but regionally as well. There is a significant degree of regional and local variation in loudness and the general nature of the music. For example, the Keith Dominion church in Perrine, Florida (about fifteen miles south of Miami), is known for loud music and highly spirited worship services, while South Carolina "state" steel guitarist Anthony Fox plays at a considerably quieter level at the Keith Dominion church in Charleston.

The church's centennial was celebrated in September 2003 by a series of events at Keith Dominion headquarters in Nashville. Highlights included an "Old-Time Way Worship Service," for which many members dressed in clothes from the 1920s and 1930s, a performance (albeit quite shaky) by steel guitar pioneer Willie Eason, a Reunion Barbecue attended by more than two thousand Keith Dominion members and their guests, all-out performances by reunited vocal groups the Beard Sisters (Keith Dominion) and the Henderson Sisters (Jewell Dominion), and a parade through several blocks of the neighborhood surrounding the Keith Dominion complex.

A noteworthy aspect of the centennial celebration was the participation by members of churches that had split off from Mother Tate's original organization. Clergy, musicians, and members of the Jewell and Lewis Dominions, as well as some of the smaller factions that had left the church years ago, participated in the event programs. They gave speeches and tributes, sang, shouted, danced, and were embraced by Keith Dominion members. Decades-old rifts were put aside as "Mother Tate's children" celebrated the centennial of the church she had founded.

Bishop Elliott died less than a year after the centennial, on May 26, 2004, while in Nashville preparing for the General Assembly to be held in mid-June. His passing marked the beginning of considerable turmoil as a power struggle ensued within the Keith Dominion organization. Among those impacted most severely by the resultant reorganization was Bishop Charles Campbell. The profound effects of the new administration upon the steel guitar tradition of the Keith Dominion are examined in the final chapter of this book.

The Keith Dominion serves its membership as an important social institution. Virtually all of the members who joined the church in the 1920s through the 1940s were born in the segregated South. The overwhelming majority of those who have attained the rank of bishop were born in Georgia, Florida, or South Carolina. Similarly, a great many musicians and clergy in the Jewell Dominion are from families that originated in Mississippi, the state that has the greatest number of churches of that denomination. The Keith and Jewell Dominion churches served to help African Americans born into poor, rural, southern families with the struggle to better themselves economically, cope with the challenges they faced as they migrated north for economic opportunity, and obtain an education. Bishops Keith and Jewell put dozens of young people through the Keith Bible Institute and the Jewell Academy and Seminary until those institutions closed in the 1960s. Many were assisted in attaining college degrees. Current church membership reflects increasing numbers who have achieved a level of affluence and a college education.

The church continues to serve as an institution through which members find help in coping with daily life. Church meetings often involve extended personal testimony and dialogue that deal with specific individual challenges. Music is a significant force in attracting young people—especially adolescent and young adult males—to church meetings, and for some, a means of participation in church functions on a regular basis. It seems that some members and clergy are willing to tolerate a degree of testing or pushing aesthetic limits of the music by young people because the older folks recognize the importance in keeping the younger people involved in church. As a conversionist church, the Keith Dominion places a high value on the willingness of individuals to undergo a process of religious conversion to affect social transformation. The church tends to be apolitical and has little interest in social reformation by means other than individual conversion and individuals living a life of holiness.

Women have been in leadership positions since Mother Tate founded the parent church in 1903. The Jewell Dominion has always had a woman as its national leader, or chief overseer. Bishop Mattie Lue Jewell served as chief overseer for more than five decades until her death in 1991. She was succeeded by her granddaughter, Naomi Manning, who served until her death in 2003. In 2005, Bishop Faye Moore of Mt. Clemens, Michigan, was selected as chief overseer of the Jewell Dominion. The Keith Dominion has had two female leaders: Bishop Keith and the current leader, Bishop Rebecca Fletcher. Women function in the full gamut of positions of rank in the Keith and Jewell Dominions, including chief helper, bishop, elder, pastor, and board member. At worship services women generally outnumber men, often by a ratio of five to one or greater. While female musicians are not uncommon, female steel guitarists are quite rare. Since I began to research the tradition in 1992 I have made a special effort to identify female steel guitarists, but have found only a handful, and of those, very few have the set of skills required to play for a full worship service.

Present membership in the Keith Dominion is estimated to be eight thousand.[32] The church Web site, www.hogc.org, lists 188 churches within the United States, which are distributed geographically as shown in table 1.[33]

Keith Dominion churches are also found outside the United States. There are eight in Jamaica; one in Windsor, Ontario, Canada; one in Haiti; and an unspecified number in Nassau, Bahamas.[34]

Jewell Dominion membership is estimated to be two thousand or less. The church Web site, www.cotlgnet.org, lists thirty-five churches within the United States, which are distributed geographically as shown in table 2, and one in Nassau, Bahamas.[35]

Generally, local congregations in both dominions are small. At many churches, attendance at a routine Sunday morning worship service might be two dozen or fewer individuals. Edifices are generally sized for large

TABLE 1. Distribution of Keith Dominion Churches

State or District	Churches	State	Churches
Alabama	6	Massachusetts	2
California	2	Michigan	8
Connecticut	6	Mississippi	3
Delaware	1	New Jersey	10
Washington, D.C.	1	New York	8
Florida	41	North Carolina	8
Georgia	33	Ohio	6
Illinois	3	Pennsylvania	3
Indiana	6	South Carolina	26
Kentucky	1	Virginia	2
Maryland	1	Wisconsin	5

TABLE 2. Distribution of Jewell Dominion Churches

State	Churches	State	Churches
Alabama	1	Michigan	4
Arizona	1	Mississippi	7
California	1	North Carolina	2
Florida	4	Ohio	5
Indiana	1	Pennsylvania	2
Kentucky	2	Tennessee	1
Maryland	1	Texas	1
Massachusetts	1	Wisconsin	1

events (the state assembly, for example) and range in capacity from about 150 to several hundred. Consequently, very few churches are filled to more than a fraction of capacity during a routine weekly worship service, but there are exceptions. At the Keith Dominion church in Perrine, Florida, for example, one hundred people may routinely attend a Sunday morning worship service, filling the temple to about 50 percent of capacity.

The skewed distribution of the number of churches per state may be partly explained by three factors: the success of evangelizing efforts, migration patterns, and how firmly other churches were established in any given area. The large number of Keith Dominion churches in Florida is largely the result of the tireless evangelizing by Bishops W. L. Nelson and J. R. Lockley. Bishop Nelson was also responsible for the state of South Carolina, which had the second largest number of churches in the Keith Dominion system for many years, but has been recently surpassed by Georgia, one of the fastest growing states in the South. The Jewell Dominion developed a stronghold in northeastern Mississippi early in that denomination's history. The effect of migration patterns is illustrated, for example, by the number of Jewell Dominion families who migrated north from Mississippi to industrial cities such as Cleveland, Toledo, and Detroit and helped establish congregations in Ohio and Michigan. The relatively small number of churches in Tennessee seems contrary to expectations when one considers that Nashville is the headquarters for the Keith Dominion and the Jewell Dominion had its headquarters there for many years. The situation in Nashville might be explained by the large numbers of other churches that are so well-established there; new churches are more easily established where other churches do not have a strong foothold.

The Keith and Jewell Dominions place strong emphasis on marrying within the church, and spouses taken from outside the church are expected to become members. Because there are so few members and many families have been members for two or three generations, virtually all members are related. Members chuckle as they explain that one should avoid making disparaging remarks about one member to another because he or she may be a cousin, aunt, or uncle of the subject individual. One way in which the close family ties are manifested is in the large numbers of people who travel great distances to attend funeral services. Church members may attend several such services each year, a good number of which might require traveling hundreds of miles.

Throughout the geographic range of the Keith and Jewell Dominions there are regional and local variations in the degree of conservatism among the clergy, which are reflected in the general nature of the worship services and specifically in the music. For example, when I attended an assembly at the Keith Dominion church in Charleston, South Carolina, in 1999, with Marcus Hardy, a Keith Dominion steel guitarist from Crescent City, Florida, we both observed that the music was not nearly a loud as what might be the norm in Florida. Mississippi congregations of the Jewell Dominion are said to be among the most conservative in that organization.

Loyalty to the church is stressed. Keith Dominion clergy frequently exhort the congregations to be loyal to the church and warn them not to stray to another denomination. The Decree Book states that the church shall not recognize those who "split out" from the Church of the Living God, including Methodists, Baptists, Congregationalists, Church of the First Born of the Living God, Colored Fire Baptized Church, Triumphant Church of God in Christ, Church of God in Christ, and all other "false and pieced up names."[36] "Spiritual fornication" is a term used among some Keith Dominion members. Chuck and Phil Campbell have explained it to me as follows. A Keith Dominion member attends worship services at some other church and experiences something he or she thinks is the Holy Ghost. If it is a Holiness or Pentecostal church they may shout, dance, sing, and otherwise express themselves in ways that may appear similar to those seen in the Keith Dominion. But, because they did not arrive at this state by following the doctrine of the Keith Dominion, it is not to be trusted as a true Holy Ghost experience and such practice is said to be spiritual fornication. Through use of the term "spiritual fornication," the clergy attempts to encourage loyalty to the Keith Dominion. Although I personally have never heard the term spoken from the pulpit, the Campbells tell me they have. However, I have often heard clergy express very clearly that they expect all Keith Dominion members to remain members of the church and not stray to another.

Members of the Keith Dominion so inclined progress through a series of ranks, which, in ascending order, include layman, deacon (or deaconess), exhorter, reverend, pastor, elder, presiding elder, general elder, state elder, bishop, chief helper, and chief overseer. Many of the ranks may be prefixed with "trial" to designate a person who is new to the position.

Training is largely accomplished internally, both "on the job" and by completing annual courses at the headquarters church in Nashville. The chief overseer most often holds a Doctor of Divinity degree. Members of the clergy who have advanced college degrees, show plenty of ambition, live a life of holiness, and are dedicated to the church are prime candidates to rise to top positions.

With the exception of the chief overseer, Keith Dominion clergy are not paid a salary (there is a small paid administrative staff at the headquarters church in Nashville). Most members of the clergy maintain a full-time job outside the church. Others work part-time, are self-employed, or have business interests that allow them the flexibility needed in order to devote a lot of time to church matters. Pastors receive offerings from their congregations, but they are not nearly enough to live on. Many pastors supplement their incomes with fees and special offerings from out-of-town speaking engagements or by serving as a guest evangelist at revivals.

Generally, Keith Dominion musicians are not paid to play for routine worship services, the exception being cases where one must travel considerable distance to play at a church that is in dire need of a musician, usually a steel guitarist. But the compensation usually does not cover much more than the expense of gasoline. Those who play for large meetings, such as state assemblies, revivals, and the General Assembly, may receive a meager amount, most commonly an offering collected from the congregation.

The chief overseer of the Keith Dominion apparently receives substantial income from the church and is treated with honor and respect almost befitting royalty or heads of state. For example, etiquette dictates that anyone who speaks over the public address system at a church meeting will begin with "Giving honor to the chief overseer . . ." During Bishop Elliott's tenure, the phrase "and the First Lady . . ." was always added.

In the Jewell Dominion it is not unusual for a pastor or bishop to live in a home owned by the church and adjacent to a church edifice. This was the case with Bishop Eunice Treadway, pastor of the Jewell Dominion church in Deerfield Beach, Florida, and her husband, steel guitarist Sonny Treadway. There is a house next door to the Jewell Dominion church in Tupelo, Mississippi, occupied by clergy. Members of the Flemons family, including steel guitarist Jerry Flemons, live on or adjacent to church property in rural Toccopola, Mississippi. During the 1940s and 1950s, several members of the Jewell Dominion occupied houses owned by the church in the immediate vicinity of the headquarters church in Cleveland, Ohio.[37] Residences on or adjacent to church property reinforce the concept of the "church family" and are a physical manifestation of the degree to which the church is a part of daily life.

Music, particularly steel guitar music, is woven deeply into the social milieu of the Keith and Jewell Dominions. Today, the electric steel guitar is the dominant musical instrument in both dominions, and steel guitar music is an important component of church meetings. The rich steel guitar tradition of each dominion was shaped by more than a century of church history and the influences of certain innovative musicians. Steel guitarists who serve in the Keith and Jewell Dominions operate in complex environments that require, in addition to a high degree of musical competency, the ability to play music appropriate to spontaneous events during various church meetings and successfully negotiate issues of power with members of the clergy.

Church Meetings and the
Steel Guitarist's Role in Them

Keith Dominion worship services follow a general pattern common to many predominantly African American Holiness-Pentecostal churches. Familiarity with some specific characteristics of the services should help the reader better understand the origins and evolution of the steel guitar tradition and the cultural milieu in which the steel guitarists, clergy, and congregants operate. What follows is a general description of aspects of Keith Dominion worship and ritual most relevant to the steel guitar musical tradition.

Keith Dominion churches meet four times each week: Wednesday night Bible study, Friday night tarry service, Sunday morning for Sunday school followed by worship services, and Sunday evening.[1] Because the Sunday morning worship service is the most heavily attended of the regular weekly meetings, it will be discussed most thoroughly. In addition to the regular weekly gatherings, each state conducts a number of special events that may include the state assembly, revivals, church anniversaries, pastor anniversaries, state baptism, Sunday school conventions, and homegoing services (funerals). Because the Wednesday, Friday, and Sunday evening meetings have no special significance in terms of steel guitar music they are not discussed here. Some of the special events are discussed in less detail following the discussion of the Sunday morning worship services.

Sunday Morning Worship Service

Keith Dominion Sunday morning worship services are scheduled to begin at 11:30.[2] While every effort is made to begin services punctually, it is not unusual for a service to start more than fifteen minutes late. There is no set time for the end of services. One of the key differences in Keith Dominion worship services as compared to those of many other churches is the general looseness with regard to time. At most Keith Dominion churches the Sunday morning service is over by about 2:00 P.M., or 2:30 at the latest. But if spontaneous events, such as extended personal testimony or someone "seeking" the Holy Ghost in pursuit of conversion occur, sufficient time is allowed for those events to naturally flow to resolution. The service is ultimately controlled by the pastor, but spontaneity is recognized as an element of the religious experience. It is not unusual for a pastor to abbreviate portions of the planned program or "order of service" to accommodate lengthy spontaneous testimony followed by conversion, for example. It is also rather common for a few congregants to arrive as much as an hour late, or for some to leave early. The combination of early departures and late arrivals results in a greater degree of movement by members of the congregation as compared to a white Protestant church, for example, where the service lasts for exactly one hour and, aside from one or two stragglers, the congregants start the service together and stay for the duration. In the end, the degree to which worship services run on time is determined by the pastor, and some are stricter in this regard than others.

Literal interpretation of the Psalms of David are cited as the scriptural basis for giving praise to the Lord by making music on all manner of instruments and dancing. Particular scriptures cited include Psalms 150:4, "praise him with stringed instruments," and 149:3, "Let them praise his name in the dance." In addition to the church band, many congregants "make a joyful noise" (Psalms 100:1) on a variety of percussion instruments brought from home and played from the pews. Among the most popular of these are the tambourine, cowbell, and hand cymbals. The old-fashioned washboard, rubbed with a bent wire coat hanger or other metal object, is rather uncommon today, but still used by a few.

The band is usually stationed at the front of the church, well to one side of the pulpit. The pews closest to the band are often occupied by boys and young men who aspire to be church musicians. Some of the younger boys may play along on plastic toy guitars and others may play "air drums" with a pair of drumsticks. Aspiring Keith Dominion musicians learn much by observing and imitating experienced church musicians.

In addition to the electric steel guitar, instruments played by members of the church band commonly include electric bass, electric guitar, a drum set, and quite frequently, a keyboard synthesizer. Older churches may have an organ, but even when an organ is present, the keyboard instrument most likely to be played is the synthesizer. The drums are church property and stay set up at the church at all times. Certainly the drums are a church fixture partially due to the effort required to move and assemble a full drum set. But more than that, drums are seen as essential to worship services. Many older members remember bygone days when the sole instrumental accompaniment was provided by one person beating on a bass drum. I have seen a worship service begun with a member holding the bass drum and beating on it while someone assembled the church drum kit, which had been temporarily removed from the church, probably for a special program held elsewhere. Percussion is a key element in Keith Dominion worship and most worshippers could hardly imagine a service without drums.

Another important element is the sound reinforcement system, or PA. Except in the most affluent churches with technically advanced facilities, the PA is used only for the vocal microphones in the pulpit area. The amplifiers for the steel guitar and other instruments are not connected to the PA. Consequently, by simply increasing the volume setting on the individual instrument amplifiers, the band can overpower the preachers and singers, whose voices are amplified over the PA at a set volume level.

Much of a worship service is led by one or more devotion leaders. Worship services begin when a devotion leader gives the call to worship taken from Psalm 100:1 and 2: "Make a joyful noise unto the Lord, all ye lands. Serve the Lord with gladness: come before His presence with singing." The devotion leader then usually leads the congregation in a slow tempo worship song such as "Thank You Lord" and the band joins in. Accompanied by the band, the devotion leader then segues into an up-tempo praise song such as "Praise the Lord Everybody" or "God Is a Good God." The energy and sense of excitement among the congregation builds. The band, in turn, plays with more energy, often with increasing loudness and accelerating tempo. Usually after about two or three minutes, singing is largely abandoned because the band has begun to play so loudly as to drown out even the strongest voice. Once the band becomes dominant and the singing ceases, the band often will take a cue from the steel guitarist to abandon the chord structure of the song they started with and go into a one-chord "drive." The repetitive, rhythmic drive portion of the praise music serves to elevate the energy of the service.

The drummer, whose instrument is not amplified, is affected by the increasing loudness of the band. Often within a short time the drummer is beating the skins at full volume and must resort to continual cymbal crashes in an effort to increase the energy level. Consequently, Keith Dominion drummers who have not played outside of church have a reputation for playing loudly and using excessive cymbal crashes. Those who choose to perform outside of church must learn to control their dynamics and use of the cymbals.

During the praise music sessions, congregants engage in "holy dancing," which among Keith Dominion congregations is usually simply called "dancing" or "shouting." The usage of "shout" among African Americans to refer to dance or dance-like movements of persons during worship services is rooted in the "ring shout" tradition. Today the ring shout is practiced by only a few residents of McIntosh County in the Georgia Sea Islands and largely forgotten by those inland; however the usage of "shout" to denote holy dancing is widespread among African Americans.[3] Some Keith Dominion congregants make a distinction between dancing and "shouting," citing the latter as vocal praise.[4] Others use the terms interchangeably or use "shout" to describe all, or nearly all, animated expressions of praise for the Lord. Every Keith and Jewell Dominion church has a generous space between the first row of pews and the pulpit area for dancing. The surface of the dance space is often wood or vinyl flooring; the remainder of the church floor is usually carpeted. Congregants may also dance in the aisles, especially in crowded situations, but generally the ushers will quickly escort them to the area at the front of the church that is intended for dancing, or shouting.

Holy dancing is done solo; many dancers explain they are dancing with Jesus. At any given moment there may be dancers who are involved on a variety of spiritual and physical levels. Some dance in an effort to become infused with the Holy Spirit, but will not arrive at that state during the course of the service. Others may become infused with the Spirit to some intermediate level, but remain more or less in control, and a few may be so infused with the Spirit that they appear to lose control over their bodies. They dance intensely, limbs twitch and jerk involuntarily, faces contort. Some may salivate heavily and their eyes roll back to expose only the whites. It is not uncommon for an individual to faint or "fall out" (at a revival there may be several persons who have fainted and lie on the floor). Although many congregants are deeply moved by preaching, music seems to play a key role in helping people become infused with the Holy Ghost to the point where they lose control of their actions. I saw a young man faint at the "Musicfest" held at the Keith Dominion church in Pompano Beach, Florida, in 2003, and preaching was not part of that event.

To help protect dancers and those experiencing spirit possession from harming themselves and others, a number of ushers are employed. Ushers are usually both male and female and can most often be identified by their white gloves or other white clothing. In some cases, female ushers are dressed entirely in white and look very much like nurses. Usually ushers wear a tag or badge that identifies them as such. For example, ushers at the Jewell Dominion revival held in Tupelo, Mississippi, on February 12, 2006, wore five-pointed star-shaped silvery metal badges about two inches wide with "USHER" stamped in the center.

Many churches feature a railing or low wall that surrounds the area where the musicians play, which serves to protect them from accidental physical contact by shouters. In situations where the service is especially "high," conditions are crowded, and there is no architectural barrier to protect the band from shouters, the ushers may provide a human barrier to protect the band. A musician—most often a steel guitarist, it seems—may become so filled with the Holy Spirit he or she stops playing to engage in dancing. I have seen Chuck Campbell so moved. At the Keith Dominion church in Ft. Pierce, Florida, I witnessed Frank Owens stop playing in the middle of a particularly intense praise session and rise from his pedal-steel guitar to shout. Clergy from the pulpit area guided Owens to prevent him from knocking down floral displays as he traveled from the band area to the dance floor (there was no architectural barrier). Bryan "Josh" Taylor, a young but very accomplished steel guitarist who has served as steel guitar mentor for Owens, sat down at Owens's instrument to continue the music at an even higher level of excitement.

Ocala, Florida, steel guitarist Antjuan Edwards told me that once when his great-uncle, Henry Nelson, played at the General Assembly in Nashville he became filled with the Holy Ghost, leapt over his steel guitar, and began to shout. Nelson's feat was especially dramatic because the band was located at the edge of the mezzanine level some twenty feet above the congregation and only a waist-level handrail prevented him from falling.

Most of the steel guitarists I have interviewed have experienced instances when they were overcome with the Holy Spirit. For example, Elder Elton Noble of Fort Pierce, Florida, vividly recalled: "One service got so high I stopped playin'. I jumped up and shot across the floor. Then I came back. The Spirit gets so high sometimes—and when you are engulfed in that Spirit—and you feeling all this power running through you and the church is in an uproar; they are already in an uproar and now it's falling on you. It's uncontrollable. So, I jumped up and I was gone. But then you got to get back to yourself and get back and sit down. 'Cause once you stop playing, the music's gone."[5]

The musicians do not really have a name, other than "jamming," for the music they play during this portion of the worship service. The word "jubilee" is sometimes used by musicians and clergy to describe the periods when the congregation dances and shouts. I have chosen to call the music "praise" or "shout" music. These terms seem agreeable to most musicians, members of the congregations, and clergy, but it should be understood that they are not necessarily terms used by them. This music and dance is not the same as contemporary "praise and worship" music and choreographed dance, which has become increasingly popular in many churches, including the Keith Dominion, in recent years.

A typical praise number may last six or eight minutes before the first "ending." Quite often the band will start up again at the urging of the congregation or clergy. A praise session may have three or four such "endings" before the music finally stops. The resumption of music and dancing after an attempt to end the praise music is a consequence of the energy generated by the musicians and the congregation. But beyond that, the repeated attempts to end the music are devices employed by the musicians, devotion leaders, and clergy to bring the congregation to a higher level of spiritual ecstasy. The multiple attempted endings are fully expected and provide a significant element in building the level of energy in a worship service.

The band members take their cues from the steel guitarist, who in turn takes his cues from the devotion leader or minister and the congregation. Unlike white country pedal-steel guitarists who usually sit staidly at their instruments and seldom look up at the audience, Keith Dominion steel guitarists frequently take their eyes off the fretboard and look up to watch the congregation and minister closely. They are animated and often engage in expressive body movements that may include rocking the torso from side-to-side or forward and back, dramatic flourishes of the picking hand, or closing the eyes and turning the head upward towards heaven.

Following the initial praise session, the devotion leader and congregation will sing a hymn such as "Father I Stretch My Hands to Thee." Often the hymn is "lined-out" or "raised," a practice that began in this country in the seventeenth century when enslaved Africans were not permitted to read. To line a hymn, the leader recites a line of the hymn and then he or she and the congregation sing the line together. The process is repeated until the hymn is completed. In many churches lined hymns are sung without instrumental accompaniment, but in the Keith Dominion the band always provides accompaniment. Generally, the band stops playing while the leader recites a line and returns when the congregation sings.

The hymn is followed by a group prayer led by one of the devotion leaders, or sometimes, a deacon or minister. During the group prayer the entire congregation, including the clergy seated in the pulpit area, kneels to pray. The person leading the prayer speaks over the PA and many congregants respond with "Yes Lord" or similar phrases of agreement. Often, after the leader finishes praying, several congregants will continue to pray aloud for a brief period. Again, spontaneity is a key concept. The prayers, although not sung to a melody, often have a musical quality, as congregants employ rhythm, dynamics, and various pitches as they pray. If a large percentage of the congregation prays aloud (as is often the case), their prayers fill the edifice with a powerful, multi-layered sound. Generally the musicians do not play during prayer and are expected to kneel or bow and pray along with the congregation. Sometimes they take advantage of the interlude to quietly tune up or make other adjustments to their instruments and equipment.

Following the prayer there will generally be another praise or jubilee session initiated by a devotion leader. This praise session may achieve a somewhat higher energy level than the first one, as the congregation and musicians may have received inspiration from the hymn and prayer. Again, the band and devotion leader may employ one or more false endings before the praise session comes to a more-or-less natural conclusion.

During the course of most worship services, probably most often during one of the jubilee or praise sessions, there will be at least one incidence of a member of the congregation who spontaneously rises from his or her seat on a pew to initiate a song—usually a fast spiritual such as "I'm a Soldier (In the Army of the Lord)" or "Can't Nobody Do Me Like Jesus." The steel guitarist and the other musicians are expected to know the song, find the key, and begin to provide accompaniment immediately. Often the person who initiated the song will sing off-key and out-of-time. Led by the steel guitarist, the musicians must draw the singer, who usually is quickly joined in song by other members of the congregation, into pitch and consistent rhythm.[6] The best musicians can accomplish the task very quickly and quite seamlessly. Less accomplished musicians may fumble around considerably and never get it right, ultimately failing in this function. Once the accompaniment is solidly established, most of the congregation has probably begun to sing along. The steel guitarist and rhythm section are expected to increase the energy level of song, which in turn will inspire the congregation. The ability of a steel guitarist to accompany spontaneous singing successfully is a quality that is valued highly by ministers and congregations, and consequently, a skill that steel guitarists conscientiously hone.

Following the second praise session, each devotion leader gives testimony over the PA, often dramatically citing specific areas in daily life in which Jesus Christ has provided guidance. If there has not yet been any spontaneous singing led by a member of the congregation, the devotion leader may then ask the congregation if there is a song they want to sing. Without fail someone from the congregation will respond by leading a song as the entire congregation and band join in. After the congregational singing, the devotion leader leads the congregation in group testimony and then asks if there is anyone who wishes to come forward with personal testimony. Usually one or more people testify dramatically as to how their faith has been challenged and how the Lord has helped them or their family, sometimes miraculously so. The testimony may involve a serious health challenge, an automobile accident, legal problems, financial difficulties, or all manner of personal struggles. The testifier may weep and tremble and often will ask the congregation to pray for him or her, or for loved ones.

The testimonies are followed by one ore more offerings. In Keith Dominion worship services the steel guitarist leads processional music for the offertory. The Jewell Dominion apparently ceased to practice offertory procession several years ago.[7] To begin the Keith Dominion ritual, ushers march to the front of the church with the collection plates, which they place on a table. Next, the ushers lead the congregants to file from their seats row-by-row, walk past the plates, deposit their contributions, and return to their seats. During the processions the church band provides music to stimulate a joyful, celebratory mood. Compared to the intense, driving praise or shout music, the offertory music is light and bouncy—a welcome and refreshing change for most congregants. If the music is good, the congregants smile and laugh and interact playfully, as they strut with a swagger similar to that of "second-liners" in a New Orleans post-funeral procession.

During special events, such as the General Assembly, the ushers who conduct the offertory procession (in this case all male) may dress in a uniform color theme, such as all white with gold cummerbunds. The ushers often engage in a swinging march that appears to be rehearsed but allows some degree of individual improvisation, such as twists, drops, or full 360-degree turns. Again, their movement reminds one of a New Orleans second-line dance-procession. The offertory music and swagger of the ushers serve to engage the congregants in a "celebration of giving" that will inspire them to contribute more freely and generously.

The music played for the offertory processions varies with region, preferences of the clergy in charge, and the nature of the worship service. For

House of God March

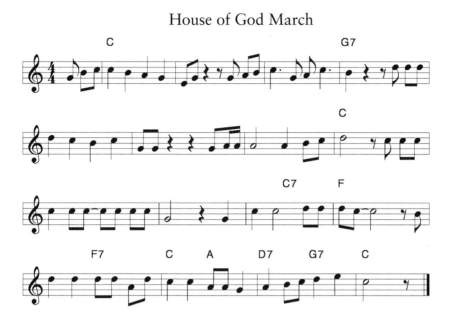

example, at the General Assembly in Nashville, the musicians understand that the congregation and the chief overseer expect to hear the "House of God March" and an instrumental medley that may include "When the Saints Go Marching In," "I'll Fly Away," "Down by the Riverside," "Children Go Where I Send Thee," and other spirituals. The "House of God March" is most often the first tune of the medley and, if the congregation is small and the offertory music is brief, it may be the only tune played for the procession. In a more liberal setting, Chuck Campbell, for example, may improvise very abstractly over any number of infectious mid-tempo boogie or shuffle grooves played by his family rhythm section during an offertory procession at a church under his father's responsibility. Such was the case with "Celebration in Giving" on Arhoolie CD 489, recorded live at the Keith Dominion church in Crescent City, Florida, as Chuck improvised freely over a I-flat III-IV chord progression boogie, which blues fans would identify with John Lee Hooker. Whatever the tune, the steel guitarist leads the band, improvising freely as his or her talent permits. Inspired improvisations are expected; playing it "straight" is almost unheard of.

The first time I heard the "House of God March" played by Aubrey Ghent at the "Family and Friends Day" assembly in Daytona Beach in

September, 1993, it sounded familiar. When I asked Ghent, some of the other musicians, and a few members of the congregation about the origins of the piece, no one seemed to know. Some referred to it as merely "the march," others called it the "House of God March." The chord changes of the "House of God March" are the same as "(Won't You Come Home) Bill Bailey," and "Just Because" (among dozens of other titles) and portions of Ghent's improvisations seemed quite close to those tunes. A little research unearthed some interesting connections.

The basic melody and chord changes of the tune are among the oldest in the repertoire of New Orleans jazz musicians. It is one of the strains (but not the whole tune) of "Tiger Rag." In a recorded reminiscence of pioneer jazz cornet player Charles "Buddy" Bolden (1877–1907), cornetist Willie G. "Bunk" Johnson (ca. 1879–1949) whistled the tune, stated that it was part of Bolden's repertoire, and demonstrated Bolden's improvisational style.[8] (There are no recordings of Bolden.) Johnson also stated that as a youngster he took music lessons at the Baptist School, located behind New Orleans University, from Professor Wallace Cutchey, a Mexican.[9] His Mexican connection is interesting to note; Mexican music, particularly that played by brass ensembles, was part of the milieu from which New Orleans jazz emerged. Today, the Mexico–New Orleans connection is frequently overlooked in casual considerations of the history of jazz.

Other interesting jazz recordings of the tune include "The Swing" by Johnny De Droit and the Arcadian Serenaders on the Okeh label in 1924,[10] and the "Dummy Song," recorded by the Hoosier Hot Shots in 1944 and by Louis Armstrong in 1953.[11] The latter two recordings are especially interesting, as the vocal melody of the "Dummy Song" is very close to the "House of God March" played "straight." It seems likely that early Keith Dominion musicians appropriated this popular tune from the folk canon and introduced it into their repertoire, and it then became known as "the march" or "The House of God March."

The tune can be traced to nineteenth century Mexico. In 1891, H. Genaro Codina (1852–1901) composed "Zacatecas," also known as "La Marcha de Zacatecas," for a competition organized by his brother-in-law, who was conductor of the Zacatecas Municipal Band (Zacatecas is the capital city of the state of Zacatecas). "Zacatecas" was an immediate success and was embraced by the political powers of the time. Codina's hometown of San José de la Isla, in the state of Zacatecas, was later renamed Genaro Codina in his honor. Today, the tune is commonly known as Mexico's "second national anthem" and enjoys worldwide popularity, especially among brass bands and orchestras. One section of "Zacatecas" is essentially the same melody as the "House of God March."

Following the offering, the church secretary makes local, state, and national announcements, most concerned with upcoming special events. At this point, approximately one hour has elapsed and the worship service is about halfway over. During the announcements the musicians may take a restroom break, and re-tune or otherwise adjust their instruments and equipment.

The pastor's sermon, or "message," follows the offering and announcements. Sermons generally last half an hour, maybe a little less, but it is not unusual for a sermon to be nearly an hour in length. A preacher begins a sermon with scriptural reading.[12] As he or she pauses between spoken lines, members of the congregation respond with confirmations such as "That's right," "Tell it," or "Amen." During this phase of the sermon the band is silent. After a few minutes the preacher will cease reading from the Bible and begin preaching extemporaneously. As the energy builds, the preacher strays from the podium and the presentation becomes increasingly animated. During this later phase the steel guitarist and other members of the band begin to work with the preacher to add dramatic emphasis to the sermon by playing short, often percussive, riffs between the preacher's vocalizations. The steel guitarist watches the preacher very closely and takes his cues from him or her. As the sermon continues to build in intensity the band becomes increasingly active in its role in helping the preacher to build the energy. The musical interludes between the preacher's utterances become longer and louder. The steel guitarist may play extended slurred moans on the bass strings, similar voice-like passages on the treble strings, or even imitate a woman's scream.

As the sermon approaches its climax, the preacher becomes highly animated, moving throughout the pulpit area, and may even come down from the pulpit into the dance area or, if using a cordless microphone, out among the congregation. Some of the most spirited preaching occurs during State Assemblies or other large events where several preachers are in attendance. In such cases it is common for the one in charge (the State Bishop in the case of a State Assembly) to allow each of four or five preachers eight or ten minutes to preach. When one Pentecostal preacher (or singer, or instrumentalist, for that matter) follows another, he or she invariably strives to generate more excitement than the one who preceded. The series of short sermons becomes a sort of preaching contest in which the preachers pull out all the stops. A preacher may leap from the pulpit to the dance floor area in great bounding steps, fall on his knees, or jump up and down repeatedly. If a cordless microphone is available, the preacher may travel down the aisle or into the pews to shake hands with members of the congregation or preach directly to certain individuals.

If the sermon is going well, by this time several congregants are on their feet, shouting responses to the preacher such as "Tell it preacher!" "Alright now!" or "Yes Lord!" Many hold their arms outstretched to feel the Spirit. The preacher then gives the band some sort of cue, which may range from a mere glance or nod to a more obvious waving of the arm, to begin playing praise music. Because the congregation is already in a spiritually aroused state, the energy builds rapidly. The praise music session that follows the sermon often results in the highest level of infusion of the Holy Ghost among congregants during a worship service. Following an especially inspired sermon, the whole congregation will be on its feet, with a good percentage dancing with abandon. The ushers are busy protecting those who have lost control of their physical actions. Often two or three ushers will join hands to encircle an individual filled with the Holy Ghost. If there are not enough ushers to protect those so infused with the Spirit, nearby congregants assume the role. Congregants not dancing will be clapping, vocalizing, and raising their hands, usually with palms vertical, to feel the Spirit.

The preacher and band may lead the congregation through several attempted endings and resumptions of the praise music. Each time the music stops the preacher may commence to preach and the band may take a cue from him or her to play more praise music until the preaching, praise music, and dancing comes to a more-or-less natural end.

The music played for the praise or shout sessions is some of the most distinctive in the Keith Dominion. Often the music has no chord changes, but rather consists of a number of phrases and rhythms played to "drive" the congregation. It is the same musical device used by "hard" gospel vocal groups such as the Blind Boys of Alabama. But while a vocal group will begin a song by singing a melody with harmonic movement and then at some point break into a "drive" section of repeated rhythmic phrases without chord changes, Keith Dominion musicians often start with the "drive" section and remain there. Henry Nelson's praise music was always one chord and drive, drive, drive. For example, immediately before starting the first round of praise music at the Mt. Canaan Keith Dominion church near Ocala, Florida, blind keyboardist Francine Jones asked Nelson what key they would begin in. His response was typical: "Get in E-flat and stay there."[13] For the highly spirited praise session and wholesale shouting that ensued for the next several minutes, E-flat was the only chord played.

Virtually all Keith and Jewell Dominion steel guitarists reiterate that when the worship service is "high" they are not in control of their playing, but are serving as a conduit for the Holy Spirit. They often record the worship service and are incredulous when they listen to the recording later. Josh Taylor, a talented young steel guitarist raised in Miami and now living in Atlanta, described his experience: "When the Spirit falls heavily it's the anointing that actually controls my playing. It's no longer me, it's the Holy Spirit within me that plays through me. When you play in the Spirit, a lot of times you won't remember what you played because when the Holy Spirit takes over and plays through you, you're actually playing new melody. And it's melody that most of the time nobody has ever heard before. And even yourself, you're shocked."[14]

Veteran Jewell Dominion steel guitarist Sonny Treadway of Deerfield Beach, Florida, offered a similar perspective: "Some of the stuff I do, I don't know I done it myself when I hear it—notes and slurs and whatever. I really can't picture it until I hear a tape and play it back again and I still can't figure it out: When did it happen? So much is coming when I'm really into it. I get set into it and my hands was shaking. Like last Sunday; it was beautiful. And I didn't have no control of it."[15]

After the sermon and the praise or shout session that follows, there is usually a call to the altar for group prayer. If the congregation is small enough, as it usually is at a routine Sunday morning service, all or most of the members will gather at the altar to pray, many kneeling. During this portion of the service, the band plays music that is sweet and melodic and slow in tempo, often "Come to Jesus." The pastor may ask if there is anyone in the congregation who is ready to receive the Holy Ghost; usually he or she has sensed if there is a member of the congregation who is at that point. If someone does come forward, the minister, often assisted by one or more members of the congregation, will assist the person in "seeking" the Holy Spirit by repeating certain phrases. For example, evangelist and minister Elder Elton Noble may tell a seeker, "Keep your mind on Jesus. Picture Him on the cross. He died for you. He has forgiven you for your sins. Just give on up to the Lord. Let Him come in. Go ahead on and receive."[16]

Some members of the congregation have a special talent for helping those who seek the Holy Ghost to keep focused. "I have worked with plenty of seekers," stated Elder Elton Noble. "When someone is there to help them keep their mind focused on what they're trying to obtain, it's much easier, and they come through much quicker."[17] Again, flexibility is a key concept: the entire congregation is expected to stay in support of the one seeking the Holy Ghost, regardless of how long it may take. The musicians generally continue to play music appropriate for the situation, usually instrumental versions of hymns or slow-tempo gospel standards. "We had one young lady say she wanted to receive the Holy Ghost on that Sunday and it was a quarter till two," Elder Noble recalled of a recent experience. "So you make way for that individual. She said she wants to get on her knees, she wants to call on the Lord. So, we accommodate her and the members stay to be help in that service. And the girl did receive the Holy Ghost on that day. I believe we left there at probably 3:15."[18]

When the call to the altar, group prayer, and any spontaneous conversions are concluded, the minister gives a final prayer and benediction and the congregation is released.

The Role of the Steel Guitarist in Worship Services

The steel guitarist leads the band during all the music played for worship services, with the exception of special pieces (choral performances, for example) that may be led by the choral conductor or keyboardist. Except for the early stages of the sermon, announcements, and personal testimony, the steel guitarist and rhythm section play constantly during the worship service. In a typical Sunday morning worship service lasting from 11:30 A.M. until 2:00 P.M., the steel guitarist may play 75 or 80 percent of the time, or almost two hours. In the Keith Dominion, the steel guitar is clearly the dominant musical instrument, more so than in any other musical tradition that comes to mind, even to the point of diminishing the importance of singers. There are many talented, even exceptional, singers in the Keith Dominion, but the steel guitar often seems to overshadow them. It is louder, outlasts the singers, and usually brings the praise sessions to a climax some time after the instruments have drowned out even the most powerful and enduring vocalists. And, in the hands of a musician adept at the rhythmic, percussive strumming known as "framming" and other techniques, the steel guitar is capable of creating syncopated, driving rhythms that can further help take a praise session to elevated levels.

Often, especially when the steel guitarist is young and relatively inexperienced, there is some amount of tension between musician and minister.

When not properly controlled, the steel guitar and its powerful amplifier have the capacity to interfere with what the minister or devotion leader is trying to accomplish. If a musician plays too loudly or shows off, most ministers will react immediately. According to Elder Elton Noble:

> Seasoned preachers and evangelists let the musicians know. And they'll speak into that mic and say, "Hey, y'all turn it down." And that draws attention to that musician, and it comes from the congregation. It can be embarrassing. It's up to that minister. You can't go in there light-footed, not using that authority, because it's not about that musician. It's about those souls out there. You have people out there that's hurting. You have people that are going through things in their home. It's not about that musician.[19]

An experienced steel guitarist knows the personality of a minister, how they work, what his or her preferences are, and has a sense of the minister's boundaries and limits.

Not every church has a steel guitarist among its members. In such cases a steel guitarist may be paid to travel from another location. For example, when Alvin Lee is not playing rhythm guitar with the Lee Boys for concerts and festivals, he has a standing invitation from the pastor at the Keith Dominion in Palatka, about one hundred miles north of Lee's Orlando home, to play for Sunday morning worship services. Steel guitarist Antjuan Edwards gave this assessment of the importance of the steel guitar in the Keith Dominion: "Like you would go in a Baptist church and maybe you look for the organ player or the piano player. And if he's not there a lot of people look funny, you know, look around. Well, in our church if the steel player's not there, a lot of people would say, 'Well, we going to have good church?' That's the kind of impact that the steel has had on the church."[20]

Revivals and Other Special Church Meetings

The tradition of Christian revivals among African Americans can be traced to the Great Awakening of the eighteenth century.[21] Generally, Keith Dominion dioceses conduct revivals at least annually. In a state with a large number of churches, such as Florida, for example, several revivals may be conducted each year. Revivals serve a number of functions. As the term implies, they present an opportunity for those who have previously received the Holy Ghost to revive or strengthen their faith. For those "backsliders" who have not been attending church regularly or have otherwise strayed from a life of holiness, revivals are a means through which they may renew their faith and commitment. For those who attend church regularly but have not yet received the Holy Ghost, revivals present an intensive, charged, large-group atmosphere conducive to becoming infused with the Holy Spirit. Newcomers are invited to attend and participate and may experience conversion. The excitement of the revival moves many people to join the church.

Today, Keith Dominion revivals are most often conducted during the evening from Monday through Friday, but occasionally may continue for two full weeks. Weeknight revival meetings usually begin at 7:00 or 7:30 and conclude by 10:30 or 11:00 P.M. On the final night, if the service is "high" and many receive the Holy Ghost, the revival may continue until after midnight.

Revivals share many of the elements present in the weekly Sunday morning worship service, including congregational singing, prayer, a scriptural lesson, a sermon, and one or more offerings. But the emphasis is on dramatic preaching and the invitation to individuals to come forward to seek the Holy Ghost. The preaching at revivals is often especially fiery and animated and frequently accomplished by a team of ministers, including the State Evangelist or special guest evangelists brought in from other states.

Revivals are among the longest and most intense Keith Dominion meetings. At peak time during a successful revival there may be more than two hundred people in attendance, and perhaps two dozen who have come forward to seek the Holy Ghost in the area normally used for shouting and dancing. Each seeker is usually assisted by one to three people who are skilled in helping seekers maintain their focus and receive the Holy Spirit. As in the Sunday morning and Friday night tarry services, those who assist utter a continuous series of verbal messages to the seekers. The general level of ambient sound necessitates that they speak directly into the seeker's ear. The seekers often become quite warm and those who attend them will cool them by waving one of the ubiquitous paper fans. Those who receive the Holy Ghost often engage in glossolalia, or speaking in tongues. Some may faint and fall to the floor. The ushers stand by them while they are down and help them rise when they are ready. At a lively revival there may be as many as half a dozen people who have fainted and lie on the floor.

Music plays an important role in revivals and most musicians are eager to play at them. Evangelist, pastor, and steel guitarist Elder Elton Noble offered some personal perspective:

Big revivals draw good musicians. Like my aunt G. C. Campbell, she comes down from Carolina. If she goes to the East Coast [of Florida] every musician on the East Coast is going to come. And if she's preaching for a week they want to get a chance to play in that service because they know it's going to be hot.

I did a revival in Perrine. I looked around; there was a lot of musicians in the house, 'cause they know that was going to be a hot week. They would like to play in that service, you know. At revivals a musician is going to play longer than he normally plays in a Sunday service. And that very well may be one of the things too that helps draw them, because they know that their playing time can be *hot*.[22]

Probably the most significant statewide event is the annual State Assembly. The term "State Assembly" can be the source of some confusion when a state is divided into regions. In Florida, for example, the East Coast, West Coast, and North Florida dioceses each have a "State Assembly," which is attended only by members of that specific diocese and the bishop who presides over it (who may reside in another state). Each state (or diocese if the state is so divided) usually has one musician designated by the Presiding Bishop as the "state" steel guitarist, who plays at the State Assembly and other statewide events. If a designated "state" steel guitarist is not available, the presiding bishop may bring in musicians from outside the state. For example, Chuck, Phil, and Darick Campbell traveled for years with their father, Bishop Charles E. Campbell, to play for his assemblies and other special meetings in Florida and Georgia. All of the Campbells are based in Rochester, New York, except for Darick, who resides in Macon, Georgia.

The largest special event is the General Assembly, which is conducted for ten days in mid-June each year at the headquarters church in Nashville, Tennessee. (The Jewell Dominion General Assembly is held at their headquarters church in Indianapolis, Indiana, during June.) For many members, the General Assembly is an annual highlight and somewhat of a pilgrimage. People take leave from work, with many putting their jobs in jeopardy so they may attend, and travel great distances to participate. The energy level of Keith Dominion services, which may be measured by the amount and intensity of shouting, increases dramatically with the size of the congregation. The Keith Dominion General Assembly often draws more than 2,500 at peak time and the energy level is among the highest the congregants ever experience. It is a great honor for musicians to be selected to play at the General Assembly and to serve at that event does much to strengthen a musician's reputation, both nationally and locally.

Measures of Success

While concertgoers and aspiring musicians may be impressed with pyrotechnic playing, the real measure of success for steel guitarists who play for church meetings is how the congregation responds. A successful steel guitarist must provide praise music that will aid the congregation to become infused with the Holy Spirit. Often the music is not especially interesting for mere listening. It is my observation that the most effective praise music in terms of building the energy of a worship service and inducing people to dance and shout is often very repetitive and rather monotonous on casual listening. In fact, it seems that the repetitive nature of the music contributes significantly to aiding the congregation in becoming infused with the Holy Ghost. "It's not the idea of playing as good as another man, 'cause everybody who plays, plays good. It's the idea of a man playing more fancier than you," veteran steel guitarist and minister Elder Acorne Coffee stated philosophically. "But on any given day if you are playing in the church for God's service, the Lord come in and everybody will forgive everybody else while they're shouting off your music. So it don't make a difference."[23]

As Elder Coffee implies, even if the skill level of the steel guitarist and rhythm section is rather rudimentary, if they are working closely with the devotion leader, minister, and congregation, the musicians will be successful in terms of energizing the congregation and helping them become infused with the Holy Spirit. Fancy playing and hot licks just do not matter that much to a congregation.

An expert steel guitarist knows how to add just the right sounds between a preacher's utterances in order to complement a sermon. The accomplished steel guitarist watches the preacher and congregation closely and is familiar with the minister's method of delivery and the structure of his or her sermons. If the steel guitarist–preacher relationship is working well, the cues that the steel guitarist takes from the minister are all but invisible to even the most attentive observer.

The successful steel guitarist must be versatile. In addition to playing fiery praise music to drive the congregation to shout, he or she must be able to render hymns and meditation music delicately and expressively. Speaking from a minister's point of view, Bishop Charles E. Campbell, father of musical brothers Chuck, Phil, and Darick, asserted:

> Now, I teach my boys, I say to them—and this is where we have had some struggle—you need to watch the floor. Watch what's going on . . .

One thing we do, if you'll notice in our services, we call "the breakdown." When you get it in high and everybody's jumpin' and getting emotional with you, we say, "Break it down. Lower it down." Put in a certain thing—and I mean you may need a hymn, or what have you—something touching that people can relate to. And they start to thinking about the Lord and themselves and how far they're down, and how they need to be lifted up, and just whatever. Just give 'em . . . at least a minute and a half of that. And then you can go into anything you want to and they'll jump, 'cause you've got 'em in that "zone" [where] everything flies.[24]

As Bishop Campbell suggests, the contrast between a poignantly rendered hymn and fiery, driving praise music can help bring congregants into a "zone" in which they have surrendered themselves to the power of the Holy Spirit. A young steel guitarist may be skilled at delivering effective praise music early in his or her musical life, but the ability to execute passionately rendered hymns and slower gospel melodies often comes much later. Being skilled at both is the mark of a mature musician.

A successful Keith Dominion steel guitarist must be able to play all the functional music needed for regular church services and special meetings. He or she must be constantly attentive to the congregation and the devotion leaders, preachers, evangelists, and others who conduct the services. A seasoned steel guitarist knows the preferences of the clergy in charge and delivers just the right music to help him or her achieve their goals at every point of the service. As leader of the church band, the steel guitarist must provide musical cues to the band members they can follow quickly and easily. A mature Keith Dominion steel guitarist working with an experienced band will do it all so seamlessly that they appear to read the minds of both clergy and congregation. They all are, as they say, "on one accord." It is demanding work that is usually made even more demanding due to a sound reinforcement system that is at best rudimentary, as well as a lack of monitor speakers for the band. Musicians who perform outside of church will invariably state that such performances are, even under the worst circumstances, much easier than playing for church meetings. However, in terms of the spiritual intensity and transformative power of the music, festival and concert performances pale in comparison to playing in church.

The electric steel guitar is an instrument ideally suited for African American Pentecostal worship services. In the hands of a skilled player the steel guitar becomes another voice, a voice that can have all the subtle variations in dynamic level (loudness), pitch, tonal color, and ornamentation of a human voice. The instrument can also create "voices"—such as the howling sound achieved by Jewell Dominion steel guitarists, for example—that are beyond human vocal expressions. The steel guitar is also capable of providing driving rhythm, a very important element of the "jubilee" or "praise" portions of a service. This rhythm is a key factor in helping dancers become infused with the Holy Spirit. While certain wind instruments such as the saxophone or the trombone, for example, may be capable of approximating the human voice, or producing a singing tone, they are incapable of producing the rich variety of rhythms available to the steel guitarist. Steel guitars, especially the pedal variety, are also capable of producing harmonized passages and rich chords. And of course, an amplified steel guitar can be as loud as necessary to elevate the energy of the service to a very high level.

The steel guitar has its origins in the Hawaiian popular music fad that began in the early part of the twentieth century and eventually made its way into African American sacred music. But the public is generally uninformed of how the Hawaiian steel guitar entered mainland popular music and eventually became an important element of a number of musical traditions, from classic country and bluegrass to various forms of sacred music. The instrument itself, although presently enjoying a revival of interest, remains uncommon—most retail music stores do not stock them—and misunderstood. It is worthwhile then, to briefly explore the origins of the steel guitar, its entry into mainland popular and secular music, and the evolution of a few of the most common varieties of the instrument.

The Steel Guitar

Steel guitar, slide guitar, bottleneck guitar, Hawaiian guitar, lap-steel, pedal-steel, Dobro—these terms are commonly used today, but what do they mean? Not even those who make or play the many variants of the instrument agree on a basic terminology. This brief chapter attempts to clear some of the confusion that surrounds the instruments employed by the musicians of the Keith and Jewell Dominions.

The steel guitar takes its name from the bar, sometimes called the "tone bar," that right-handed players hold in the left hand and place lightly on one or more strings to make notes. The first bars were made of steel, thus the name of the instrument. Although steel remains the most popular material, today bars are made from a variety of materials including glass, brass, zirconium, plastics, and ceramics. Similarly, the materials from which the instrument itself might be made include wood, plastics, brass, aluminum, and even modern synthetic composites. The materials from which the steel guitar is made have nothing to do with its name. The instrument is named for the most common bar material: steel.

The steel guitar is said to have been invented in Hawaii in the late nineteenth century, exactly when and by whom are specifics that may be debated at length. The most common claim is that Joseph Kekuku began to use a metal object to make notes on a guitar at age eleven in 1885.[1] The popular story is that while walking along a railroad track strumming his guitar he picked up a bolt and ran it across the strings of his instrument to produce the characteristic slurred, singing sound of the steel guitar. Kekuku was by no means the first person to make notes on a string instrument in this manner; similar methods have been used in Africa and Asia for centuries. In Hawaii, the instrument became known as *kikā kila* (kikā: guitar; kila: steel); in the mainland United States it became known as the "Hawaiian steel guitar," "Hawaiian guitar," or simply the "steel guitar." The term "Hawaiian guitar" is another source of confusion. Early in the twentieth century, the term was sometimes used for the instrument now known as the ukulele. Today, "Hawaiian guitar" is sometimes (many would say erroneously so) used to denote "slack key" guitar, the Hawaiian manner of finger-picking the standard guitar (usually an acoustic version) in any number of open tunings.

While Kekuku's claim to be the inventor of steel guitar may be disputed by some, it is clear that he did much to develop steel guitar technique and popularize the instrument. In 1893–94, while a student at the Kamehameha School for Boys in Honolulu, he experimented at length in the machine shop to make a bar suitable for his technique. After trying several shapes, he ultimately settled for a slim, solid-steel cylinder about four inches long. He began to realize that the *kikā kila* technique was more than a novelty and worked hard to develop a degree of mastery. On a steel guitar the strings are raised high above the frets (or position markers). When the bar is placed on the strings to make notes, the strings do not touch the fretboard. Steel guitars are played horizontally. Because the pitch of notes played on the steel guitar is determined by the placement of the bar and not restricted by fixed frets, an adept steel guitarist may execute subtle variations in pitch, seamless glissandi, and unrestricted vibrato—techniques that result in sounds that the player of a standard, fretted guitar may approximate but cannot duplicate.

Kekuku became an accomplished steel guitarist and did much to popularize the sound of the instrument, presenting concert performances to his classmates at the Kamehameha School for Boys and to the general public at various venues in Honolulu.[2] Many other Hawaiians soon took up the instrument.

Kekuku became a professional musician and, in 1904, departed for the United States mainland to work as an entertainer. Many other Hawaiian musicians came to the U.S. mainland to perform too—some before Kekuku—and Hawaiian music and dance became quite popular during the first decade of the twentieth century. In 1915, the Panama-Pacific Exposition was held in San Francisco to celebrate the completion of the Panama Canal. It proved to be a major showcase for Hawaiian music and fueled an interest that quickly blossomed into a popular music craze of unprecedented magnitude.

More than seventeen million visitors attended the Panama-Pacific Exposition during its seven-month run.[3] The territory of Hawaii viewed this as an important opportunity to present and promote its culture, land,

and products. The main attraction at the Hawaii Pavilion was the show that presented Hawaiian music and dance. The music created a sensation, as untold thousands heard Hawaiian songs and instruments for the first time. The steel guitar was one of the signature sounds of the music and the lush vibrato, harmonized legato passages, and chords played with sweeping glissandi became elements of the popular concept of a "Hawaiian" sound.[4] Tin Pan Alley responded with a flood of "Hawaiian" songs that further increased the momentum of the worldwide Hawaiian music fad. Hawaiian steel guitarists appeared on thousands of recordings, toured extensively, and performed for radio broadcasts. Many, including Joseph Kekuku, established permanent residence in the mainland United States. The business of teaching Hawaiian steel guitar was also established, as many artists opened studios or endorsed instruction method books for publishing companies.

The popularization of Hawaiian steel guitar throughout the continental United States resulted in syncretism with African American musical forms. Hawaiian popular music played and recorded on the mainland often included jazz and blues. Similarly, the sound of the steel guitar was heard in African American jazz, blues, and gospel. Black musicians often used the neck of a glass bottle, or a piece of metal tubing placed over one finger of the left hand—often the pinky—to make notes in the "Hawaiian" manner. The techniques became known as "slide" or "bottleneck" guitar. (Some players modified the instrument to raise the strings higher above the fretboard to get a cleaner sound when using the slide technique, others did not.) This arrangement also allowed musicians to fret notes with two or three fingers of the left hand. Unlike their Hawaiian counterparts, who played the steel guitar placed horizontally on their lap, the bottleneck players held their guitars in the conventional vertical position.[5] There has been much debate as to how much Hawaiian popular music influenced African American bottleneck guitarists, and certainly much of their music does not have the languid, legato sound so often associated with Hawaiian music. But as we shall see, more than one early "sacred steel" musician had a direct connection to Hawaiian popular music.

The earliest steel guitars were simply acoustic guitars modified for the purpose by installing an adaptor nut (the nut is the grooved piece, near the tuning pegs, that the strings rest on) to raise the strings above the fretboard. When played in an ensemble, the relatively quiet sound of the acoustic guitar is easily overcome by louder instruments and strong voices. In the quest to produce a louder, brighter sound and to help sustain notes of longer duration, acoustic steel guitars were fitted with strings made from steel rather than the traditional gut. By the 1920s, instruments made specifically to be played as steel guitars were produced commercially. To produce a strong tone, most steel guitarists wear picks on the thumb and some of the fingers (usually the first two) of the right hand.

In a quest to make the acoustic guitar louder, brothers John and Rudy Dopyera of the National Company introduced a few prototypes of a revolutionary guitar in 1926.[6] The "tri-plate," which became more popularly known as the "tri-cone," featured three six-inch diameter aluminum resonator cones, which functioned as mechanical speakers, housed in an art deco-inspired, shiny nickel-plated body of German silver (a copper-nickel-zinc alloy). These loud, highly playable, and smart looking instruments were accepted enthusiastically by musicians. Among the first to play the National tri-cone was Sol Hoopii (1902–53), one of the most highly regarded steel guitarists of his, or any, generation. He recorded "Farewell Blues" / "Stack O'Lee Blues" (Columbia 797-D) with one of the prototypes in October 1926.[7] As a result of that recording, the tri-cone rocketed into popularity virtually overnight. National went into commercial production of the tri-cone in 1927.[8] The first instruments were fitted with thick necks designed for Hawaiian-style playing from the lap by stopping the strings with a steel bar. By 1928, "Spanish neck" models were introduced for playing in the conventional manner of stopping the strings by pressing them onto frets with the fingers of the left hand (for right-handed players).[9] The square neck National tri-cone quickly became the favorite of many top Hawaiian steel guitar performers and recording artists. National expanded their line of instruments to include single-cone resonator guitars with bodies made of wood, steel, brass, and nickel-silver.[10] The National resonator guitars had a unique, strong sound that has endured. Today, players and collectors alike value vintage Nationals highly, and several companies produce reproductions similar to the classic Nationals of the 1920 and 1930s. The success of the metal Nationals has also contributed to confusion surrounding the term "steel guitar." Many people today refer to any metal-bodied guitar—even those made of brass or German silver—whether played in the Hawaiian manner or not, as a "steel guitar."

John and Rudy Dopyera later broke off from National to make resonator instruments under the brand name Dobro (today the trademark is owned by the Gibson Guitar Company). Dobros always have been and continue to be made with either square necks for Hawaiian-style playing or round, fretted necks for conventional "Spanish" style playing. Today the wood-bodied, single resonator Dobro is commonly identified with bluegrass music played in what might be described as a "modified Hawaiian technique" that incorporates the frequent use of bluegrass banjo rolls, hammer-ons, pull-offs, and blues licks. Common usage of the term "Dobro" today usually refers to this bluegrass application, regardless of whether the instrument is a genuine Dobro or a resonator guitar made by some other company or an independent luthier. Ironically, while the Dobro, or resonator guitar, played with a steel bar and seen so often in bluegrass bands, is probably the most common type of acoustic steel guitar heard in the mainland United States today, it is rarely referred to as a steel guitar.

Electric steel guitars were first commercially produced in 1932 by the Ro-Pat-In Company, which would later become Rickenbacher, then Rickenbacker.[11] The first electrics were Hawaiian models, a fact that gives testimony to the popularity of Hawaiian music and the steel guitar at that time. Electrification brought two very important enhancements to the instrument: increased dynamic range (loudness) and increased ability to sustain notes of long duration. While there was some resistance to the new sound of the electric Spanish-neck guitar played in the conventional manner, Hawaiian-style players, that is, steel guitarists, quickly embraced the new technology.

Stopping the strings with a steel bar, rather than with the fingers, introduces certain physical limitations. Accomplished guitarists who play in the conventional manner learn how to use the fingers of the left hand to form a large number of chords and play harmonized passages on two or more strings. Playing the steel guitar with a rigid bar is analogous to using just one finger of the left hand to make notes on a standard guitar. To deal with this limitation, virtually all steel guitarists tune their instruments so the open strings form a chord. The steel guitarist is limited to the available intervals he or she can make by holding the bar straight across the strings or, using a more advanced technique, by turning, or "slanting" the bar at a precise angle to change the musical intervals available. The earliest steel guitar tunings were simply major chords. As steel guitar technique developed, many players explored a variety of tunings.

Increasing the number of strings also added to the harmonic possibilities of the instrument. For the most part, strings were added to increase the variety of harmonic intervals rather than merely to increase the range of pitch. For example, an eight-string C6 tuning might be G-A-C-E-g-a-c-e, where the top, or first, string is the same pitch as that of a conventional guitar and the bottom G-string is a minor third above the low E-string of standard guitar tuning. In this tuning, by plucking selected strings or strumming across three or more adjacent strings, a steel guitarist may play major, major 6th, minor, and minor seventh chords without having to slant the bar. A closer look at the C6 tuning reveals intervals of a major second between strings 4 and 3, a minor third between strings 3 and 2, and a major third between strings 2 and 1—important intervals for playing two-part harmony and for easily rendering melodies.

Because the electric steel guitar does not require a large, resonant body to produce sound, it made practical another important development in the evolution of the instrument: multiple necks, each in a different tuning. The multi-neck instruments featured two to four necks, usually eight strings each, thus greatly broadening the harmonic possibilities.[12] Multi-neck, solid-body electric steel guitars were uncomfortably heavy to be played on the lap, so they were usually fitted with telescoping legs, which offered another important advantage: the steel guitarist could stand while playing. Playing from a standing position gave the steel guitarist increased mobility and visibility and allowed the player to become more animated—a big plus for performing artists.

As the electric guitar evolved so did controls, amplifiers, and other devices that affected the timbre and loudness of the sound. The first electric guitars had no controls at all; loudness was controlled at the amplifier. Very soon a volume control knob was added, followed by a tone control knob. Players of electric guitars, both steel and standard, soon discovered they could affect the properties of notes by manipulating the volume and tone controls while playing. Picking a string with the volume reduced during the attack then increasing the volume by rolling the knob with the third or fourth finger of the picking hand immediately after picking made the notes swell with a voice-like (some say violin-like) quality and helped notes sustain a reasonable level of volume for an increased duration of time. A similar manipulation of the tone control—bass tone during attack, then rolled to treble tone after attack—produced an effect popularly known as "wah." Some musicians even manipulated the volume and tone controls simultaneously. Later, foot-operated volume pedals and combination volume/tone pedals were developed. (These pedals were *not* what put the "pedal" in "pedal-steel" guitar.) Today, many Keith Dominion steel guitarists incorporate manipulation of the volume and tone controls mounted on their instruments into their playing. Henry Nelson was a master of the knob-spinning techniques. Nelson's son, Aubrey Ghent, and Darick

Campbell are examples of contemporary Keith Dominion steel guitarists who are adept at the technique.

Over the years, the variety of effects available to electric guitarists has continued to grow. In addition to reverberation and overdrive (a form of distortion), the most common effect favored by Keith Dominion steel guitarists is the wah pedal. Most often they use the wah pedal at a fairly constant level to affect the timbre of notes, as opposed to the more common pedal pumping, which produces the wah-wah effect. Lorenzo Harrison, who conventionalized the steel guitar style in the Jewell Dominion, was a master of using the wah pedal as a tone control. He began to use the Morley Rotating Wah pedal in the early 1970s, which enabled him to produce a piercing, howling sound that seemed to penetrate to the very core of congregants' souls; this is the sound that nearly all Jewell Dominion steel guitarists try to replicate today. Chuck Campbell and other steel guitarists brought Harrison's use of the wah pedal sound—or something close to it—into the Keith Dominion soundscape.

As mentioned earlier, one of the limitations of the steel guitar was the number of chords available, even when using instruments with multiple necks and applying virtuoso bar slanting techniques. As early as the 1930s, steel guitar makers began to experiment with mechanical designs that permitted the musician to easily change the pitch intervals between the instrument's strings without having to employ the difficult slanted-bar technique or stop to re-tune. The earliest designs incorporated simple lever-operated mechanisms that provided the steel guitarist with two or three different open-chord tunings; however, changing to another tuning could only be accomplished when the instrument was silenced. Further developments resulted in pedal-steel guitars, which incorporated a more complex mechanism operated by foot-pedals and knee-levers that made it possible to change the pitch of each string independently while playing. But the pedal-steel guitar was not especially well-received for some time.

In 1954, Bud Isaacs played a pedal-steel guitar solo on country star Webb Pierce's hit recording "Slowly," in which he used the pedals to change the pitch of one or two strings while the strings were sounding, a technique that contributed to the twangy sound associated with electric country music.[13] Isaac's solo simultaneously rung in the acceptance of the pedal-steel guitar in country music and marked the end of popularity of steel guitars played without pedals among country musicians.[14] By the 1970s, sales of non-pedal steel guitars had diminished to just a few units. By 1981, no major manufacturer was making any type of steel guitar—with or without pedals. Since that time, electric steel guitars have been made by a handful of independent companies.[15]

Although the electric steel guitar has been played in Keith Dominion services since the late 1930s, to my knowledge the earliest appearance of the *pedal*-steel guitar in the Keith Dominion was when steel guitarist Robert "Bobby" Tolliver (1928–) played one for services in Dayton, Ohio, in 1952. While many of his peers took an interest in the new instrument, most stayed with their non-pedal steel guitars during the 1950s and 1960s. By the early 1970s, the pedal-steel guitar became popular among Keith Dominion musicians for two reasons. First, because the non-pedal instruments were not being manufactured and were becoming increasingly difficult to find. But more importantly, the technical advantages of the instrument were being applied to the Keith Dominion musical tradition in a manner that fit the music. Although there were (and still are) many challenges and negotiations surrounding the pedal-steel guitar and the music made on it, the music was largely accepted by the musicians, congregants, and clergy. Today, the pedal-steel is the instrument of choice of most of the younger musicians and many of the senior steel guitarists in the Keith Dominion. However, a number of mature steel guitarists among them choose the "lap," or non-pedal, variety, and even more play both lap-steel and pedal-steel. Nearly all the steel guitarists in the Jewell Dominion play lap-steel guitars. Often they use pedal-steel guitars that have had the pedals and pitch-changing mechanisms removed.

The pedal-steel guitar configuration used by most country musicians is two ten-string necks: one in a hybrid tuning known as "E9 chromatic" and the other tuned to C6, often with an added 9th (d) on top and a low 4th (F). Keith Dominion pedal-steel guitarists favor instruments with one neck of ten to twelve strings (Robert Randolph is presently using a thirteen-string neck). Although there is some variety in tunings, most Keith Dominion pedal-steel guitarists use a tuning based on E major or E7. Modern pedal-steel guitars permit the guitarist to raise or lower the pitch of any string as much as three halftones, although two halftones is the more common limit. In addition to using foot-pedals to change the pitch, levers that dangle from the underside of the instrument chassis are operated by the player's knees. The normal practical limit is five knee-levers: left-knee left, right, and vertical; and right-knee left and right. Right-knee vertical movement is reserved for the foot-operated volume control. (Some instruments are fitted with two sets of left knee levers, for a total of eight.) The maximum number of foot-pedals is a function of the space available on the instrument. Seven is a popular number, but instruments with nine or more have been built. All pedal-steel guitars are made in small shops, and custom orders for instruments with foot-pedals and knee-levers configured to the client's specific requests are common. All the knee-levers and pedals are fully programmable (mechanically) according to the musician's preferences. The steel guitarist (or technician) may set up each individual knee-lever or foot-pedal to increase or decrease the pitch of a particular string by one, two, or three halftones as dictated by the limits of the particular design. The possibilities are virtually endless.

Terminology

In an effort to minimize confusion, I have developed the following definitions for use throughout this book. The reader should remember that these definitions are peculiar to this author and that others may define the terms differently.

- *Steel guitar*—An acoustic or electric guitar played in the horizontal plane by stopping the strings with a bar of hard material held in the left hand (for right-handed playing).
- *Bottleneck* or *slide guitar*—An acoustic or electric guitar played in the vertical plane using a "slide" made of hard material, such as metal, glass, or ceramic, held in the left hand (for right-handed playing) to stop the strings. Notes fretted by the fingers of the left hand may (or may not) be used in combination with notes made by stopping the strings with the slide.
- *Lap-steel guitar* (also known as *Hawaiian steel guitar*)—An acoustic or electric steel guitar that does not have pitch-changing pedals or levers. Included in this category are acoustic resonator guitars (including Dobro brand instruments), multi-neck steel guitars, steel guitars fitted with legs, and steel guitars played from stands. Although it may seem inconsistent and awkward to refer to a multi-neck instrument on four telescoping legs played from a standing position, or a Dobro strapped to a musician who plays standing, as lap-steel guitars, the instrument itself (aside from the legs or strap) is essentially the same as an instrument played from the lap. The term "lap-steel" is widely used by many steel guitarists—but by no means all—and music journalists today.

- *Pedal-steel guitar*—A steel guitar fitted with pitch-changing pedals and/ or levers. Pedal-steel guitars are electric instruments. Some makers have fitted pedals, usually operated by the palm of the right hand, to acoustic steel guitars, but such instruments are generally considered experimental and are not at all common. Because of the great popularity of the pedal-steel guitar in country and western music, many people mistakenly refer to any electric steel guitar, especially if it is mounted on legs, as a pedal-steel. Consequently, musicians who play the lap-steel guitar may use the term "non-pedal" steel guitar to explain their instrument. To further complicate the issue, many lap-steel guitarists use a foot-operated volume control pedal or a wah pedal. The volume and wah pedals are not the "pedal" in pedal-steel guitar.

The electric steel guitar seems perfectly suited to Pentecostal worship. Certainly, the Keith Dominion and Jewell Dominion musicians have adapted the instrument well for their purposes. They have developed tunings, equipment setups, and playing techniques to serve the needs of every aspect of church meetings, from delicately rendered musical backdrops during periods of meditation to poignantly played hymns, from swinging offertory march medleys to roaring, jubilant praise music. In the process they have created a unique tradition of expressive steel guitar music.

The Eason Brothers

Brothers Troman and Willie Claude Eason are perhaps the earliest Keith Dominion steel guitarists to impact the music of the church on a national scale. Their father, Henry Eason, was born in 1878 and their mother, Addie Eason, was born in 1889. Henry, Addie, and their parents were born in Georgia.[1] Troman (1905–49) was the oldest of fifteen children, and Willie was the tenth.[2] The 1910 and 1920 U.S. Censuses locate the Eason family in a community known as Lickskillet (later named Ebenezer), about five miles southwest of Ellaville, the seat of Schley (pronounced "sly") County, Georgia, and about fourteen miles north of Americus.

Henry Eason was a tenant farmer. He probably grew cotton, corn, or peanuts as cash crops and raised a variety of vegetables for family consumption. Most families in the area grew sugar cane, which they ground in a mill turned by a mule, and cooked the juice into cane syrup, the popular source of sweetening. Most people in the area kept hogs too, and nothing was wasted; they ate "everything but the squeak." If the Easons had joined the Keith Dominion by that time—when they joined is unknown—they almost certainly would not have raised hogs, as the Decree Book forbids consumption of pork. Surely they raised chickens for eggs and meat. The gently rolling farm land in that part of Georgia is productive, but working the soil with mule and muscle was difficult, and the typical tenant farming arrangement offered no hope of getting ahead.

Details of Henry Eason's life prior to 1910 are lacking. It is possible he was the Henry Eason, an African American born to Georgia-born parents in Georgia in February 1878, counted in the 1900 U.S. Census.[3] He lived in Satilla Mills, Camden County, in the southeastern corner of the state, below Brunswick, some 275 miles from Ellaville. He was one of about two dozen men working in a turpentine operation and living in company barracks. This Henry Eason is one of the few listed as a turpentine "operator," which means he probably ran the still or other equipment. Most of the other men were listed as laborers. Like most of the others, Henry Eason was married but did not have his wife with him. The business of making turpentine was rough work and living conditions—single men housed in crude company barracks, often miles from town—made it even more difficult. If Henry Eason, the husband of Addie Eason, was the Henry Eason working turpentine in 1900, then moving to a tenant farm in Schley County would have been progress in terms of standard of living. Even if there was little hope of advancing economically as a tenant farmer, he would be with his wife and family and be his own boss.

As is the case with many African Americans of their generation, the antecedents of Henry and Addie Eason are difficult to trace. Eason is a common name in Georgia and white Easons were among the pioneering families in Schley County. One of them, Edmond D. Eason, settled in Schley County between 1840 and 1850. His son, William Thomas, owned a large plantation north of Ellaville and built a fine home at the crest of what is still known as Eason Hill.[4] However, I have not been able to trace Henry Eason's family to slave owners.

On June 26, 1921, Henry and Addie Eason were blessed with their tenth child, Willie Claude. He was delivered by Ella Baisden, a midwife from the La Crosse community, about ten miles as the crow flies from Lickskillet. Baisden was illiterate and signed the birth certificate with an "X."[5] In the summer of 1921, while Willie was still an infant, or in his words, an "arm baby," the Easons moved to Philadelphia, Pennsylvania, seeking economic opportunity and freedom from the racial oppression of the South. No details of their migration survive.

Troman Eason married Agnes McFadden and they had five children: Leroy, Ella Mae, Delores, Barbara, and Vivian. The 1930 U.S. Census shows them living at 1437 North Eleventh Street, Philadelphia. In this time of the Great Depression, Troman was fortunate to be working as a "washer" at a laundry. In 1930, ten members of three families lived under one roof, pooling their resources to survive: Troman, Agnes, and their four children; his sister, Ida, her husband, a daughter, and two in-laws; and three adults from the McFadden family.[6]

Sometime in the mid-1930s, Troman Eason heard a radio broadcast that would change his life as well as the lives of many others. The sweet, singing sound of the Hawaiian steel guitar broadcast over the radio compelled him to telephone the radio station and arrange to take lessons from the musician he had heard. His teacher is remembered by his oldest surviving daughter, Ella Mae, and was remembered by his brother Willie only as a Hawaiian named "Jack." Two of Troman's daughters are still living: Ella Mae Berry (b. 1927) and Barbara Foxworth (b. 1937). Both were born in Philadelphia and have lived there all their lives. Ella Mae recalled how her father began to play Hawaiian steel guitar.

> I remember this fellow Jack would come on every afternoon around 2 o'clock playing this Hawaiian guitar over the radio. I don't remember the station because that was way back in the '30s. He used to come on the radio every day. That's how my father got interested. And he called into the station and he had a talk with the gentleman to say that he was interested in playing. He went to the radio studio where this fellow would be playing every day. That was downtown, but I can't recall the station because I was a little young girl then. So, the next thing I know, my father went down there and then he came home with this wooden Hawaiian guitar at first, then he moved on up to the steel Hawaiian guitar [probably a metal, National brand instrument], then he moved on up to the electric Hawaiian guitar. And he was teaching. My father was teaching others. That's how all this began here in Philadelphia because my father was the first black man to play this Hawaiian guitar.
>
> Barbara was born when he was going down taking lessons. He started a little before then because I remember when she was born we had a city nurse would come out every day to wash [my] mother up and get [her] ready. And this city nurse, she got interested in playing too. She was a white girl. And she was taking lessons and different ones were taking lessons from my father.[7]

While positive identity of Troman Eason's teacher is not possible, evidence suggests that he was Jack Kahauolopua (ca. 1906–?), who, along with his brother Jimmy (1904–75), taught Hawaiian steel guitar in Philadelphia and played engagements in the area.[8]

One of Jimmy Kahauolopua's former students proved a valuable source of information about the Kahauolopua brothers. Ralph Kolsiana (1912–2002) was a career Hawaiian steel guitarist of Dutch, Brazilian, and Peruvian extraction. He was born in Oahu, Hawaii, and moved with his family to Philadelphia when he was a boy. In 1932 and 1933, he studied acoustic Hawaiian steel guitar with Jimmy Kahauolopua in Philadelphia.[9] The Kahauolopua brothers both used the spelling Kahanolopua for business purposes, eliminating the "auo" vowel combination that many non-Hawaiians find difficult to pronounce. (Anglicizing surnames was a fairly common practice among Hawaiian performers.) Kolsiana remembered that Jimmy and his brother Jack, who played both standard guitar and Hawaiian steel guitar, were reputed to be the best Hawaiian musicians in the Philadelphia area, if not the Northeast, at that time. Kolsiana learned his lessons well: in 1933 he landed a two-year engagement at the Steel Pier in Atlantic City, New Jersey, then went on to play Hawaiian steel guitar professionally for six decades. Among his more colorful gigs were private parties hosted by Al Capone in Miami, Florida, and New York City, for which Kolsiana's group played Hawaiian music behind a curtain as Capone and a few friends made love to women.[10]

The studio at which Jack and Jimmy Kahauolopua taught was the Honolulu Conservatory of Music at 709 Chestnut Street. It was part of a system of teaching studios some have called "the Amway of Hawaiian guitar" because of its pyramid structure. The Oahu Publishing Company of Cleveland, Ohio, was founded by Harry G. Stanley in 1926, and became the most popular and enduring of Hawaiian guitar teaching studios; it continued to operate until 1985. Oahu established some twelve hundred teaching studios throughout the United States and Canada, as well as a few in other countries. The company estimated its instructors taught more than two hundred thousand Hawaiian, Spanish, and tenor guitar students.[11] The numbers are especially impressive when one considers that the company's heyday was in the 1930s, the depth of the Great Depression. Most teaching studios supplied by Oahu were named the Honolulu Conservatory of Music. The Oahu plan was comprehensive: lessons were offered from beginner to advanced levels; student guitar clubs, often called the Honolulu Guitar Club, were organized; students purchased Oahu brand instruments and amplifiers through the teaching studios; faculty and students played for live radio broadcasts; and the related Guitar Publishing Company produced a monthly magazine, *The Hawaiian Guitarist,* which was re-titled *The Guitarist* sometime in 1935.

Jimmy (James) and Jack Kahauolopua are listed in the 1920 U.S. Census taken in Honolulu as two of the seven children of Joe and Kealoha Kahauolopua. I have found no evidence of Jack Kahauolopua on any public records after the 1920 U.S. Census, and the members of his family in Hawaii to whom I have spoken do not know what became of him after he moved from Honolulu to the mainland. The magazines published by Oahu present the only written evidence of Jack Kahauolopua I have unearthed. Early issues of *The Hawaiian Guitarist* and *The Guitarist* included radio listings for stations that featured regular broadcasts of Hawaiian music.[12] The Honolulu Melody Boys were listed in the February 1934 issue of *The Hawaiian Guitarist* as playing for a total of five fifteen-minute weekly live broadcasts over four Philadelphia radio stations.[13]

Although I have not been able to determine the identities of the individuals who played in the Honolulu Melody Boys, several issues of the Oahu magazines contain reports from the Philadelphia correspondent that suggest Jack Kahauolopua was a member of the group. (It is possible that Jimmy joined the group later.) Apparently, the Honolulu Melody Boys was composed of the Philadelphia Honolulu Conservatory of Music faculty members, and perhaps, advanced students. Selected students frequently joined the Honolulu Melody Boys for radio broadcasts. Mary Stiffel, "Philadelphia studio reporter," wrote the following in the February 1935 issue of *The Guitarist* under the heading "Two Students from Quakertown":

> Among our youngest students is little Ronald James of 2525 Massey Street, Philadelphia, Pa. Ronald, who is eight years old and is in the third grade at school, is another protégé of Jack Kahanolopua.
>
> When Ronald stands beside his guitar he looks like his shadow, but when he sits down to play—well, that's something worth hearing, and I wish some of our many readers and friends could hear him. Little Ronald has only been taking lessons for a short time, but he has made several radio broadcasts with the Honolulu Melody Boys, and from what I gather is due for many more. In fact if Mr. James' young son continues to advance much faster, I'm afraid he'll be teaching Mr. Kahanolopua instead of Mr. Kahanolopua teaching him.[14]

In the April 1935 issue of *The Guitarist,* Stiffel reported under the heading "Philadelphia Philanderings": "Mrs. Rose Fites of 3005 S. Sydenham Street, Philadelphia, Pennsylvania, is another student of Mr. Jack Kahanolopua, instructor at the Honolulu Conservatory of the Philadelphia branch. . . . Mrs. Fites has made her radio debut with the Honolulu Melody Boys, which is really something to be elated over."[15]

Jack Kahanolopua was also was mentioned in the November 1935 issue of *The Guitarist,* in an article that reported the activities of the Honolulu Guitar Club of Philadelphia: "Saturday night, August 17, Mr. William Pace, managing instructor of the Philadelphia Studio, was tendered a surprise birthday party by the Honolulu Guitar Club at the home of Mr. and Mrs. Goldsmith Riley. At 8:30 P.M. a special radio program was broadcast in his honor over station WPEN by the 'Sunrise Hawaiians,' and was directed by Jack Kananolopua, assistant instructor."[16]

Although one cannot be certain, the article above seems to imply that the Sunrise Hawaiians was a student group. The Oahu Publishing Company used radio to reach audiences locally and nationally, and to build interest among students and potential students in the listening audience.

Radio was *the* nonprint mass communications medium in the 1930s and an opportunity to be heard over the airwaves must have been exciting. The company sponsored the Oahu Serenaders, a professional group that was broadcast from Cleveland over the CBS Coast-to- Coast Network, and encouraged local instructors and students to play on the radio.

Jimmy Kahauolopua is much more evident in public records than his brother Jack. On his application for a Social Security account dated January 10, 1938, Jimmy listed the Honolulu Conservatory of Music at 709 Chestnut Street as his place of employment. Exactly when Jimmy became an employee there is unknown. The entry for "Give date you became an employee (if you began employment after November 24, 1936)" was: "18 (card lost)." Apparently Jimmy had established a Social Security account before January 10, 1938, but lost his card.[17] According to the Social Security Death Index, Jimmy died in Honolulu in January 1975.

Lessons printed in "diagram arrangement" (commonly known today as "tablature") were at the heart of the Oahu system. Copies of Oahu arrangements from the 1930s in good condition are in great supply today, no doubt because so many were distributed. The diagram method showed the fret number over which to place the bar on a particular string or strings to render the melody and harmony. (Because of the diverse tunings used by steel guitarists and the directness of the diagram or tablature system, tablature remains the most common method for teaching steel guitar today.) Troman's younger brother, Willie, clearly recalled Troman playing from tablature, and in fact, Troman eventually used the method to teach him some melodies.[18]

Troman Eason's daughter, Ella Mae Berry, remembers her father teaching Hawaiian steel guitar to the public nurse that came to care for his wife when her younger sister, Barbara, was born on May 6, 1937. Therefore, he had to be playing for some time—probably at least several months—before then. The fact that Jack Kahauolopua was teaching at the Honolulu Conservatory of Music on Poplar Street in August 1935, and one might assume, taught there when the November 1935 issue of *The Guitarist* was published, strengthens the likelihood that he was Troman's teacher. Troman Eason's residence at 1437 N. Eleventh Street was about two miles from the teaching studio; he could have easily taken public transportation for his lessons, or even walked. The Oahu plan included rent-purchase instruments. Beginning students got to keep their guitar—an inexpensive acoustic model—after fifty-two lessons. When electric instruments became popular in the late 1930s, the Oahu Publishing Company sold a full line of electric steel guitars and amplifiers.

The covers of printed lessons published by Oahu often included clever illustrations, complete with proverbs, quotes by famous persons such as Mark Twain ("The music of the Hawaiians, the most fascinating in the world, is still in my ears and haunts me sleeping and waking"), or exhortations to practice diligently. The back covers often included more of the same as well as cartoons, personal testimony from successful students, and advertisements for instruments, picks, cases, music stands, and other accessories. The catalog of diagram arrangements included a significant percentage of Christian sacred music, and those folios usually featured a spiritual message on the back cover. The printed lessons of the 1930s, as well as the pages of *The Hawaiian Guitarist* and *The Guitarist* magazines, often included messages to motivate the student to complete the Elementary or Beginner's Course, continue training to complete the Professional Theatrical Course, and take the Manager Instructor's Course. Teaching Hawaiian guitar was touted as an excellent way to overcome the hard times and achieve economic independence:

> Possibly you are considering becoming a lawyer, physician, druggist, electrician or stenographer, or any one of a hundred other occupations that we could mention. We think you will readily agree that these occupations are already badly overcrowded. Universities are graduating thousands of lawyers and doctors every year who can find no employment, and the universities themselves cannot locate the graduates, which they turn out.
>
> In the Hawaiian Guitar field we find conditions different. . . . For the person who has the energy, for the person who is willing to work, for the person who has foresight and ability, who completes these courses of instruction, we can truthfully and honestly say that your earnings will be twice or three times as much in this line of endeavor as if you had prepared for some other vocation.[19]

Although little is known about what attracted Troman Eason to the Hawaiian steel guitar, if he studied with Jack Kahauolopua at the Honolulu Conservatory of Music he surely would have been exposed to Oahu's motivational rhetoric.

Troman taught his son, Leroy (1926–98), Hawaiian guitar. Troman's younger brothers, Willie and Henry (1926–70), took an interest in Hawaiian steel guitar, too, and Troman eventually gave them some instruction, but not as much as he gave Leroy. Ella Mae Berry recalled: "My brother was the first one that he taught. Leroy was the first one that he started giving lessons to. He was before Willie, before Henry too. He was more of a singer. He played too, you know. He would go on concerts with my father, I mean duets together, when he was small. But Leroy didn't really play with the Hawaiian music. He was taught it, but he didn't play with it. He was more of a gospel singer."[20]

In about 1930, Willie Eason was crushed by an elevator while visiting Troman at work at the Progressive Laundry in Philadelphia. He was hospitalized for an extended period and recalled that he had to wear a body cast for several months. On news of his injury, his aunt, Elder Lovie Stakely of Americus, Georgia, is said to have turned her dinner plate upside down to fast and pray for his recovery. When he recovered, the family considered it a miracle. He began to play sacred music on the piano, and later, on the Hawaiian steel guitar, as testimony of God's healing.[21]

Troman visited his parents and siblings frequently at their home at 1415 North Randolph Street—about three-quarters of a mile from his residence. When Troman visited he usually brought his instrument with him and often one or two musician friends as well. Willie and his younger brother, Henry, were drawn to the beautiful music Troman and his friends played, especially the plaintive strains of the electric Hawaiian guitar. In his early teens at the time, Willie was forbidden to touch his brother's instrument (Troman was sixteen years older than Willie). But when Troman would go out for a while, or otherwise leave his steel guitar unattended, young Willie would sneak some time on big brother's instrument. Not having the benefit of instruction, he was left to use his own abilities to find a way to make music on the steel guitar. Troman was not interested in taking time out to teach Willie. Finally, at the urging of their mother, Troman taught him the basics of reading tablature. Willie remembered the first melodies he learned using the method: "I even learned how to read 'Home Sweet Home.' Yeah, learned how to read it on the Hawaiian guitar and I played 'Home Sweet Home.' 'Nearer Oh My God to Thee' was my second song. After I learned that—I was brought up in the Holiness Church, Pentecostal, so it just started to come. I just had the rhythm already there. It was already there."[22] It is interesting to note that "Home Sweet Home" and "Nearer My God to Thee" were both included in the catalog of Oahu Publishing Company diagram arrangements for Hawaiian steel guitar.

Troman eventually separated from his wife, Agnes, and moved to Brooklyn, New York, shortly after she gave birth to their last child, Vivian, in 1939. In Brooklyn he led a three-piece group that played for secular social engagements, such as Elks Club dinners, as well as for worship services. Willie recalled that Troman played lead Hawaiian guitar; Plummer played "tenor" Hawaiian guitar;[23] Henry Smith picked the Spanish, or standard, guitar; and a fellow named Loveland, whom he remembers as having a humpback, played the accordion. Troman sang lead and the other members sang backup or harmony.

Willie referred to both Troman and Plummer as "professors" of Hawaiian guitar. Although neither Willie nor Ella Mae remembered the name of Troman's group, Ella Mae recalled he was billed as "Professor Troman Eason" on posters and handbills. Reference to Troman and Plummer as "professors" suggests the possibility that they may have completed the Professional Theatrical Course or even the Manager Instructor's Course offered by the Oahu Publishing Company, but I have found no evidence of that. In fact, there is very little documentation of Troman Eason other than U.S. Census records and his death certificate; not a single photograph of Troman has surfaced, and he and his group never recorded.

Troman Eason died of a ruptured gastric ulcer on October 5, 1949, at Kings County Hospital, Brooklyn.[24] He was estranged from his family and left no possessions. Ella Mae remembered that when her father died the family tried to get his instruments from his landlady. "When he died and we tried to get them instruments from the house the lady made pretend he pawned them. But we know he didn't pawn them because my father wouldn't have did nothing like that. So I think she had them over there and wouldn't let them go. She claimed he pawned them but I know better than that. He loved his music too well. I know he wasn't that poor he had to pawn no guitars. She just held them. At that time he was playing a double-neck. He had a single-neck too and the double-neck."[25]

Both Ella Mae and Willie Eason's widow, Jeannette, reiterate a story that circulates among Keith Dominion congregations: women drawn to Troman's music were the cause of him leaving his wife and family, and led to his ultimate demise. They believe he was poisoned by a jealous lover. Since Troman died in a hospital, it seems reasonable to assume that the cause of his death was properly identified by the attending physician. Whether fact or fiction, the story serves as a cautionary tale for Keith Dominion musicians and their wives to warn of the power of music to attract lustful women who can ultimately destroy the musician and his family life. Similar stories of blues musicians who met an early demise after taking up "the devil's music" are part of African American oral tradition.

Although no recordings of Troman's music exist, there are many people alive today who clearly remember his playing. They describe his music as sounding "hillbilly" or Hawaiian. They use adjectives like "exact" and "precise" to describe his technique. Ella Mae compared Troman's approach to the instrument to that of Keith Dominion steel guitarists that have followed. "My father read music. He was taught music. A lot of these guys coming along, they don't read music. They just pick up. They play by ear. My father was a strictly *Hawaiian* player."[26]

Keith Dominion pedal-steel pioneer Elder Acorne Coffee, who was born in Philadelphia in 1936 and lived there most of his life, presented his personal definition of vernacular music as he described Troman's playing: "Troman played by notes. We'd play by ear. Troman played like these guys when these hillbillies play. Troman played church music like that. We played just like we speak broken English; we'd play broken music."[27]

Willie eventually got his own guitar, a silvery metal National acoustic resonator model. He was inspired by Philadelphia musician Walter Johnson, who played the same type of instrument for church services broadcast live over radio. As Willie later recalled,

> I not only heard him on the radio, I seen him in person. This is what gave me the enthusiasm too of gospel, you know, the way he would play. I can tell you the song he mostly enthused me with when I'd hear him play on the radio or whatnot. . . . You know what his main number was? I'll never forget it: "Nothing Between My Soul and My Savior. Keep the way clear, there's nothing between." The pastor would sing, Reverend F. D. Edwards, his main song, and I sing it a lot of times, but I do it on piano: "I Tell It Wherever I Go. I was dying with only just one word to say. I'll speak it for Jesus, then I'll breathe my life away. I tell it wherever I go."[28]

The first time he saw Walter Johnson play was a revelation for Willie. In addition to being inspired by Johnson's steel guitar technique, he also observed how he had raised the strings of his instrument above the fretboard to get a clear sound, something Willie had yet to achieve on his acoustic guitar. Fiery preaching by the Reverend Edwards added to the excitement. Willie continued:

> He was playing at a church. Don't forget, I wasn't nothin' but a kid. I had to be like about fourteen or fifteen years old. He'd come over the broadcast with the Reverend F. D. Edwards in Philadelphia, in South Philadelphia on Reed Street. He had an old saying, you'd hear him on the radio: "We've got the devil on the run!" . . . That was one of his main things that he'd use, that phrase. And the service be going so good, and it's way up in the air, he'd come on and he'd say, "We got the devil on the run here!" That's right. And Walter Johnson would play "Nothing Between" and "There's Not a Friend Like the Lonely Jesus."

I saw him in Philadelphia, at Reverend F. D. Edwards's, at the church. And that's how I saw the strings raised. I had to put the thing [extension nut] under to raise the strings. I saw the way he was playing his, but the strings was raised. And I wouldn't get no sound. I wondered what was wrong, till I saw Walter Johnson and I got a chance to get close.[29]

Willie remembered Walter Johnson playing with the guitar lying horizontally in his lap, Hawaiian style, rather than held vertically in the "bottleneck" or "slide" style. Johnson didn't sing; he played only instrumental music. Willie described Johnson's manner of playing as consisting of predominantly single-string leads, occasionally harmonized by a second note, and punctuated by rhythmic strumming, a natural approach for an untutored African American gospel or blues musician.[30] A flyer for a 1940 performance by Walter Johnson in Ardmore, Pennsylvania, about eight miles west of Philadelphia, which I obtained seven years after Willie Eason first described Johnson to me, is included among the illustrations contained in this book. It clearly shows Johnson playing a metal guitar on his lap. The flyer lists Blind Connie Williams as among the other artists who appeared on the program with Johnson. Williams performed as a singer and guitarist on the streets of Philadelphia for years and Eason remembered him well when I showed him the flyer. In 1961, Pete Welding of Testament Records recorded him singing twenty-three songs, including "Tell Me Why You Like Roosevelt" and "Oh What a Time," both of which Willie Eason recorded for black gospel labels in the 1940s. Eason's recordings are discussed more thoroughly in the next chapter. The recordings of Williams have been reissued as Testament CD 5024, *Philadelphia Street Singer Blind Connie Williams: Traditional Blues, Spirituals, and Folksongs*.

Those familiar with African American folk blues and gospel music are often curious to learn if Willie Eason was influenced by another acoustic steel guitarist named Johnson, the popular recording artist Blind Willie Johnson. Over the years, I asked Willie Eason many times if he was familiar with Blind Willie Johnson. He consistently responded that he had not heard of him. I have also asked the question to other senior Keith and Jewell Dominion steel guitarists and received the same response.

Willie Eason eventually purchased an electric Hawaiian steel guitar and amplifier and began to play at church musical programs and on street corners. Often Troman's son Leroy, who was five years younger than Willie and a talented singer, would join his uncle Willie. As Willie developed his performance skills he began to attract some notice locally. His big break was not long in coming.

In African American culture it is common for gospel singers and some instrumentalists to celebrate an "anniversary" in observance of their longevity as performers or church musicians. The date of the anniversary may or may not accurately reflect their first acknowledged performance as a soloist or member of a recognized ensemble. Quite often a convenient date is chosen, say, for example, the first Sunday of every March. The anniversary celebration may occur at the musician's home church, or if that edifice is not large enough to accommodate the event, at a larger church or rented hall. The scale of the event is usually a function of the degree of esteem in which the musician is held among peers, clergy, and congregations. When a musician has an anniversary, he or she invites his or her musician friends to perform and is expected to reciprocate when requested to perform at their anniversaries. Attendees contribute cash offerings for the honoree, and the total amount collected often exceeds a thousand dollars. Sometime in the late 1930s—probably 1939, soon after Troman had left his wife and moved to New York—young Willie played electric Hawaiian steel guitar following a performance by Troman's trio at Troman's anniversary celebration in a large Baptist church in Brooklyn. The full roster of talented musicians included Charlie Storey, a powerhouse singer known as "the Mayor of Brooklyn." The church was packed to capacity. Willie began his performance of "Just a Closer Walk With Thee" by speaking the lyrics slowly while playing slurred passages on the top string of the steel guitar to make the instrument "talk"—to echo a line he had sung or complete a phrase from which he intentionally omitted some words. After talking a verse or two, he picked up the tempo, sang in his soulful baritone, added rhythmic backbeat strums, and continued his call-and-response steel guitar leads. The congregation went wild, and rose to give the adolescent artist a standing ovation and shout "amens." The members of Troman's trio, all trained and polished performers, could hardly believe the response Willie received with his home-grown approach. But Willie clearly understood what set his performance apart:

> He called it "one-string melody." That's what my brother called it. . . . He had a trio: two Hawaiian guitars, one was like a tenor. I know the fellow that played it—Plummer, that was his name. . . . I played "Closer Walk," see, but I make the guitar say the words, and that's what they couldn't understand. They playing all that pretty melody and everything, and they're picking out all these harmonics. Plummer asked my brother—I remember that, I was nothing but a kid—he says, "How in the world? We playing all this sweet music and

all this pretty music. How's he getting away with this?" But I was playing the *words*. And that makes the people sound, "Ooh, the guitar's talking."[31]

Willie's performance at Troman's anniversary celebration was the milestone event that would launch his career playing and singing for street-corner ministries and church services. It was Willie's first major public performance of his unique combination of compelling vocals and "talking" steel guitar style. Willie's manner of playing, although very much his own, reflected the influences of Troman's disciplined "Hawaiian-style" approach and Walter Johnson's unschooled technique.

Troman's Hawaiian-style influence is evident in Willie's precise intonation, use of slanted bar technique to execute smooth legato double-stop passages, and the playing of artificial harmonics, often in combination with glissandi, or slides, over several frets. (Willie referred to the latter technique as "runs.") Based on Willie's verbal descriptions of Walter Johnson's playing, Johnson's influence is manifested in Willie's extensive use of slurred voice-like passages, often played on a single string, and rhythmic strumming on the back beat. All the characteristics of Willie Eason's style can be found in the playing of contemporary Keith Dominion steel guitarists. The execution of voice-like slurred single-string passages has been developed to a very high degree of artistry by a number of steel guitarists, Aubrey Ghent, brothers Chuck and Darick Campbell, and Josh Taylor being among the most notable. The use of slanted bar technique among Keith Dominion steel guitarists today is minimal, but some lap-steel guitarists, such as Aubrey Ghent, use it nearly as frequently as Willie did. Keith Dominion pedal-steel guitarists use the pitch-changing foot pedal and knee levers of their instruments to achieve a similar effect.

Willie Eason's practice of rhythmic strumming is continued by Keith Dominion steel guitarists. Among the electric steel guitarists who play in the variety of musical genres in which the steel guitar is heard today, Keith Dominion musicians strum their instruments more than any of the others. Rhythmic strumming of the pedal-steel guitar is virtually unheard of outside the Keith Dominion. Interestingly, among many Keith Dominion musicians—even some of the most cosmopolitan—the word "strum" is not in their vocabulary: they say "fram," instead.

While Willie's steel guitar playing was compelling enough, what propelled him to the legendary status he would ultimately achieve was the total package: his powerful and expressive voice, his animated face, the dramatic gestures and flourishes as he played and sang, his engaging personality, and his ability to quickly connect with an audience. Surely many of these elements were established by the time of his first performance at Troman's anniversary celebration, but Willie was still just a teenager and had a lot to learn about performing for church congregations and the general public.

As he matured, Willie Eason became a consummate performer and church musician and played a tremendous role in the formative years of the Keith Dominion steel guitar tradition. He was one of the first to place the instrument in a position of central importance in worship services and other church meetings. His commercial recordings and association, both as a performer and concert producer, with the most renowned gospel stars of his day elevated his status far beyond that of any of his Keith Dominion contemporaries. His engaging and dynamic personality further boosted his reputation beyond that achieved by mere musicianship. He was a powerful performer and an unforgettable person.

Jewel Dominion congregation, Corinth, Mississippi, ca. early 1930s. Members hold a banjo-ukulele, two resonator guitars, an unidentifiable percussion instrument, and a flat-top guitar. Courtesy Jewell Archives.

Bishop Henry Harrison with Kay lap-steel guitar and amplifier, ca. early 1940s. A "Red Letter Edition" Bible sits atop his amplifier. Courtesy Aubrey Ghent.

WALTER JOHNSON
STEEL GUITAR ARTIST

at CALVARY BAP. CHURCH
Rev. HEDGEMAN   ARDMORE, PA.
on
THUR. MAY 9, 1940-8:30 P. M.
assisted by the Following Quartets

FAMOUS MORNING STAR   ISRAEL LIGHT
EOLEUM GOSPEL SINGER   KING OF KINGS
CONNIE WILLIAMS - BLIND GUITAR ARTIST
SELECT SOLOIST
ADMISSION   25c

Walter Johnson was one of Willie Eason's earliest influences. He saw him perform and heard him over radio broadcasts with the Reverend F. D. Edwards. Author's collection.

Willie Eason with his new Buick, Philadelphia, Pennsylvania, 1948. His clothes matched the baby blue car. Courtesy Jeannette Eason.

Willie Eason with Epiphone lap-steel and amplifier, Philadelphia, ca. late 1940s. This was the cover photo for a songbook he sold as he traveled. Courtesy Jeannette Eason.

Henry Nelson ca. 1960s. Courtesy Johnnie Mae Nelson.

At Henry Nelson's homegoing (funeral) his steel guitar was placed in front of the casket. He was buried with his fingerpicks on. Queens Village, New York, 2001. Photo by the author.

Henry Nelson's son, Aubrey Ghent, plays for services at the House of God No. 1, Ft. Pierce, Florida, 1998. In Ghent's hands the lap-steel sings like the most passionate gospel vocalist. Photo by the author.

Ghent's apprentice, Elton Noble, plays for the call to the altar, Crescent City House of God, 1999. Photo by the author.

Towering at six feet-two inches, Chief Mattie Lue Jewell ruled with authority for more than half a century. Courtesy Opal Louis Nations.

Fred Neal accompanied here by his son, Lemuel, Los Angeles, California, ca.
1960. By most accounts, Fred Neal was the first Jewell Dominion electric steel
guitarist. Courtesy Lemuel Neal.

Bishop Lorenzo Harrison,
by far the most influential
Jewell Dominion musician,
with his triple-neck steel
guitar in the late 1950s.
He later settled on a
single-neck eight-string as
his preferred instrument.
Courtesy Jewell Archives.

The Jewell Gospel Singers recorded for the Aladdin and Nashboro labels. *Left to right*: Lorenzo Harrison, steel guitar; Harvey Jones, guitar; Corroneva Burns, drums; Bobby Powell, piano; Candi Staton; Naomi Harrison Manning; and Maggie Staton. Nashville, Tennessee, 1951. Courtesy Harvey Jones.

"Gospel Cruiser" bus used by Lorenzo Harrison and the Jewell Gospel Singers, ca. 1960s. Courtesy Jewell Archives.

Sonny Treadway crafted the body of his instrument from found wood and fitted it with a Fender fretboard and pickups, and Sho-Bud tuners. Jewell Dominion church, Deerfield Beach, Florida, 2006. Photo by the author.

The "Footie's Gospel Train" name painted on Reginald "Footie" Covington's steel guitar and his use of a vintage Morley Rotating Wah pedal reflect Lorenzo Harrison's influence. Philadelphia, 2000. Photo by the author.

Little Willie and His Talking Guitar

When Troman Eason began to play the electric Hawaiian steel guitar for Keith Dominion services in Philadelphia, Bishop J. R. Lockley (1893–1971) enlisted him to travel with the Gospel Feast Party, a troupe of musicians, preachers, and dancers he organized in the late 1930s to perform at church services, revivals, and assemblies from New York to Miami. Lockley served as chief helper to the national leader, Chief Overseer Bishop Mary F. L. Keith. His dioceses included the state of New York, Philadelphia—where the Eason family worshipped—and the west coast of Florida. As proprietor of a used car lot in Brooklyn, Lockley always managed to drive a big car, often a black Cadillac. When the Gospel Feast Party traveled, he towed a flatbed trailer piled high with musical instruments covered by a canvas tarpaulin behind his Cadillac.[1]

Troman ceased to travel with the Gospel Feast Party after just one or two trips, as he found being away from home for extended periods was too difficult for him and his family. Lockley had witnessed young Willie's ability to engage a church congregation with his strong, spirited singing and voice-like steel guitar playing. He had seen Willie draw large crowds that filled his guitar case with greenbacks as he played and sang on street corners in Philadelphia. Although Lockley was not present at Troman's anniversary celebration when Willie received a standing ovation, news of that momentous occasion spread quickly to him. Sometime in the winter of 1938–39, he requested permission from Willie's mother to allow her son to travel south with the Gospel Feast Party. A deeply religious woman who recognized her son's talents as a gift from God, Addie Eason gladly honored her bishop's request. Willie's public school records state that he was withdrawn from Central High School in January 1939.[2] It is logical to assume that Mrs. Eason withdrew her son from school just before he departed to travel with Bishop Lockley. Bishop Lockley and other members of the Gospel Feast Party stayed home to observe Christmas and the New Year's Eve "night watch" service, and did not depart for their southern sojourn until some time after New Year's Day.

At that time, the Gospel Feast Party band consisted of Willie on electric steel guitar, the bishop's son, J. R. Lockley Jr. ("J.R."), who played upright bass and vibraphone, electric guitarist Roosevelt Eberhardt, and drummer Moe Harper. In the late 1930s and early 1940s, most Keith Dominion churches were small and austere. Musical instruments were generally limited to simple percussion such as tambourines, washboards, and cowbells brought from home by congregants who played them from the pews. A more prosperous church might purchase a large bass drum, or if it was especially well-off, a piano or organ. Not only was the electric steel guitar new to Keith Dominion congregations, full drum sets would not come into general use in the Keith Dominion until the 1950s, or even later in some locations. The Gospel Feast Party, with its full complement of musicians playing professional-grade instruments, created a sensation wherever it held its fiery worship services. Bishop Charles E. Campbell saw Lockley's compelling entourage when just a boy growing up in Florida. "He had his singers that could sing and he also had his dancers," recalled Campbell. "So when he hit the scene, he had the whole thing. And you talk about a service! White and black would come to see the performance because they loved to see them get happy and dance."[3]

Traveling with the Gospel Feast Party to play for spirited worship services and revivals was an awakening as well as an adventure for young Willie Eason. As he left the urban Northeast to venture below the Mason-Dixon Line, he was shocked to encounter for the first time drinking water fountains and restrooms labeled "white only," as well as other Jim Crow practices in the South. Still, it was an exciting experience and a rite of passage for him.

Bishop Lockley limited Eason's compensation to meals and lodging, an arrangement that Willie soon found intolerable, so he left the Gospel Feast Party. Willie recalled:

> I was coming up in a time when musicians didn't get paid. Bishop Lockley and all, they just used me. After I found out what they was using me for—with the big tent services and all, and I wasn't getting nothing out of it, and they're taking up all these offerings and whatnot—it was like, you're going to hell if you don't play. Like frighten you and scare you up. And I got in all that strain. But I found out it was altogether different as I got older. I was a teenager and on into my twenties. But after I got married, I knew I had to go

out and make a living. That's when I started making a living with it, *really* making a living with it. That's when I got on the road and started traveling. Had my own car. Bought my own first house at twenty-two years old. Yeah, in Philadelphia, 1203 Flora Street. So that's what made me go to the streets. I made my living from the streets. And not only that, I'm the father of fifteen children, and I fed all them children.[4]

Bishop Lockley was angered by Eason's departure from the Gospel Feast Party and took action to sanction him. At a meeting at the Keith Bible Institute in Summit, Tennessee, on August 22, 1943, the Supreme Executive Council of the Keith Dominion passed a measure, at Lockley's recommendation, to restrict Eason's performances as an independent musician. As recorded in the Decree Book, the measure stated that talented musicians were not permitted to play within ten blocks of a Keith Dominion church. Furthermore, if a musician performed in a program produced or hosted by a church member, the chief overseer would receive ten percent of the gross receipts and the musician would get 50 percent of the net after expenses.[5] Eason's method of dealing with the rather harsh restrictions was to hit the road to avoid Bishop Lockley, at least temporarily.

The measure recorded in the Decree Book provides early documentation of the power struggle between the clergy and musicians that continues today. The clergy may be in charge, but the musicians have the power to help induce the congregation into an elevated state of spiritual ecstasy. Music is a good draw, and a larger congregation means more souls to save for Christ and more money from offerings. And good musicians can play music for the offertory that will put the congregation in a spirit of jubilation, or even playfulness, which usually results in increased donations. (The infectious, wah-drenched boogie, "Celebration in Giving," played by the Campbell Brothers at the 1998 North Florida State Assembly in Crescent City and recorded on Arhoolie CD 472, *Sacred Steel Live!* is an excellent example.)

Eason married Alyce (pronounced "Alice") Nelson of Ocala, Florida, in 1941.[6] She was the attractive oldest daughter of Keith Dominion bishop W. L. Nelson (1895–1973), a very important figure in the Keith Dominion. Bishop Nelson served faithfully under Mother Tate, and was the right-hand man of her successor, Bishop Mary Keith. He worked tirelessly to establish new churches in his dioceses, which included the East Coast of Florida; South Carolina; South Pittsburgh, Tennessee; and Jamaica, British West Indies. The combined efforts of Bishops Nelson and Lockley evangelizing throughout the Sunshine State resulted in Florida having more Keith Dominion churches than any other state, peaking at more than fifty.[7] Willie inspired Alyce Nelson's younger brother, Henry (1929–2001), to take up the steel guitar, and in time, Henry Nelson became one of the most influential steel guitarists in the Keith Dominion.

One of Willie Eason's most productive street corners in Ocala was at the intersection of Twentieth Avenue and Broadway, in front of Buddy B's, a popular west Ocala juke joint. Young Henry Nelson was usually nearby, soaking up Eason's every nuance on the Hawaiian steel guitar. At Buddy B's, Eason was frequently requested to play and sing "Flat Foot Floogie (With the Floy Floy)," a hit recording for Slim (Gaillard) and Slam (Stewart) on the Vocalion label in 1938. Many Keith Dominion congregants remember it as "Flat Foot Susie." Henry Nelson's older sister, Mary Linzy, recalled how Eason responded to the requests by playing just a few bars of the popular number.

> That was a little joke for him. Sometimes he would throw a little joke in there to make the people laugh when they come around him on the street. And see, that was one of those blues, "Flat Foot Susie with the Floy Joy" [sic]. And he was really referring to seeing some of them shouting. People were shoutin' on them corners when he played. But sometimes he would get his little joke to going. They requested, and sometimes he would do his little guitar with that, and that would just tickle them to death. But he don't go no further. Just for them, his group—whoever's around—get everybody happy.
>
> He's never, never, never played the blues—always songs he made, put together. And they were religious songs. And he would take the old religious songs—we had a book of 'em for our church—and he would play that and sing 'em all. I have to give him credit for that. He didn't know anything about any blues playin' anyhow.[8]

Indeed, all indications are that Eason never played blues.[9] He certainly never recorded any, despite, according to his recollections, requests from Savoy Records and others. To my knowledge, he had no blues in his repertoire. The rumor that he played blues on the street corners was used against him by many clergymen and churchgoers throughout his lifetime; however, a number of ministers, undeterred by the allegations and gossip, employed Eason to play for worship services and revivals. After all, he was a good draw. He could be counted on to raise the energy level of a worship service and to inspire increased contributions to the offertory.

Eason's relationship with the Keith Dominion, and with Bishop Lockley in particular, changed over time. Even under the restrictions placed by the Supreme Executive Council in 1943, Eason was still sought by some Keith

Dominion ministers to play for worship services and other church meetings. He attended the Keith Bible Institute and was ordained as a minister in 1944.[10] He eventually reconciled to some degree with Bishop Lockley, and the bishop hired him to play and sing for many worship services, assemblies, and other events over the years. But after he made his initial break as a teenager from Lockley's grip, Eason was never again in the fully submissive position he had assumed during his youth.

By the time I began to interview Eason in 1994, his recollection of details of his involvement with the Keith Dominion in the 1940s was sketchy at best, and in the following years he became impaired by Alzheimer's disease. Because of Eason's impaired memory and my lack of access to Keith Dominion records (which, I am told, are very limited), I have relied on the personal recollections of a few individuals to reconstruct Eason's activities during the 1940s. With regard to his tenure in the ministry, Mary Linzy recalled that Eason served as a pastor at the Keith Dominion in Knoxville for a short time around 1944. After he resigned as pastor, he ceased to be a member of the Keith Dominion but continued to play and sing for many Keith Dominion worship services.[11] Bishop Lockley continued to call on him to play with some regularity for more than two decades. Eason also journeyed south to the annual State Assembly in Americus, Georgia—the Keith Dominion church nearest his place of birth—to play for his aunt, Bishop Lovey Stakely (the one who had fasted and prayed for his recovery from injuries sustained in the accident at the laundry where Troman worked), many times over the next forty or fifty years.

Early in their marriage, Alyce accompanied Willie as he traveled throughout the East and to Chicago to perform musical ministries on street corners and in farm labor camps, and to play for church worship services, revivals, and assemblies. Once they started having children, she stayed home in Philadelphia to care for their family. Eason needed an assistant to collect and count the money and help with the domestic aspects of life on the road. At first, his older sister Earline, a gifted organist and preacher, traveled with him. Later he hired Troman's daughter Ella Mae, who was six years Willie's junior. Willie and Alyce had four children: Willie Claude Jr., Alvin, Dalton, and Lauretta. By the mid-1940s, Eason had moved to Chicago, where he owned several rental units. He had also begun to produce gospel "programs," or concerts, which presented local and nationally known artists. But Alyce refused to move to Chicago. She became pregnant by another man and she and Willie were divorced in 1953.[12]

Ella Mae continued to accompany Eason on road trips for a while after he married his second wife, Jeannette Davis. In all, Ella Mae spent about four years traveling with him. She fondly recalled her days on the road with her beloved uncle:

> Oh, I loved it. Sometimes I lay down and reminisce what a good time we had. I enjoyed being with my uncle, traveling with him, because he treat you royal. He loves me and I love him. Made a lot of friends and seen some parts of the world I probably would have never seen if it wasn't for him. If I be travelin', I met a lot of people. When we'd go into the churches I enjoyed playing along with him. I played the piano, or either organ, along with him and I enjoyed the service. He can preach a little bit too, you know. He can go. He's a gifted young man. He can cook. He used to throw some nice picnics.
>
> He would do like street service, street playing. People would come by the hundreds, they'd gather. When he'd start playing guitar, they would come from everywhere, stand and listen at him play. And quite naturally, people would want to give donations. So I would go and pass a box around and he would make hundreds and hundreds and hundreds of dollars a day because we would have three to four stops a day.[13]
>
> It was in the '40s. I would say from '46 all the way on up until the '50s. He would go from Chicago, Indianapolis, Ohio, just travel the roads. Sometime we would go out during the week, everyday sometimes, as long as it don't rain.
>
> We'd head south in the wintertime, because usually in the winter up here you don't be out on that corner. We traveled all through the southern lands, Florida and all. In the South it was around Florida—Ocala, Orlando, Jacksonville, Apopka, Miami—and Georgia. I went to Ellaville and Plains, Georgia, with him. I've been all through there. The people would come out and listen. I went to Macon, Georgia. They would come and pick him up and take him on to the radio station. I've been to Nashville, Tennessee, and Chattanooga with him. Sometimes they would have tents up—different tents, you know—and he would sing under the big tent. Usually we stayed in hotels. Once the people see you're going to stay more than a week, once the people find out that he's in town, they would open their doors to us.[14]

Eason was a talented, animated, and engaging performer. His vitality and love of life was infectious. He quickly won the hearts of audiences—and usually, local law enforcement—wherever he busked. Ella Mae continued:

> He was the gift of the streets. They loved him to death. And that personality, that'd make you really love him. He'd get hundreds and two hundreds on a street corner. I mean people *come*. They come out the alleys, everywhere. Policemens would stop. He would stop the traffic. Some kind of way the cops would fix it where he could continue to play. They would have to protect him

and bring the people in so they wouldn't block the traffic and everything. They were very kind because they enjoyed him themselves. The white and the black, they enjoyed that music. At that time he was singing "Pearl Harbor, What a Time" and "Tell Me Why You Like Roosevelt." And he would play that guitar and make the guitar repeat the words, you know, and that would knock the people out, just him doing that. He was somethin' else in his younger days. And he could play the piano and he could sing. "Little Willie and the Talking Guitar," that's what they called him.

He made good money, now. He was able to provide for his family. Sometimes he'd make as high as a thousand dollars a day. Somebody would come up and give him a ten or twenty dollar bill to play "If I Could Hear My Mother Pray Again." That was big money in those days. See, the people be cryin' because they feel good. And it wasn't nothin' for them to throw a five or ten or twenty dollar bill, and they'll pay him twenty dollars to play it again, because a lot of money was travelin' around the streets at that time, especially during wartime.[15]

In time, Ella Mae ceased to travel with Eason. But her fondness for her uncle Willie remained strong and she enjoyed visiting fairly frequently. "I'd say I spent a good four years travelin'. Then it was time for me to get serious and get my life together, which I did. And we always stayed in touch. When he was living over in New Jersey I would come over on the weekends or what have you. Over in Teaneck, New Jersey. Even since he's been in Florida, we'll jump up and fly into Florida, my sister Barbara and I, anytime."[16]

The "Roosevelt" and "Pearl Harbor" songs Ella Mae refers to were by far Eason's most popular numbers on the streets. "Tell Me Why You Like Roosevelt" was composed soon after the death of FDR. It chronicles the late president's life, emphasizing actions that made him "the poor man's friend." Similarly, "Pearl Harbor," also known as "Oh, What a Time," reports the bombing of the United States naval base there and provides a historical overview of much of World War II. Both numbers were six or seven minutes in length. Eason performed them in a melodic "talking" or "rapping" style. (The origin of both songs, which raises some interesting issues, is discussed later in this chapter.)

Ella Mae's recollection of the amount of money her uncle made on the streets is exaggerated compared to what he remembered. Eason recalled bringing in about five hundred dollars on a good weekend when he worked the streets of big cities such as Chicago, New York, and Philadelphia in the 1940s and 1950s—still, several times the average working man's wages. Specifically, he remembered that a five dollar bill was about the largest denomination any one person might contribute. He recalled a few individuals who would drop a five in his case every time he played their repeated requests for a certain song, usually "Roosevelt" or "Pearl Harbor."[17]

Although the police frequently helped Eason with crowd control and traffic flow, sometimes he would be asked to move. He vividly remembered a situation in New York:

> In Jamaica, Long Island, they used to sit me up in a high-bed truck, because there was so many people, just all around me. I entertained them from the guitar and they just loved to hear me playing. Sometimes I'd just have a prayer with them. I was on this corner and people wanted prayer so bad, and I guess they thought I was "the man." And, you know, they was all standing there. Some people had got seats, brought their chairs and all. This was off a vacant lot, but I had them all standing in the street. This police came along and he says, "Look"—he was amazed—he said [Willie speaks in a low voice], "Can't you make 'em come in? You done stayed on this corner long enough. Can't you go to another corner?"[18]

Eason deftly worked the crowds to maximize his earnings. He recalled making more money busking on the streets than top male gospel vocal quartets of the day, such as the Soul Stirrers, earned performing concerts.

> If I made fifty dollars, fifty to seventy-five dollars on a corner and I see the crowd weakening, I go to another corner. And I knew all my main corners. Like in Chicago, Forty-seventh and Prairie, Forty-seventh and Langley, these are main corners. At Thirty-fifth and Prairie—that's where I stood—I was singing there and the police got tired of keeping the people out the street. He said, "Hey look fella, you done made enough on this corner. Go to another one."
>
> Even the Soul Stirrers—Harris and Medlock—those were the two main leaders. That was before Sam Cooke joined the group. They say, "God"— you know, they looked at the people throwing all that money at me—they said, "God. You make more money than we make. We don't make no kind of money like that." Yeah, and they'd look down at my guitar case—it was like maroon velvet inside—and all that money be down there where the people be throwing it.[19]

Eason's audiences were sometimes a force to be reckoned with. The following anecdote demonstrates the affection Chicagoans had for Little Willie and His Talking Guitar. Eason believed Oscar De Priest, a highly esteemed Chicago politician and the first African American elected to Congress in the twentieth century, was responsible for his expedited release from jail.[20]

One day I was singin' at Forty-seventh and Langley. And these policemen in Chicago, they want you to grease their palm. They're bad about it, *real* bad. And I didn't bother with no police. So this black policeman come up, and he always carried a angry face, but this time he gonna bother me— talkin' about I have to move it—'cause he had saw me on a couple other corners. So he caught me on this corner, Forty-seventh and Langley. Started tellin' me I goin' to have to wrap it up and move. So he annoyed the crowd. Almost was a riot. It got real bad. So there was an arrest. I went down with him to the precinct. And I don't know who it was in the crowd, they got in touch with Oscar De Priest, that's right, and explained to Oscar. And he called the precinct and explained to the captain and told him who you have down there, and they released me. The captain wouldn't tell me anything. "Naw, we just been asked to release you, that's all." That's right.

And I went right on back on that same corner where the policeman was and played. The guy was shocked! He was shocked. I went on back on that corner and went to playin"[21]

Eason's second wife, Jeannette Davis, was born in Longwood, Florida, near Orlando, in 1937. Her father was a Pentecostal minister. The entire Davis family traveled "on the seasons" along the eastern seaboard from Florida to the mid-Atlantic states, following the crops to pick fruits and vegetables. Jeannette was feisty and a hard worker. She was known as "Shadow" because she moved quickly and elusively. She also says she was fast enough to catch wild rabbits for the family table bare-handed, a skill she learned from her mother. She could sense the presence of snakes in a field, and farm labor crew leaders frequently asked her to check a field for snakes before they would permit their crews to begin work.

Jeannette played piano and sang in the family youth gospel ensemble, which was first known as the Singing Davis Family, and for a while, the Golden Harps.[22] She met Willie in 1952, at a musical program that featured both Eason and the Singing Davis family. The event was held at the Keith Dominion church in Ocala, near Ft. King Street and Broadway, where Bishop W. L. Nelson served as pastor.

When Willie and Alyce separated in 1953, considerable strife ensued. Bishop Nelson, Eason's father-in-law, attempted to have him jailed for failure to pay support for Alyce and Willie's five children. Alyce had her estranged husband's shiny, pea-green 1952 Cadillac impounded. Eason was able to get his car released and was making preparations to head back to Chicago to tend to his rental properties. He was brokenhearted and sobbing. Jeannette Davis, only fifteen at the time, was moved by his distress.

When I seen him crying, well that night—I lived with my aunt down the street—I went and wrote him a letter tellin' him that I would make you a better wife. I'm trying to console him, without realizin' I'm proposin' to him. I only went to the fourth grade, so you can imagine what that note was like. At the same time, I had no boyfriend. Sex was nowhere in my life. I was the support of my father and my mother and my sisters and my brothers, workin' in the fields right out from Ocala. So I wrote the letter and I told him—he kept the letter until we got burned out—I told him I would make him a good wife, keep his shirts, his handkerchiefs clean, and his shoes shined, for him to go sing on the street.

What I done, I took the note—his coat was on the porch over a chair—so when I come up from my aunt's house, I took the note and I pushed it down on the inside of the pocket. And I went on and I helped set the table, put the biscuits on the table and everything. And my mother and father went into the kitchen, so that give me a chance to tell him in his ear, "Look in your inside coat pocket." But after I said that I was runnin' all the way back to my aunt's house. I was so afraid—you know how people will go to your parents—that he would say, "I wonder what kind of note was that your daughter told me to look at in my pocket?" Oh, God. I would have been a dead person.

He got up to Gainesville and went to gas up and he said to hisself, "Wait a minute. That little girl told me she put a note in my pocket." He said he stood there and he read it and he started laughin'. He said it gave him encouragement to keep on going to Chicago. When he read it he said, "Oh gee, she ain't nothin' but a baby." 'Cause don't forget, he was thirty-one and I was fifteen.[23]

Eason had begun to produce gospel concerts in 1945. By 1953, when Jeannette slipped the note in his pocket, the Singing Davis Family was among the groups frequently included in the gospel programs he presented. Eason kept in touch with Jeannette's father as the family traveled to follow the harvests, and he often produced concerts that featured the Singing Davis Family at venues in the general area where the family was doing farm work. Jeannette continued to court Willie, and in time, they developed a romantic relationship.

In the winter of 1956, the Davis family was back in Florida, working and living near Lake Mary, a few miles north of Orlando. Willie and Jeannette had decided to get married in February, so he drove down to Lake Mary from Chicago. By then Eason was prospering not only as a street musician, but as a landlord, booking agent, and gospel concert producer. Jeannette vividly recalled Eason's grand arrival at the humble Davis home in Lake

Mary and the impression he made on her family of fourteen hardscrabble farm workers.

> He had just bought a brand new '56 Cadillac when he drove down. Now, the Cadillac was "goddess gold" and yellow, two-tone. The '56 was brand new off the floor, but then he had some [chrome] "v's" over the back bumpers. He had sent all the way to Hollywood, California, to get the extension of the trunk with the chrome tire on it. The [windshield] visor was on there. And in the front he still had the small v's right there on that fender over the tire. It had fender skirts. The interior was white, white leather. I'll never forget it. It was *gorgeous*. My father almost fainted when he seen it. His payment was $356 a month. That shows you how much Willie was makin'.
>
> When he come down he had my weddin' suit, my blouse, my corsage, my pearls, my shoes, my stockings in the trunk of that car—everything. He paid good money at a very exclusive store. When he stepped out his clothes matched *everything*. When Willie got out that car, he had on one of these—I know you've seen 'em—a Stetson hat, but it's made out of cowhide. So, you know how the brown is in the cowhide and then the beige is in the cowhide? That's the kind of hat he had on. It wasn't no wide brim hat like the guys wear now, it was smaller. He had on shoes to match, gold shoes, with a little alligator goin' through it. And he had on beige pants with a shirt with beige in it, but it looked more like silk. Oh, when he got out he *shined*. He didn't have no tie on, he was sportin', you know, free man.[24]

Jeannette's father was an abusive alcoholic who did not work regularly. His usual contribution to his family's subsistence was the fish he caught in local rivers and lakes and the occasional few dollars he made from selling fish when he had a surplus. Because Jeannette was the chief source of income for the Davis family, her father was reluctant to let her marry and leave the family to live with her new husband. He violently opposed the union, sometimes striking Jeannette for mentioning her intention to marry Eason. Jeannette was too young for legal marriage in Florida without her father's permission, so she and Eason "eloped" to Folkston, Georgia. Oddly, Jeannette's father accompanied her and Eason on the trip to Folkston. Jeannette recalled that after the ceremony her father cursed all the way home.

Shortly after the marriage, Eason had to return to Chicago for a few days to tend to his rental properties. Jeanette recalled that her father had his eyes on Willie's Cadillac: "We got married on the fifteenth of February. He took off on the seventeenth and flew to Chicago. He left the car there in the yard with me, and he got someone else to take him to the airport.

Well, my father was so happy that Willie left the Cadillac. He figured, you know, he wanted to play big shot and drive it around. . . . He asked me for the keys. I said, 'Willie didn't leave me no keys.' But I had went and hid the keys in the dirt under the house, to make sure that he couldn't find 'em, in a jar."[25]

When Eason returned to Lake Mary after taking care of his business in Chicago, he fell victim to the manipulations of his father-in-law, who insisted that Jeannette was needed at home to provide support for the Davis family. Eason's solution was to evict most of the tenants from his rental property at 1918 West Adams Street—one of three multi-family rental properties he owned in Chicago—and move the entire Davis family in. The only way he could afford the move was to let his pride and joy, the brand new customized 1956 gold and yellow Cadillac, go back to the finance company. Eason cried all night long over the loss of his new automobile. The Davis family had two cars: a 1951 Pontiac, which Jeannette had bought by secretly working extra and saving for more than a year, and an old 1941 Buick. Eason worked on the cars himself to get them in mechanical condition for the long journey north. After toiling several days, he pronounced both vehicles roadworthy. All sixteen people packed themselves and their belongings into the two old cars and lumbered along to the Windy City to start a new life. When his friend guitarist Roosevelt Eberhardt saw the sacrifices Eason made and the generosity he extended towards the Davis Family, he shook his head and remarked, "Eason, there ain't that much lovin' in the whole world."[26] In Chicago, Eason provided financial assistance and housing for the Davis family for about two years before he finally tired of it and curtailed his contributions.

When Eason came to south Florida during the winter months he often stayed with "Mother Pearl," a Pentecostal healer and disciple of Mother Tate, who operated an independent Christian mission in Pompano Beach, a few miles north of Ft. Lauderdale. There he played for worship services at Mother Pearl's mission in exchange for rent. In the South, where the towns were smaller, he could not make his entire living playing on the street corners as he was able to do in the teeming northern cities; however, he had a keen eye for economic opportunities and made the most of his circumstances. Eason recalled:

> When I go to Miami, I work more or less from Pompano to Miami, and you pickin' up Dania and all in there, Perrine. You pickin' up all these small towns. But I would go back—Pompano was my main source. That's where I'd stay, with Mother Pearl. What I'd do I'd take a load of them women fishin'. I'd

take 'em over to Lake Okeechobee [about sixty-five miles, one way]. While they're fishin' I'd go down to the "cane belt" where they got the sugarcane at. And I'd give a guy fifteen dollars. He'd let me put as much sugarcane as I could get on there. That's right. I'd go in the field and I'd cut the cane. Only thing I was scared of and I'd watch out for was snakes. And I'd cut that cane. I'd cut that cane and load it down. Them stalks would be so long sometimes they'd be still draggin' the ground. If I done took four of them women down there, I'd ease back there to the bridge at Pee-hokee [Pahokee] around Lake Okeechobee there and pick those women up and I'd head back to Pompano. Next morning I'm up and I'm out through the quarter selling sugar cane. Yeah, see, I was always a hustler.[27]

Jeannette sometimes traveled with her husband to south Florida. Being sixteen years younger, she remembered more details about his enterprises there.

Willie sold the cane for twenty-five cent a stalk. But he would have close to three to four hundred stalks of cane on that wagon, a '51 Oldsmobile station wagon. Mother Pearl—who came up under Mother Tate, that's who we would be stayin' with, there in Pompano—what she would do, she take three or four women, and Willie would take them down, and they would pay him like five dollars a head to take them fishin' at Lake Okeechobee. He'd go and get his cane, bring it on back and then go back, pick up my car, and then go back and pick them up. Then he'd have the cane there when he would go through the migrant quarters sellin' it twenty-five cent a stalk. He would get rid of it between Friday and Saturday mornin'. And Friday afternoon he would hit a spot singin' and then Saturday he'd go to Miami and sing there in Liberty City, 'round that area. Lot of history behind that gray-headed man.[28]

The sixty to eighty-five dollars net profit Willie made from selling a load of cane was big money in the 1950s in southern Florida. At that time, fifty dollars a week was a good wage for white skilled labor and considerably more than most black men could hope to make. As Willie recalled: "I'd sing on the weekend. Friday and Saturday when people get paid, I'm down in Miami on the corner because Miami's the big thing now, the big city. People are workin'. I hit the farm section Friday, and Saturday too. Like when the people come out the field, I know which camps been out there and made that money, picked so many baskets of tomatoes and pole beans and all of that. And you keep up with that stuff, because that's how I was makin' my livin'."[29]

Eason remembered dozens of anecdotes from his years of traveling to perform on street corners and in farm labor camps, homes, and businesses.

He relished telling them in his dramatic, animated manner, often imitating the voices and actions of the characters.

> If I'm on a street, what I'd do, like I come to your door, this is your house, and I told you, "I'm a gospel singer and I'd like to render a service in song, if you don't mind." I'd offer to pay for the electricity so I could plug in my amplifier, but most of the time people would not let me pay after they heard my music. And I made a lot of people happy.
>
> I'll never forget, in Jacksonville, Florida, on Ashley and Davis, I went to this project where these people lived. And you know back in those days they had these aprons. They were in the kitchen and they were making this dough flour. They roll it, you know, to make the bread and stuff. I hit a good fast number, like "I Never Heard a Man [Like This Man Before]," and I start playin' the guitar and they say, Ooh, listen to that instrument! It's sayin' the words! Well, this is what I want to get them to say, how I get my rousin'. And this lady come out and she said [Willie exclaims in falsetto], "My goodness! I wanted to go to church and I couldn't get to church and God sent the church to me!" And she's just shoutin' and the flour goin' everywhere, you know!
>
> One time I was playin' "Just a Closer Walk With Thee." When I started doin' this, this lady says—she was half high—she said, "Don't do that no mo'." So I just do it for devilment, you know. I go way down there and I said, "Daily walking close to thee," and I go way up on the fine keys [high on the E-string] and I come back. She says, "I told you not to do that no mo'!" And the guitar was in my lap and she sat down on the guitar. And do you know three or four men couldn't hardly pull that lady up off there? She said, "I told you not to do that! I told you not to do that!"[30]

Jeannette remembered Rattlesnake Bill, a colorful character they encountered occasionally, who worked his routine in farm labor camps and "colored quarters."

> He was a real Indian, number one. And he'd do what they call medicine shows. And he would have his rattlesnake venom and he would be telling people how good it is, what it will make you do. He'd say, "Men, you're not doin' nothin'. No wonder your wives are unhappy. Why don't you put a little of this on the back of your back?" And some way—this guy was big and tall—he'd hold his stomach in and his pants would drop right down on his hips. Not off his hips, but when you seen the pants drop the crowd would say, "Haawh!"
>
> The rattlesnakes that he had, we found out that they had the fangs removed. He handled a lot of snakes. It was like teaching the kids and people that would come up to his show about the snakes, what they could do and what they couldn't do. During the middle of the show, when he got everybody

laughin' and all and women is standing around, he would pull something out like this thing you used to see kids playing with—a spring that looked like a snake—and he'd say, "This box right here is what you need." And he'd open it and this thing fly out into the crowd, and people would be runnin' and screamin'.[31]

On the street corners, Eason usually worked alone, but fairly frequently he was accompanied by other musicians, such as Troman's son, Leroy Eason, and guitarist Roosevelt Eberhardt. Sometimes he teamed up with ministers such as Elder B. B. Barber, herself a steel guitarist (but, according to Eason, not a very good one), or Sister High. In 1960, he struck up a temporary alliance with a smooth-talking, muscle-bound giant of a young black man called "Strongman" in Lawnside, New Jersey. Lawnside was a popular destination because local laws allowed alcoholic beverages to be sold on Sunday, a practice prohibited in some surrounding areas at the time. Eason remembered:

> Everybody had a little stand. It was a little resort, like. We sold sausage, frankfurters, and hamburgers from the stand and, you know, drinks, hot sausage. We was famous for our good hot sausage. See, I used to play my guitar sittin' outside the stand, to draw the crowd up to the stand. Their favorite songs was "Tell Me Why You Like Roosevelt" and "Pearl Harbor." It was like a new thing at that time. They just loved to hear that and they had me singing it over and over. I had to cut the verses short. I couldn't sing all them long ones. Well, I could, but the thing about it, it takes so long getting all them verses out. So I found out the verses that they liked to hear and that's what I started singing.
>
> And Strongman happened to be wandering the crowd, came up, and he liked us from the first start. He was seven feet. He was like, muscle bound. What he done, he come and asked me could he put on his little show? It would help draw my crowd right on, you know, because it's a rest-up for me. So I let him come on and show me what he could do. He'll take a glass and chip it up fine and eat the glass. If he didn't, you don't know where it went. He had a special act. He'll wait till on a Sunday—like you advertise him for a couple Sundays. And the crowd's hollerin', especially the women and girls. They like that big macho man and they go wild over him, you know. He'd pick up 500 pounds with his teeth. Don't forget, I weighed two hundred-and-somethin' pounds—around 260 or 280. My brother weighed somethin' similar to that, that's Henry. What he'd do, he'd take a rod in his mouth and let us hold on and he'd get right between the two of us. He'd keep moving until he get in the center. He'd make sure before he'd do it. And then he'd just lift both of us off the ground by his teeth and walk ten feet. That was one of his acts.

He'd take a twenty-penny nail and run it through a two-by-four board with his fist. He'd grip hisself, you know, he'd get hisself together before he'd do that. That's right. And everybody, the crowd, be in suspense. But when he hit that board that nail go through. He'd let you, anybody, come try and pull it out. You can't move it. At least three-quarters of an inch would be sticking out the other side.

What he'd do, he'd get an offering, something like I was getting. He originated out of Chicago and he found me. He used to stand on the corner and listen to me sing. We just called him Strongman. He told me, but there ain't no way in the world I could remember that man's name. Even if I laid down, I might have to dream it and if it come to me, then I could say it. He was a young man. Not only that, when he talked, he can hold his crowd in suspense, then with what he'd do he'd hold 'em. Yeah, he was educated good.

He let a tractor-trailer run over his chest. This man is out of the ordinary. You think it's trickery, but it ain't no trickery. He'd let everybody examine him. He went as far as holding the tractor-trailers. Yeah, he'd make the wheels spin. But he'd set himself up for that, you know, and then the people they be waitin' for him to do that. You can't do that! He'd make 'em go into arguments and everything, build it up like that. Yeah, they'd go into arguments. There ain't no way this guy can do that. And then they'd start bettin'.[32]

Women were attracted to Eason. He and Jeannette discovered rather early in his career as a street musician that his tips increased if she was kept out of sight. If the crowds were large and Jeannette was needed to collect the money, she posed as his younger sister. Eason recalled one overture in particular: "One lady—we was out at Lawnside Park, New Jersey. I don't know what song I was playin'. She said, "Don't do it. Don't do it." You know what she done? She took off her underwear and she dropped 'em right on my guitar. And the crowd—jammed, big crowd like that, all these people standing around—she said [imitating an excited woman], 'Here it is. You can have what go in 'em too!' I'm tellin' you, I done seen so many crazy things in my life!"[33]

As Eason played for church worship services, revivals, large assemblies, and on street corners, his reputation became larger than life. Chuck Campbell related some of the stories he heard from his parents and uncles, all of whom grew up in Florida, as well as from other sources among the Keith Dominion community.

My father's always been a minister, my mother's been a deaconess in the church. Some of my uncles weren't saved but, you know, they had integrity. And they said Willie Eason would make the thing [steel guitar] talk so until you'd swear that it was someone singing. Or the instrument would talk so much and then they'd ask him to it put down and let it walk. And sometimes he'd let it go and it would just vibrate, and you could actually see the steel moving.

Another great tale that I heard from some ministers in Georgia was: You guys play great, but Willie Eason was the best by far, the greatest that ever did it, because one time Willie made it talk so much that he stood the guitar up on the wall and the next thing they know the guitar had walked around the corner.

I heard one story of him playing on the street corners. They'd start the collection off. He'd have some of the kids or some of his friends help. He'd play and they'd dance around or they'd start the collection off, in the hat. He had so much money that he had to stop the people from paying him. And they would have to stop because the hat was full. They couldn't accept no more. It was that much money.[34]

As Ella Mae Berry stated, Eason did have biracial appeal. But Chuck Campbell found it difficult to believe that Eason received the royal treatment reiterated among Keith Dominion members: "Another story, coming from a prejudiced time, is that the white people would just beg for Willie to play. And they treated him like a king, although we're in the Deep South, because of what he did on the street corners. So you'd hear these stories and they'd be so large that you'd say, 'Come on. You know, you're in the Deep South and the white people fallin' all over Willie Eason because he played the steel so well?'"[35]

Eason's legendary musicianship became for many a standard that could never be achieved. Chuck Campbell continued:

A story that was told from the pulpit was that Willie would play the song so well that all the congregation would just be crying. He played the song so well that the people would actually stop singing because they wanted to hear Willie's steel sing the words. Now that story is very believable, but we [brothers Chuck, Phil, and Darick] were never hardly able to reach that pinnacle. And so, when a minister would talk about that, it's always setting such a high standard that you as an aspiring musician would never reach that level where everybody stops singing and you're just the total show.

The other one was that Willie Eason could play so well that he would make the people just pay money in the offering and help the cause of God so much as a musician. You know, after the people would rejoice and shout and have praise, they'd stop everything and then Willie would just pull on those strings and the congregation would just start paying money, and that's how the offertory march was formed.

Our Bishop J. T. Thomas used to be on that Gospel Feast Party. He was the bishop in New York before my father, and he was in Brooklyn. And he would have us stop and he'd say [Chuck imitates Bishop Thomas's high-pitched voice], "Now you play somethin' real soft and mellow. I want you to hit on that E-string like Little Willie used to do. And when Little Willie would hit on that E-string the people would just start payin' money and cryin' and payin' mo' money. That's the way I want you to play somethin', really mellow on that E-string." And I'm sitting here as a musician asking, how does he know about an E-string? So the whole thing was, if the offering didn't come up as good as it should be, it was because we weren't as good a musician as Willie Eason. I don't know of any Keith Dominion musician that hasn't heard of Willie Eason and that wasn't compared to him.[36] Some people would put Henry Nelson in Willie Eason's category, but of course, Henry Nelson couldn't sing like Willie.[37]

Eason was multitalented. Playing the steel guitar and singing were just two areas in which he excelled. Campbell continued:

Willie Eason comes into Florida and plays the steel, and of course, every-body's falling out. But then he looks over and they've got a piano that is broken down, that nobody could play. They're ready to throw the piano out. And Willie jumps on the piano and they think they have a brand new Steinway because nobody ever made the piano talk. He not only made the steel talk but he could make the piano talk. After Willie got done the whole congregation says: We don't need a new piano, we just need somebody that can play it.

This is one from Acorne Coffee. Willie was kind of unassuming, come in walking pigeon-toed, looked like he can't do too much. When he sits down [to play], everybody falls out because you never heard nothing like this. Now, to some of them's credit, maybe it's the first time they ever heard it or maybe it's the first real good steel they ever heard. But they've never heard nothing as good as this. And then, on top of that, Willie would go out, he could cook, he could barbeque. He knew how to work on cars, he could play the piano, he could direct choirs, and if you needed it, Willie could preach. Now, I know Willie could do all these things, but not only could he do them, he was the best at everything[38].

Eason made seven 78-rpm records: four on the Queen label, two for Aladdin, and one for Regent. His earliest recordings were made for Queen in June 1946, probably at King Recording Studios in Cincinnati, Ohio.[39] Syd Nathan was the brash, gravel-voiced, cigar-wielding founder of King Records, a company that produced a large catalog of music for con-sumption by the working class. The King recordings included hillbilly, honky-tonk, rhythm and blues, and soul music by artists who ranged from Grandpa Jones to James Brown, from Cowboy Copas to John Lee Hooker. In 1945, Nathan formed Queen Records, primarily to record black music, but deleted the label within a year.[40] When I began to interview Eason in 1994, he was unable to recall any details of his recording sessions, not even the names of the vocalist and guitarist who accompanied him. In time, he did recall some of the circumstances of a trip to Cincinnati that may have resulted in the Queen recordings.

Eason took three people with him to Cincinnati to play music ministries on the streets: his good friend, Roosevelt Eberhardt (1915–71), played guitar, Troman's twenty-year-old son, Leroy, sang, and Troman's nineteen-year-old daughter, Ella Mae, collected the money.[41] Ella Mae and Leroy stayed with an aunt, and Eason and Eberhardt found lodging in a rooming house. Eason recalled that the trio sang and played from atop the flat roof of a garage for hearses at a funeral home. The elevated improvised stage allowed the musicians to be easily seen and heard and they quickly drew a large crowd. As was often the case, local law enforcement cooperated. Eason recalled that the police set up barricades to protect the crowd from automobiles and direct the flow of vehicles and pedestrians.[42] Although he did not recall how he was engaged by King Records, or any of the session details, one can easily imagine that reports of the group causing all the excitement down at the funeral home—and wherever else they might have played—reached Syd Nathan quickly. Billed as the Gospel Trumpeters (not to be confused with the Trumpeteers), Willie Eason, Roosevelt Eberhardt, and Leroy Eason recorded four records in Cincinnati: "Oh Lord What a Time!" parts 1 and 2, Queen 4130; "Remember Me Lord" / "No More, No More," Queen 4131; "Standing on the Highway" / "Does Jesus Care?" Queen 4145; and "I Thank You Lord" / "If I Could Hear My Mother Pray Again," Queen 4146.

One could make a case for the Queen sides being Eason's most compelling recorded works. They were his only recordings that included a rhythm guitarist, and Eberhardt's energetic guitar work—it sounds like he was playing an acoustic arched-top instrument—complements Eason's fills, strums, and solos perfectly. Freed from being the sole provider of rhythmic accompaniment, Eason was able to sing more freely and play hotter steel guitar. Eberhardt played with punch and syncopation and created a jazzier mood by sometimes employing sixth chords, which were especially effective on "Oh Lord What a Time!"

With one exception, Eason's steel guitar work on all his recordings, including the Aladdin and Regent sides, was limited to introductions, tags, and accompaniment in the form of fills and rhythmically strummed chords. On the up-tempo "If I Could Hear My Mother Pray Again" he played two hot sixteen-bar solos. Similarly, Eberhardt demonstrated his instrumental prowess with a tasteful, syncopated solo on "Never No More," another up-tempo song. Listening to these two recordings one can imagine the excitement the trio generated as they played—unrestricted by the constraints of making commercial recordings—to large crowds as they busked from Chicago to Miami.

With the exception of "Oh Lord What a Time!" the Gospel Trumpeters shared vocals according to a simple formula: Leroy sang the lead during the earlier part of the song, while uncle Willie sang backup, usually a repeated baritone phrase or a response to Leroy's lead lines. In the later portion of each song the roles were usually reversed for a while, as Willie sang lead and Leroy sang backup. On "Oh Lord What a Time!" Leroy sang lead all the way through and Willie sang a response during the chorus. "Oh Lord What a Time" is a two-part narrative delivered as a rhythmic "rap" at a fairly brisk tempo. The clever lyrics chronicle the sneak attack on Pearl Harbor, much of the rest of World War II, and wartime life at home in the mainland United States.

The surprise attack by the Japanese on Pearl Harbor thrust the United States immediately into World War II, dramatically changing the lives of Americans virtually overnight. The well-crafted lyrics of "Oh Lord What a Time!" presented a popular view of the traumatic event and life back on the home front. The attack on Pearl Harbor launched a period of unforgettable experiences for Americans and "Oh Lord What a Time!" was an effective means of expressing the shared fears and hardships of wartime life.

Eason's next recording session was in June 1947, when he made two records with the highly popular Soul Stirrers quartet singing backup as he sang lead: "Pearl Harbor," parts 1 and 2 and "Why I Like Roosevelt," parts 1 and 2. "Pearl Harbor" was essentially the same song as "Oh Lord What a Time!" recorded on Queen 4130, with only very minor differences in the lyrics. "Why I Like Roosevelt" presented a biographical sketch of the late Franklin D. Roosevelt that included commentary on life during the Great Depression and FDR's efforts to place African Americans in important positions in the military and public service. Recording with the wildly popular Soul Stirrers added to Eason's credibility as a recording artist and served to confirm his reputation as a performer known throughout the eastern United States. To match the smooth harmonizing of the Soul Stirrers, Eason sang lead in a reserved, rather smooth voice.

The Roosevelt song, and to a lesser degree the Pearl Harbor song, be-
came staples of the canon from which Eason drew for street performances.
Over the years he probably made thousands of dollars in tips from the
Roosevelt song alone. Otis Jackson, a gospel music composer, singer, and
concert promoter who operated out of Philadelphia, Pennsylvania, and
Jacksonville and Orlando, Florida, is usually credited with composing both
the Roosevelt song and the extended version of the Pearl Harbor song.
It is interesting to note that as a member of the Evangelist Singers, Jackson recorded "What a Time" (one part) and "Brand New" as Hub 3012
and "Tell Me Why You Like Roosevelt," parts 1 and 2 as Hub 3011 and
Chicago 116 in April 1946.[43] Eason and the Gospel Trumpeters followed
in June 1946 with the extended version of "Oh Lord What a Time" on
Queen 4130, and in June 1947 Eason recorded "Why I Like Roosevelt,"
parts 1 and 2 with the Soul Stirrers for Aladdin. Eason and the Gospel
Trumpeters were the first group to record the extended, two-part version
of the Pearl Harbor song. Of course, Jackson may well have had a two-part
version when he recorded in April 1946. But if he did, for some reason he
or the record label decided they did not want to record both parts. When
pressed, Eason did not claim to have written either song, but said both
"were out there," that is, they had (at least in his opinion) become part of
the public, or folk, repertoire among African Americans. Jackson and Eason
frequently crossed paths, most often as producers of gospel concerts, and
they developed an adversarial relationship. Conflict over recording and
performing the Roosevelt and Pearl Harbor songs may have contributed
to the animosity between them.

Eason's next recording session was in Atlanta for Regent Records on
April 30, 1951. Regent was under the umbrella of Herman Lubinsky's
successful Savoy label, which included jazz and rhythm and blues as well
as gospel. Eason recorded six sides at the Regent session: "There'll Be No
Grumblers There" and "I Want to Live So God Can Use Me," were issued
as Regent 1043, while "Everybody Ought to Pray," "Jesus Is My Only
Friend," and "Roosevelt, a Poor Man's Friend," parts 1 and 2 were not
released. On Regent 1043 Eason performed unaccompanied; apparently by
that time Roosevelt Eberhardt did not travel south with him. In contrast
to his recordings with the Soul Stirrers, Eason's voice had grown rough
from singing daily outdoors (a problem he often mentioned during our
conversations over the years). This recording captures the Willie Eason
that one might have heard playing unaccompanied on a street corner. On
both "There'll Be No Grumblers There" and "I Want to Live" we hear
examples of his "talking guitar" as he omits words from vocal phrases

and uses his instrument to fill the voids—very much the same sound and performance style, albeit at quicker tempos, that he presented when I met him in 1994.

Willie and Jeannette Eason moved from Chicago to Philadelphia in 1959. They bought a six-room home at 1938 North Sixth Street, which Jeannette recalled was in a pleasant neighborhood at the time. Willie also bought a Sunoco service station at Sixth and Norris, which he and his brother Henry operated. Eason continued to produce gospel concerts, or "programs," as they were more commonly known, until 1960.[44] In the early years, the programs featured local acts such as his wife's family group, the Singing Davis Family. Eventually he featured the top professional touring acts of the day, such as the Blind Boys of Alabama, the Dixie Hummingbirds, the Chosen, the Reverend C. L. Franklin, the Davis Sisters, the Dixie Hummingbirds, the Trumpeteers, and the Blind Boys of Mississippi. Unfortunately, all of the Easons' publicity photos, posters, flyers, and other materials relating to the concerts were destroyed when their home burned down in 1982.

Willie and Jeannette Eason were resourceful in finding a variety of ways to earn a living in contexts that ranged from inner city neighborhoods in New York, Philadelphia, and Chicago to farm labor camps in the South. A copy of a flyer (of quality too poor to reproduce here) from a program Eason produced on July 27, 1959, coupled with recollections by Jeannette Eason, give valuable insights into how Willie and Jeannette operated, and some of the complications they encountered in the production of a gospel music program.

The event was an evening gospel concert cruise that featured Willie Eason and renowned recording artist Sister Rosetta Tharpe in a guitar duel. There were also three other acts on the bill. Eason produced the event and took all the financial risk; however, he deliberately did not mention himself serving in that function. The flyer stated: "The Victory Baptist Church (Rev. Woodward, Pastor) Presents Just What You Have Been Waiting For!" Jeannette explained, "You had to use a minister and Willie didn't want to include himself, so he got [the Rev. Woodward] to sponsor. But [Woodward] didn't pay any money. Willie gave him a donation, 'cause he had a pretty large church, quite a few members. Willie played there quite a few times."[45]

The concert was billed as "The Biggest Battle of Songs and Guitars Ever to Be Held! $500 to the Best Guitarist." Regarding the prize money, Jeannette quipped without hesitation, "That was just a gimmick."[46] The flyer further stated "Also on board will be the Staple Singers of Chicago, Ill., plus the North Phila. Juniors and [in the smallest font] the Holy Wonders."

The Staple Singers, however, did not appear for the program, and Jeannette does not remember why.

Ticket prices were $2.00 at the Gate, or $1.75 for an "advance donation." The flyer further stated: "Tickets Now on Sale $1.50 Only until July 6th." The numerous ticket sales locations listed gave testimony to the Easons' marketing experience: "Tickets at Both Paramount Record Shops, Kae Williams Record Shop, Ida's Restaurant [1903 Columbia Ave., operated by Willie's sister, Ida], Treegoobs [a large Philadelphia record store], Ferry Auction Market, Peedie Lou's, Willie Eason, 1938 N. 6th Street [his residence], Eason's Sunoco Station, 6th and Norris, Downbeat Record Shop, 1914 Columbia Avenue, and all Usual Places." Eason also paid some of his rental property residents (or discounted their rent) to distribute flyers. "He always had help by some of his tenants," Jeannette recalled.[47]

On the evening of the concert, a large audience boarded the cruise ship. But the propeller drive transmission would not engage. The ship was stuck at the dock. "The boat never sailed," Jeannette remembered. "Between him and Rosetta, the owner of the boat told Willie, 'Well I'm not going to just see you fail. I'll go down and I'll rock the boat.' It wouldn't go in gear, but he could rock it. He just made it look like, from rocking the boat, in the bottom of the boat, it made it look like the boat was sailing."[48] Although it seems difficult to believe, the audience aboard was apparently so engaged by the performances that they did not notice, or care, that the vessel never left the dock. Jeannette explained: "The crowd was beautiful. They didn't even know it wasn't moving. Him and Rosetta with that "Ninety-nine and One Half Won't Do," my God they played that song, I would say, about six times. Rosetta, she just *turned it on,* you know. She would make her guitar talk, he would make his talk. And the crowd was just going up!"[49]

Otis Jackson was living in Philadelphia at the time, where he frequently competed with Eason as a gospel concert producer. Jeannette recalled that Jackson tried to stir discontent among the cruise concert audience as they disembarked. "What he done, he come out at the last minute and was telling people, after he discovered the boat didn't go out, to get they money back. But it was too late then. Everybody coming off the boat passed right by us and said, 'Oh, Mrs. Eason,' said, 'we ain't never had a ride like that before. Oh, that ride was smooth.' But it never left the shore."[50]

Jeannette vividly recalled there was trouble with the Holy Wonders, one of the opening acts:

That's the ones Willie almost put in the Delaware River, the Holy Wonders [laughs]. Now they wanted to come out and demand that he was supposed to give them $250 just for opening up the program. It was about seven of them, and by that time I had my pocketbook and the forty-five, and I'm headed toward the Cadillac on the dock. They rushed up to Willie, and he had hit [the leader of the Holy Wonders] and knocked him down. And Willie said, "Look, I didn't promise you no money and tried to get you to venture out and you was on the program it's true," he said. "But I told you my expenses was too much . . ."

I went on to the car. And when they looked up, they looked at that forty-five and I said, "You hit [Willie] and you going to be in the river." Well, before I could get that out [laughs] Willie hauled off and hit the leader. I mean, made the change come out his pocket [laugh]. And the other guys are saying, "Oh man, we'll get you." They tried to follow us. We was living at 1938 North Sixth Street at the time. They tried to follow us for a couple of blocks, but they gave up.[51]

While living in Philadelphia, the Easons continued a seasonal enterprise they had started while residing in Chicago: they made artificial rose corsages for Mother's Day and sold them on the streets. Family members labored for days to create hundreds of corsages from a material known as "wood fiber." Willie packed his car with the goods and headed for Chicago, where family members and hired help, including some of his tenants, sold the corsages on the streets. And of course, Willie would play and sing to attract a crowd. Jeannette remembered that their net profit was always between $2,000 and $3,500.[52]

The Eason's then bought a five-acre farm with an eight-room house in Dorothy, New Jersey. They quickly tired of the incessant work to operate and maintain the farm and the long commutes into the city and Lawnside, New Jersey, where they operated a concession stand on the weekends. They sold the farm in 1960 and moved to Brooklyn, New York, and, at Nostrand Avenue and Quincy Street in Bedford-Stuyvesant, opened what would be the first of several "Fat Willie from Philly" barbecue restaurants. The Easons soon realized that a "sit-down" restaurant was not for them, sold the property, and opened a series of take-out restaurants, all named "Fat Willie from Philly." The restaurants were contained in larger buildings that included several rental units and residential space for the Easons. In 1967, the Easons moved into a spacious ten-room house at Twenty-eight Church Street in Teaneck, New Jersey.

Jeannette ran the restaurants and, during the week, Willie managed the rental properties, collecting the rents and maintaining the buildings. On the weekends, Willie played and sang for worship services and busked for tips on the streets. Throughout the 1960s, he was usually accompanied by his good friend, Roosevelt Eberhardt, the guitarist who played on Eason's Queen recordings in 1946. Bishop Lockley also called on Eason fairly regularly to play for worship services at Keith Dominion churches under his jurisdiction in Philadelphia and New York. After their evening gigs on the streets or in church, Eason and Eberhardt often engaged in their favorite pastime. "Them two guys was crazy over the western movies," recalled Jeannette. "Honest to God, they would go to one movie, move from that one, if something different was playin' in the next one, they'd go to that one. Sometimes Willie and Roosevelt didn't get home until closing time, four o' clock in the morning."[53] Eason and Eberhardt continued to perform together for Lockley until shortly before Eberhardt's death in 1971. Bishop Lockley died in December of the same year.

Eason served as a musician and choir director at Gethsemane Baptist Church in West New York, New Jersey, from 1968 until 1981. On weekends he traveled frequently with the Gethsemane group to perform for gospel programs throughout the region. On October 20, 1979, the Gesthemane Senior Choir held a fortieth "anniversary" program at the Zion Baptist Church in Jersey City, New Jersey, to celebrate his four decades of service as a gospel musician. Performers on the program included Brother Charlie Storey (known as "the Mayor of Brooklyn"), the Mighty Bethel Specials, Thomasina James, Brother Leroy Eason, and the Eason Singers. Buses were chartered to bring patrons from Brooklyn and Philadelphia.[54]

Jeannette recalled that in addition to playing for legitimate worship services and gospel music programs, Willie played for charismatic preachers who worked various scams such as phony healings and faking the ability to sense detailed information about the lives of total strangers, who were actually "plants" in the audience. The more successful among the charlatan preachers attracted large congregations from whom they collected sizeable cash offerings. They paid Willie as much as $250 to provide music for their "worship" services.[55]

In 1982, the Easons' large home in Teaneck, New Jersey, burned to the ground, destroying all their belongings, which included a treasure trove of memorabilia. They then moved to 29 Hickory Road in Ringwood, New Jersey, where they resided until they relocated to St. Petersburg, Florida, in 1986.

Both Willie and Jeannette were born into large, poor, farming families in the rural, segregated South. Through years of hard work they rose above their humble beginnings and accumulated considerable wealth. They owned and operated three successful barbeque restaurants simultaneously and owned a total of 280 rental apartments. They enjoyed fishing from their twenty-two-foot inboard cabin cruiser, drove fine cars, and lived comfortably in large homes. At the root of their accumulated wealth was money Willie made from playing his steel guitar and singing on street corners and for various religious services as a young man. This was the seed capital that financed all later economic ventures.

Unfortunately, the Easons made two disastrous investments when they moved to St. Petersburg. First, there was the Sunshine Skyway Motel, the biggest loss, then a "Fat Willie from Philly" take-out barbecue restaurant that quickly failed. They had also bought a large waterfront home at 6960 Fourth Street South, but had to sell it after the motel and restaurant failures.

The Easons raised a large family. In addition to eight children of their own, they informally adopted several children and young people who were in need of a home. Jeannette says she has raised or provided extended care to thirty-two children.

When I first met Willie and Jeannette in 1994, they were living quietly in a nice home in the Pinellas Point neighborhood of St. Petersburg. Willie, then seventy-three, was recovering from surgery for aneurisms in his legs and he walked with the aid of a cane. He was still able to play the steel guitar and piano with considerable facility and expression. He sang with passion, conviction, and strength. Michael Stapleton and I recorded him in his home for the Florida Folklife Program's *Sacred Steel* album. He enjoyed a minor career revival performing at the Florida Folk Festival and other public venues. In 1995, the Florida Department of State honored him with the Florida Folk Heritage Award for his lifetime contributions to gospel music. In 2000, he was similarly honored by Keith Dominion steel guitarists with the Sacred Steel Heritage Award at the first Sacred Steel Convention. He was included in the Arhoolie Foundation's *Sacred Steel* documentary video, which was released in 2000, and on a segment of *Egg: The Arts Show,* produced for broadcast over PBS stations by WNET, New York.

Early in 2000, Eason began to show symptoms of Alzheimer's disease. Although he could still play the steel guitar in tune, his tempos were severely slowed, his mind wandered. He made a few attempts to perform publicly, but could not deliver a coherent performance. Following a series of strokes, he died of pneumonia in St. Petersburg on June 16, 2005. A wake and funeral services were held at Norwood Baptist Church on June 24 and 25. Steel guitarist and Keith Dominion minister Trial Elder Elton

Noble of West Palm Beach served as emcee for the wake. Several members of the Eason family delivered heartfelt readings and sang passionately. Willie Eason Jr., the oldest son born to Alyce Nelson, rendered a hymn on his father's old Epiphone lap-steel guitar.

Willie Eason's influence, by virtue of his engaging live performances throughout the East and his seven recordings, was huge. While some Keith Dominion steel guitarists, especially those from the Detroit area, where Eason never performed, may argue that he had no direct effect on them, his indirect influence is undeniable. He was, without a doubt, the most influential early steel guitarist in the Keith Dominion. As explained in chapter 8, he also influenced Bishop Lorenzo Harrison, who established the steel guitar style of the Jewell Dominion. Moreover, Eason was the musician who inspired Henry Nelson to take up the instrument. Nelson went on to have a major impact in shaping the Keith Dominion steel guitar tradition and solidifying the instrument's role in church meetings.

Henry Nelson

The Liberace of Sacred Steel

Willie Eason's brother-in-law, Henry Nelson, was a major contributor to the Keith Dominion steel guitar tradition. Eason inspired Henry to play the steel guitar, and like his inspiration, Nelson's charismatic personality contributed much to his success. While Willie Eason operated outside the Keith Dominion for much of his life, Henry Nelson—except for a hiatus in the Church of God in Christ—was solidly ensconced in the Keith Dominion, resulting in his having a larger impact than Eason on the functional music played in church meetings.

Henry's father, Bishop W. L. Nelson (1893–1973), was a dedicated clergyman who worked tirelessly to establish dozens of Keith Dominion churches. Dioceses under his responsibility included the Florida East Coast; South Carolina; South Pittsburg, Tennessee; and Jamaica, British West Indies. W. L. and Gelene Boyd Nelson had eleven children, but only eight survived. Two boys died in infancy and a third was killed by an automobile as he played in the street. Alyce, who would become Willie Eason's first wife, and two of the boys who did not survive, were born in Daytona Beach. The Nelsons moved to Ocala sometime in the late 1920s, where seven more children were delivered by midwives in the Nelson home at 1826 West Broadway. (Today the street is a four-lane highway known as West Silver Springs Boulevard, State Road 40.) Charles was born first, then Mary. Henry Randolph Nelson was born on January 10, 1930; the midwife signed his birth certificate with an "X."[1] After Henry, came Irma, Pauline, Audrey Pearl, and Cecil. Only three of Bishop and Gelene Nelson's children survive in 2010: Mary Linzy and Audrey Pearl Gillum, both of Ocala, and Pauline Parkey, of Tallahassee. The oldest surviving member of the Nelson progeny is Mary Linzy, who was born in 1928. A widow and retired school teacher, she has been in very poor health for several years.

Mary Linzy is a rich source of memories of Nelson family life in the 1930s and '40s and informed much of what follows.

The Florida East Coast Diocese for which Bishop Nelson was responsible extended along the five hundred mile stretch from Jacksonville to Key West. For the most part, his works were concentrated along the Dixie Highway—known today as Old Dixie Highway—which closely parallels present-day U.S. Route 1. The Florida East Coast Railway ran parallel to and a short distance west of Dixie Highway. Many African Americans came to Florida's Atlantic coast to fill the need for agricultural labor. Citrus fruits and spring vegetables were raised in the northern and central parts of the state, and winter vegetables and tropical fruits—mangoes, avocados, guavas, and papayas—in the south. Blacks established communities generally along the west, or "other," side of the railroad tracks.

Tourism also provided jobs for blacks in hotels and homes to work as cooks, porters, and domestics, especially in the southern portion of the state. South Florida's steady population growth provided employment in building construction, lawn care and landscape maintenance, and domestic labor. Many African Americans from the northern areas of Florida moved south for economic opportunity because jobs there were generally easier than the agricultural jobs available in the central and northern portions of the state, often paid better, or even presented prospects for self-employment.

In the early 1930s, the bishop, his wife, and his four oldest children—Alyce, Charles, Mary, and Henry, all of whom were pre-school age—packed into an old Model T Ford Mother Tate bought for him for fifty dollars.[2] He made his rounds, visiting existing congregations and starting new ones, which were frequently the result of conversions at revivals. A newly established congregation often met at a member's home, or out in the yard. In some cases a congregation gathered under a "bush arbor," a general term used by Keith Dominion members to denote any space shaded by vegetation.[3] The next stage might be to rent a building, often a storefront. As the congregation gained stability, the members would establish a building fund, purchase land, and erect a permanent edifice. Bishop Nelson participated in the construction of two churches in his hometown: Ocala Number One, located a few blocks from his home in west Ocala, and Mt. Canaan, about five miles east of town on Baseline Road, near Silver Springs.

In the 1930s, much of Florida was sparsely settled. Traveling throughout the state by automobile was an adventure for anyone, but especially so for young African American children from north-central Florida. A good portion of the Ocala area is gently rolling country shaded by large moss-draped oaks. Much of the region is covered by dense expanses of pine and hardwood scrub. Ocala lies well inland, about thirty-five miles from the Gulf of Mexico coast and twice that far from the Atlantic. The region is dotted with black-water lakes and blessed with several cool, crystalline springs, the most renowned being Silver Springs, which has been a large tourist attraction for decades.

In contrast, southeastern Florida is flat. The climate, flora, and fauna are distinctly subtropical. Saltwater bodies—the Atlantic Ocean, Indian River, and any number of bays and estuaries—and the teeming fishes, crustaceans, and birds that spring from them, are always nearby. The Florida Keys, a chain of small islands, some only a few yards wide in places, stretches south and west from the southern tip of the peninsula through azure waters for 120 miles to the tropical terminus at Key West.

Mary, Henry, and their siblings experienced many new sights, sounds, and scents on the journeys south through subtropical Florida with their parents. They tasted luscious tropical fruits for the first time and experienced a mixture of fear and wonder as they watched herds of hundreds of land crabs—each holding high a claw as big as a man's thumb and index finger—cross highways and invade neighborhoods. They trembled with fear as Bishop Nelson's sputtering, rickety Model T traversed stretches of the Overseas Highway to Key West that were submerged by seasonally high tides. Decades later, Mary Nelson Linzy still vividly remembered the adventure of journeying to Key West:

> There was mangoes for sale on the streets, and guavas. The older people would take the guavas and make jelly, and that would be food with bread for the children to hush their mouth. We were with him when he went down that way. He would stay till he visit all the churches. And sometime it would be a week at some, but the members would house us.
>
> In Key West I remember the crabs a-walkin' the streets. And we went in a playground across from the house where we stayed and they came and said, "Hurry up and come on back in." They could hear the crabs coming, and we didn't understand what they meant. We had come out to the playground. But as soon as we got inside and shut the door, a drove of them crabs were going over toward the Gulf. And they said, "They will catch you and hold you 'til the lightning and thunder come." But anyway, we enjoyed being in the area.
>
> And the bridge was a little ol' narrow bridge go across that water. And

daddy didn't worry about it, he didn't seem to be afraid. If he was, he didn't mention it. But my mother, she was sitting there holding her brow most of the time. "We gonna fall over," she'd call to him. "We gonna fall over here." But we made it, and had no accidents. That was the only scary part.[4]

Bishop Nelson's territory included South Pittsburg, Tennessee (near the Tennessee-Georgia-Alabama border). He and his family also made annual trips to the General Assembly in Nashville. Traveling across the mountains in the old Model T was also quite an adventure for young Mary:

All the trips down to Key West would be the most scariest—other than crossing the Lookout Mountain—'cause at the time, crossing the Lookout Mountain was two lanes. And with the Model T, they told him to stay off the brakes 'cause they would burn up. But the curves was worse than what they are now up there, so he had to do something. When it was going like this, I would always get in the bottom of the car and close my eyes, going down especially. 'Cause he had to cross Mount Eagle, and Signal Mountain. But you don't have to cross but one now, going into Nashville. Signal Mountain was steeper. He started down, and hit them brakes, and they did start burning sure enough. And he pulled—you know once you're going down the mountain you see water—and he popped right in there, and he thought he'd just put some water in 'em. They could cool down and he would get on down. There was some northern white people coming behind him. They stopped. You know, when you got a bunch of children, everybody try to help you then. They stopped and told him, "No, no, don't put the water in there." So somehow or another they scraped enough dirt under them rocks in Tennessee to put down in there, and cool it off. And then they stayed behind, because going down is when you really had problems real bad. And then when he got down, they followed him into Nashville, and tell him where he could get some work done on the brakes, and [the white man] took care of the price of what it was. [The congregation] never knew it, but it still didn't stop him from doing his church work, crossing the mountains.[5]

Despite such hazards, life on the road had its rewards, asserted Linzy: "One thing I liked about it: the travels. It was a thing that most children don't get to do 'cause the parents will leave them. And they didn't worry about where we were gonna sleep or what we was gonna eat, because the membership always prepared that. And they loved us so much. They'd load the car when we got ready to come home, with things they thought that we would like. They would bake cakes and turkeys and everything, and pack the car."[6]

Back in Ocala in the 1930s and early 1940s, the Nelsons led a rural lifestyle. There was no electricity. Water was drawn from a well by a pitcher pump and the family toilet was an outhouse. Bishop Nelson worked full time in the clergy; neither Mary nor Audrey Pearl remembers him ever having a job outside ministering in the Keith Dominion. Like many country preachers, he was not paid a wage or salary but supported his family on contributions from the congregations he served. Because cash was scarce, the church membership often paid him with produce. The Nelsons also grew a few vegetables in their home garden and raised chickens. Linzy recalled some of the constraints of rural life:

> The only meat you might have would be on Sundays for Sunday dinner. It's not like you have it every meal and all that now. It would be chicken, 'cause my dad raised them from the eggs. He didn't like to buy the chickens at the market. And if he bought one, he would clean it out with castor oil and food, and pen 'em up. And after so many days they had been cleaned, they would kill them and eat them. But we didn't have refrigeration like now; you had ice boxes with a block of ice about fifty pound, twenty-five pound. It would last long enough to keep the meat till time to cook it Sunday. Didn't worry about it no other part of the week. Wasn't nothing wrong with that. Everyone was healthy.
>
> My mother loved them greens. Dad had a hand plow 'cause the lot was big enough for him to use the back end. Got a big wheel and a little spade behind that plows it up. Had them boys [Henry and Charles] out there pushing. And all that was to show them how to make a living. But the membership, they would bring produce in on Saturday out there at Mount Canaan, like corn, peas. Get enough corn, Preston Mills had a grounding machine in front of our house across the street and everybody would bring their corn up there and make the grits and the meal. And it was a big ol' thing.[7]

Bishop Mattie Lou Jewell, the chief overseer of the Jewell Dominion, lived in West Ocala part time. Mary Linzy remembers that in the early 1940s Bishop Jewell built a large church on Broadway. The bishop was innovative in making her worship services appeal to potential new members, especially young people. Among the young people she attracted was Lorenzo Harrison, who would establish the dominant steel guitar style in the Jewell Dominion and eventually become vice president of that denomination. Linzy recalled:

> When Jewell came in and built her church right down from our house out there, that's when she had these young people in there with their music, and they were doing the natural born dance steps, like you go to a ballroom, and all of that. Young people, she had all the young people. They do it any way

they want. And that was just drawin'. It was like a side show to me. Yeah, now you know that would bring 'em in. Somethin' to do.

And wasn't too much action coming here in Ocala on our side of town, so all the young people got to tellin' bout the good time they have in there. And that's how Lorenzo Harrison met Nettie Mae [his first wife]. She was one of the main ones to start her little dances. Lorenzo got stuck on Bishop Jewell's daughter [actually, her adopted granddaughter], Nettie Mae. The Harrisons left our church and joined in there with them. And that's how Lorenzo got involved with them. Got in there with Bishop Jewell, and then he started with his music. Everything he needed, she would get.

They had a thing inside [the church] that was like a train comin' in from heaven with angels on it, comin' in to get you. It was working by electricity. Ms. Jewell had that set up, and you couldn't go in the back end of the church outside because all the electrical stuff was out there. She had got her electricity all hooked up, and I think it was more of a battery powered thing. The people was talkin' about Jesus coming in the church and doing this, that, and the other, so everybody was going.[8]

Henry Nelson often said that he began to play the steel guitar when he was seven, which means he took up the instrument in 1937. He also vividly recalled that Willie Eason was his inspiration. Nelson would have been nine when Eason traveled south to Florida with Bishop Lockley and the Gospel Feast Party band in January 1939. Regardless of the exact year, the electric guitar—indeed electric power itself—was new and exciting to African Americans in Ocala. In those hardscrabble times, one or two acoustic instruments played with rudimentary skill by local members for worship services was an attraction. A band of a half-dozen skilled musicians from the urban northeast playing professional-grade instruments—including Willie Eason on the singing electric Hawaiian guitar—for services and revivals was a source of wonder and considerable excitement. Nelson recalled the Gospel Feast Party band:

Bishop Lockley would have a musical team; there was a gospel band. Bishop Lockley's son [J.R.] used to accompany Willie Eason with the vibes. They were *dynamic*. Went to Miami and my goodness, they had to fight their way out of there. That was back in the early forties before the war. They used to drive a big Cadillac limousine that would be loaded with instruments and those boys. When they'd drive in town, they always had a little trailer in the back that would be the music [instruments].

Moe Harper was the drummer out of Brooklyn. They have tom-toms now, but in those days they used gourd heads and each gourd had a different tune for the drummer, and that was his tom-tom. They'd take a gourd from the garden and cut that big head off and they would formulate the sound to the size of the gourd head. He had a lead guitar player out of Brooklyn, too. His name was [Roosevelt] Eberhardt—electric guitar. Whenever a bass player wasn't there he would tune [down] the bass strings of the lead guitar and he'd hold it up.[9] You couldn't tell the difference between that and the bass. They had an upright bass in those days. They'd attach a pickup on the back of the bass. That's the only way you could get it electrified.

In those days you wouldn't have as many plugs in the wall as you have now. They used to have just one straight line and they would plug that in the middle of the church and everything would come from that line. It was *dynamic*. People would come from far and near to hear the electric guitar. It just amazed me as a young man. I just wanted to do everything I saw.[10]

From an early age, Henry Nelson had expressed an interest in making music. His sister, Mary, remembered him making a "guitar" by wrapping rubber bands around a tobacco can and taking it to church:

He started with a tobacco can. You know how they had to roll up the cigarettes? Us being on the highway, it would be a lot [of tobacco cans] in the ditch in front of the house. He got one and loaded it up with rubber bands, and come in church, and he beat that thing. And he'd peek at [the congregants] until he start to annoy, and mama said, "Leave that boy alone."

But that's when he first started, and then they got him a Spanish guitar, and he was playin' it like a Hawaiian, and he kept on his own. He did piano the same way. We would tell him how he'd mess up the service, but mama would say, "Let him play. He got to learn."[11]

Linzy's recollection illustrates aspects of the informal learning process and the interaction of congregants with young musicians still prevalent in the Keith Dominion today. Musicians typically begin to play at an early age, often before adolescence. Rhythm, the most fundamental element of music, definitely comes first with Keith Dominion musicians. For many, the drum set is their first real instrument. "We all started on drums," stated steel guitarist Chuck Campbell.[12] While Campbell's generalization is somewhat exaggerated, certainly many—maybe most—Keith Dominion steel guitarists are competent drummers, or played drums early in their musical careers. Emphasis on rhythm is instilled in Keith Dominion steel guitarists from an early age. Aspiring musicians use a rhythmic approach, frequently "framming" the instrument (strumming it percussively) when first attempting to make music with the steel guitar. As a steel guitarist's skill level in picking melodies, riffs, and slurred notes increases, the amount of framming generally decreases, but it remains an important part of technique for many.

Linzy's recollections of her mother's tolerance for young Henry's developing musicianship reveal the supportive and nurturing environment often experienced by young Keith Dominion musicians at their local church. As a young musician struggles with a solo performance, congregants will often give words of encouragement such as "Take your time, son." Paradoxically, a congregation may be quick to let a musician—young or old—know if he or she is not making a positive contribution to the service or is exceeding aesthetic bounds.

Young Henry's enthusiasm and budding musical ability were noticed by his father. He also impressed Chief Overseer Bishop Keith as he performed after dinner on his tobacco can-and-rubber band "guitar" when she visited the Nelson home. He recalled her saying, "Bishop Nelson, this boy got something going good here. I can preach behind this."[13]

Bishop Nelson soon purchased Henry a stylish black and white National electric lap-steel guitar and amplifier from Ace Music in Miami. Delighted with his shiny new instrument, Henry played for hours on end with youthful exuberance. "I wore that guitar out, especially where you put the strings on at," he recalled. "It was wood and I used to peel that wood with them picks. I would run that wood hot."[14] Young Nelson wanted Willie Eason to give him a few pointers, but Willie was constantly on the move, so Nelson had to learn on his own. "I wanted Willie to teach me but he stayed so busy. When he found it out I was already pulling a service by myself. My father was so interested in me learning that he made every effort he could. I don't even remember rehearsing at home. It was just a gift from God that I came through with it."[15]

Bishop Nelson recognized his son's gift and exercised his ministerial powers to guide him. Henry Nelson recalled the sense of mission his father instilled:

> My anointing came by him laying hands on me when I first started playing when I was seven years old. He anointed my hands [with olive oil]. And he said "Henry, if you keep this in the name of the Lord, play for Him, it'll make room for you." And to this day, no blues, no rock and roll. That haven't been. Been approached a million times to do it. No way. I say, "God, He'll paralyze my hands." I do believe that, and which He will do. And I been working with Him and obeying Him too long to change now. Can't teach an old dog new tricks.[16]

As an adolescent, Nelson began to establish a reputation as a "ladies' man." He was tall and handsome, had wavy hair, and spoke in a soft, charming voice that often bordered on a lisp. Henry and his brother Charles attended Howard Academy, the segregated public school established soon after Emancipation to serve African Americans in several counties surrounding Ocala. Both Nelson brothers played on the Howard Academy football team, the Wild Bulls. Because their social activities were closely regulated by codes of behavior delineated in the *Decree Book,* they kept their football playing a secret from their parents. Mary Linzy described how that secret finally came to light:

> Those boys had been playing all the time. They would put those togs under the house, what they practice in. Put em' under the house, and they could come in the door then. [Our parents] wouldn't know a thing.
>
> So one morning my mother went to wake Charles up, and his leg was out from under the cover. And where they had stepped on him in that game that night with them things [spikes], [the wound] was opened. 'Cause see, the coach put a red powder puff—you know, what the ladies put powder on their face with?—right down in the hole to pad it, and somehow or another the wrapping had come off. And she yelled. It woke him up. And that's when they really found out Charles and Henry had been playing a couple of years.
>
> Well, my father wouldn't have allowed it because of the laws of the church. You know, in our Decree Book it's all listed what you're not supposed to do. So, Bishop Keith revised it by letting them know that was a physical activity for your body. Nothing sinful about that. 'Cause dad had them to talk to her after he found this out, and she okayed it. So he didn't worry about it no more. . . . And they were in the top three or four for Howard High School, both of them.[17]

Soon after taking up the steel guitar, Henry was able to contribute spirited music to his father's church services. By the late 1940s, he began to travel with his father to play the steel guitar at church meetings throughout Bishop Nelson's dioceses in Florida, South Carolina, North Carolina, Tennessee, Georgia, and Alabama. Henry recalled:

> I was my father's chauffeur. And I drove everywhere he had to go, all up through Alabama and Georgia. We had a Buick, a '39 Buick. In them days cars were so expensive, and he had to buy a big car that lasted a long time. It was a second-hand car.
>
> It was bad during that time. Daddy wouldn't go in some parts of Georgia in the daytime because of racial problems. A lot of places we had to go at night or early in the mornin'. In Georgia, they'll call you a nigger: "Get out

of here you nigger." I went to a place in Georgia, around Douglas, Georgia. I pulled into the station. A guy walked up to the window and I told him, "Fill it up and check the oil." The guy told me, he said, "What'd that nigger say?" I said, "Fill it up and check the oil." He said, "Don't you know we don't serve niggers gas here, in this station?" Well, I threw it in [low gear] and I pulled out of that station. Dad said, "Son, we need some gas in here." I pulled in the station on empty and I pulled out the station on empty. He didn't even get the nozzle in the tank. They were *so mean*, especially to black people. People didn't stand a chance.[18]

Times have changed and racial tensions have eased, but the drive north on U.S. 441 through the low, flat pinewoods of southern Georgia is still a long, lonesome stretch. It took tremendous faith and courage for Bishop Nelson and Henry to travel throughout the South in a time when Jim Crow was the law of the land and African Americans were still occasionally lynched.

In addition to racial discrimination, early in the days of the Holiness-Pentecostal movement participants in this highly demonstrative form of worship were often viewed with curiosity, fascination, and fear by both whites and blacks. Nelson recalled a variety of reactions to Keith Dominion worship services and to his steel guitar playing:

Holiness had just started and people liked that movement. They loved the music. It's a going religion in those days, and it just so happened that when we would play they had never heard no instrument like that. I would have nothing but the [steel] guitar and we'd beat on the back of a tub and that was my bass. Now, my mother always did beat the bass drum with a stick with a big ball on it. And she'd beat it so—she had a small ball on one end a big ball on the other end—you would think it was a whole [drum] set. She was left handed. And she'd follow everything I played. She'd flip that thing [the drumstick]. She was dynamic, my God! We'd church all night long. People didn't know when to stop.

People would come to see it. They were afraid of the religion because we would "get happy." We had the anointing. The Holy Ghost itself came into existence and so many people were afraid of it because of what it does: you are no more controlled by yourself; you're controlled by God. It is a *happening*. It is an honest-to-goodness happening. And those days when it was coming about, the Baptist and Methodist people, they were fighting. They would say that we were "hoodooers" and they called us "holy rollers."

[The Keith Dominion] started in 1903 in Greenville, Alabama. That's where my father found my mother. That's where he found his rib, in Greenville, Alabama, and got me in the picture. In those days there was a lot of prejudice among the Negroes of the religious part of their lives. And they were prejudiced otherwise. Because when the whites would come to the meetings they would always stand around and daddy would invite them up. He had quite a name throughout the Greenville, Alabama, area, especially. He would come in with the word of God and convince them that when the word of God get on you there is no difference in nothing. The spirit of God is on you, you have no control by yourself.[19]

Discrimination against African American Holiness-Pentecostals created difficult physical circumstances, but the Keith Dominion congregations were determined to worship in their demonstrative manner. Henry Nelson recalled some of the challenges of those early years:

In those days they wouldn't even rent a building to us. That's when the bush arbor times came. Down in a place called Corner Flat, Alabama.[20] That's where I played under the first bush arbor. And they had to run the [electric] cord a long way. A *long* ways! We would start playing, people would come from everywhere.

They didn't have no road coming up to the place where we had the bush arbor. And they were too tight in those days, they wouldn't give you nothing because what you represent. "That's them holy rollers?" Oh, the dust, even under the bush arbors. They didn't have the sawdust to put down. It was just natural dirt and the benches didn't have no backs. It was just a side to hold the [offertory] bowls on top. The spirit would get so high [and the dust would get so thick] you couldn't even see one another in the bush arbor. Those were the days. Those were the days.

The reason they named us the holy rollers is because we believe in coming down to the altar and calling the name of Jesus and receiving the Holy Ghost. Once they got down there, the power would be on them and they would be moving around, and to keep them covered they would have blankets to put over them, and sheets. That was the purpose of it. And they'd joke about it: "That man's in there rolling with my wife," and all that stuff. The inside of it was the fact that they was seeking Christ and He was visiting them. When you get to a certain point and believe in Him, He automatically comes in and you can't help yourself moving in all directions. Sometimes there would be fifty or a hundred down there. It's a big job for the [ones helping those seeking the Holy Ghost]. That's where they gave us the name of holy rollers.

Those were the rough days. They used to shoot out the lamps on the table. They used to take the air out of the tires. Most of the transportation they was using then was horse and buggy. We would always have to leave somebody— three or four deacons—outside to watch the horses. [The horses] would get spooked. When we would get high going in the service, it wouldn't take but one horse to spook and they'd run wild. I could see them traveling around all in South Carolina.[21]

Nelson recalled an especially memorable service in Pamplico, South Carolina, when congregants packed into the country church for an assembly danced and shouted until the foundation collapsed: "The church sink in the ground with so many people! All the [foundation] pillars went down! The next day I had to jack it back up. Ooh, I could see it now. That place would get so fired up under the learning of God until it was *dust* in there. It was just like a haze."[22]

In 1955, Henry Nelson married Hattie Ghent (pronounced "jent"), the only child of Keith Dominion minister Elder Eugene G. Ghent and Mattie Ghent of Fort Pierce. For a while Nelson worked for his father-in-law, who was a labor crew chief for a local Indian River citrus operation. In 1956, Henry and Hattie Nelson moved to New York, where Henry attended Brooklyn State Hospital Nursing School. They moved back to Florida, then separated. Henry returned to New York and Hattie remained with her parents in Fort Pierce. On October 17, 1958, Hattie gave birth to a boy she named Aubrey. About two weeks later Hattie Ghent Nelson died of complications resulting from the birth. Distraught at the loss of their only child, the Ghents forbade Henry Nelson to visit his son. Aubrey was given the surname Ghent and raised by his maternal grandparents. Although not raised by his father, Aubrey Ghent became a master lap-steel guitarist who plays in a manner that reflects considerable influence by him.

In 1959, Henry Nelson met Johnnie Mae Varnado (1943–), the fair-skinned sixteen-year-old adopted daughter of Elder Charles Henry Varnado (1894–1979).[23] In March 1962 they were married at the Bethlehem Church of God in Christ (COGIC) in Jamaica, New York, where Elder Varnado served as pastor.[24] Henry worked as a truck driver with his father-in-law at Berger Machinery. He and Johnnie Mae had five children.

Nelson joined the COGIC and played the steel guitar, accompanied by his wife on piano and organ, at the Bethlehem COGIC as well as for worship services, revivals, and gospel music programs at other churches in the area. He earned quite a reputation playing in the metropolitan New York area and eventually caught the attention of one of gospel music's biggest stars when he performed on a program at a Methodist Church in Brooklyn that featured Mahalia Jackson. He recalled that when Jackson heard the voice-like strains of his steel guitar she inquired, "Who was that? Where is that talking machine?"[25] Jackson invited Nelson to participate in a recording session at the Columbia Records studios and on February 2, 1959, he joined her group to record "To Me It's So Wonderful." The sound of Nelson's steel was buried by the other instruments and voices in the mix; it is barely audible in the recording. However, as was the case with Willie Eason's recorded collaborations with the Soul Stirrers, Nelson's appearance on Mahalia Jackson's recording put the stamp of approval by a mainstream gospel artist on his work, albeit to a much lesser degree than in Eason's case.

On August 22, 1968, Henry Nelson suffered a gruesome industrial accident at Berger Machinery, which was later graphically described in the memorial booklet distributed at his funeral, or "homegoing" service, at New Greater Bethel Ministries, Queens Village, New York, April 14, 2001.

> After making an attempt to make a correction inside one of the machines, the machine backed over his body, twisting him where the top portion of his body faced the back, blew his eyes out of his head, punctured his left lung, crushed his kidneys, broken his ribs, broken his pelvis, broken the veins around his heart and he bled profusely from his ears, nose and mouth. His working years for man was put to rest while lying in New York Hospital. His father, the late Bishop W. L. Nelson, told him to do like Abraham and make a covenant with the Lord. His covenant was if the Lord let him live, he would play for him and tell what God had done for him everywhere he would go. He kept his covenant and began traveling with his father to different assemblies and conventions playing his Hawaiian guitar and telling how God healed his body. He also played and chauffeured for the Chief Overseer, Bishop J. C. Elliott and he assisted many others during revivals, assemblies, etc. nationwide.[26]

It took two or three years for Nelson to recover from the accident sufficiently to lead a more-or-less normal life, and he received Social Security disability benefits until his death.[27] As he recovered, he became very active as a steel guitarist and considered playing sacred music his full-time occupation.

Nelson had not played at the Keith Dominion General Assembly for an extended period, since 1958 or 1959. The year of his return to play at the General Assembly is a subject of some debate, but Chuck Campbell has made a convincing case for it being 1973 (the details are discussed below). Johnnie Mae Nelson remembered that Henry did not rejoin the Keith Dominion until her father died in 1979, but thought that he may have traveled south to Nashville to play for the General Assembly as early as 1973.[28] During Nelson's hiatus, Ted Beard and Calvin Cooke played regularly at the General Assembly. Both Beard and Cooke were raised in families that had been members of the Jewell Dominion. The steel guitar music of the Jewell Dominion was largely shaped by Bishop Lorenzo Harrison. The music played by Beard and Cooke reflected Harrison's influence and contrasted to Nelson's one-chord drives, which were punctuated with copious amounts of rhythmic "framming." The music played by Beard and Cooke was more melodic and usually followed a three-chord (I-IV-V) harmonic structure. During Nelson's absence from the General Assembly for more than a decade, his music was replaced by that of Beard and Cooke.

According to Chuck Campbell, Nelson returned to the General Assembly in 1973. Although Nelson was still a member of COGIC, orders came from Chief Overseer Bishop J. W. Jenkins that he would play at the General Assembly. After all, he was the son of the late Bishop W. L. Nelson, who had established and presided over the churches of the East Coast of Florida and South Carolina, which together constituted about half of the total number of churches in the Keith Dominion system. Congregants from those states, especially the older folks, were accustomed to Henry Nelson's music and responded demonstratively to his steel guitar playing. At the 1973 General Assembly he played on "Florida night," which featured instrumentalists, vocalists, choirs, and preachers from his home state. Campbell recalled that Nelson's playing largely failed to move the congregation: "His style just doesn't work well and we [the musicians] think the 'old style' is still dead. The older people are saying they're glad to hear 'real House of God music,' not Jewell and rock-and-roll. Ted and Calvin both dismiss Nelson's return as political and not because of his skills. It's said: He won't last. Ha!"[29]

As he contemplated the 1973 General Assembly twenty-nine years later, Campbell believed there were two factors that contributed to Nelson's difficulties. First, because Nelson had not played regularly for Keith Dominion services, particularly large congregations, for some time, he was not playing and interacting with the congregation at full potential. Second, and more important, he had too much accompaniment. The organ, bass, guitar, and saxophone interfered with Nelson's driving, one-chord music. His syncopated, rhythmic frams were buried in the mix of instruments.

His return to the General Assembly in June 1974 was quite a different story. Nelson and his stellar rhythm section succeeded in moving the congregation to a high level of spiritual energy. Chuck Campbell recalled:

Nineteen seventy-four is the year Henry Nelson along with [guitarist] Larry Taylor and [bassist] Harold Braddy, who was out of jail, took over. Playing with Larry and Harold left him to do the rhythm drives. They had a groove and serious bass lines. . . . We also found out this year how much better Henry was with choirs and soloists, as the newer, modern, complex-chord choir songs by Edwin Hawkins, Andraé Crouch, and James Cleveland were being sung. Lastly, Henry was on tour around the church playing all the state assemblies, so by General Assembly time he was in demand.

One reason I modeled after Calvin was that Ted's Nashville style worked well with a lot of accompaniment, but in a drum and steel service [like one might encounter at a local weekly worship service] his style didn't work for me. Henry's style works great, even without drums.[30]

It is important to keep in mind that large assemblies on the state level are attended by hundreds, and the annual General Assembly in Nashville draws well over two thousand on peak days. Local weekly worship services are much smaller, often attended by fewer than thirty. At a small church, a steel guitarist may have only a drummer as accompaniment for a worship service. As a young man playing at small churches within the dioceses under his father's responsibility, Nelson developed a full, rhythmic sound out of necessity. Today Chuck Campbell appreciates Nelson's approach, which he has described succinctly: "He was emulating the rub board, the bass drum, the hand clapping, and the moans that we'd hear from a regular service, with just this one instrument."[31]

For the next twenty years, Nelson continued to play steel guitar for worship services, revivals, and assemblies at Keith Dominion churches throughout the United States. After his father-in-law's death in 1979, Nelson quit the COGIC and was fully reinstated in the Keith Dominion.[32] In addition to his tremendous talent, two factors facilitated the spread of his musical influence. First, because he did not have a "day job" he did not have to be concerned about requesting absence from work to play out of town. He was available to go anywhere on short notice and stay as long as necessary. Second, as the son of the recently deceased Bishop W. L. Nelson (1895–1973), who had established dozens of Keith Dominion churches and served the organization faithfully for nearly half a century, he was ensconced within the inner circle of power.

As a young man traveling with Bishop Nelson, Henry had established a reputation as a steel guitarist who could "move" a worship service. He traveled widely to play for worship services, revivals, and assemblies, not only with his father, but with Keith Dominion Chief Overseer Bishop J. W. Jenkins. After his father's death in 1973, he continued to serve under Bishop Jenkins. When Bishop Jenkins died in 1990, Nelson served under his successor, Bishop J. C. Elliott of Sarasota, Florida. Playing under bishops Nelson, Jenkins, and Elliott for state assemblies, revivals, and special events—including the biggest gathering of all, the annual General Assembly—meant Nelson was heard by the largest congregations as he played for the most spirited services held in the most prestigious circumstances. Consequently, Henry Nelson's influence was widespread. He was especially influential in Florida and South Carolina, where his father had established so many churches, as well as in "downstate" urban New York, the region of his own residence.

Henry Nelson also cultivated a charming persona. He was a sharp dresser and knew how to "work" a congregation. Prior to a service he would visit with congregants, exchanging pleasantries and shaking hands. He complimented the ladies, paying special attention to elderly women. Before he even hit one note on his steel guitar, he held the congregation in the palm of his hand. His suave manner prompted brothers Chuck and Phil Campbell to refer to him as the "Liberace of the House of God." Phil Campbell fondly recalled Nelson's sartorial appointments and charm:

> The diamond rings. He had the matching shoes and the matching socks. He had the two-tone vest on. He'd have the tie; he'd have the clip. He'd have the gold pendant. He'd have the chain with the cross. He'd have—everything would just be *impeccable*. He was impeccable. I guess that's the word: always impeccably dressed.
>
> In fact, he'd have his son carry his guitar in for him and set everything up. Then he walks in down the middle of the aisle and he takes his place like a big performer. And he sits down and, you know, his hands just flowing [Phil gestured with a flourish]. And this is the way he played.[33]

Testimonies to Nelson's influence abound among Keith Dominion steel guitarists. James Hampton, a lap-steel guitarist from the Charleston, South Carolina, area who lived in the Bronx, New York, as a young man, recalled, "He's one of the main players that I looked up to. He is a great inspiration to me. I'm glad he was here to show us. He wasn't there in front of us, but we were listening. Everybody's got a part of Henry in them."[34] Southpaw Anthony Fox serves as the official "state" steel guitarist in South Carolina. Fox enjoys playing pedal-steel, but often plays much of a worship service on his six-string lap-steel, so he can deliver the "Nelson sound" that so many congregants prefer. "[Henry Nelson] is the *main* steel player that has influenced my style on the six-string. I think he is the greatest," declared Fox. "I really admire his style of playing. That's what got me to where I am on the six-string."[35]

The Nelson style dominated in Florida too. "We all grew up on Henry," emphatically stated Alvin Lee of Perrine. "Everybody played like Henry . . ."[36] And Elton Noble of Fort Pierce remarked, "That's all you heard from New York, Ocala, Fort Pierce, Vero, down south in Miami. . . . Henry Nelson was a household name, I'm going to say that, especially among the steel players."[37]

Phil Campbell offered his perspective on Nelson's contribution to the tradition: "Willie Eason had melodic performance and all those things, but when it comes to Keith Dominion praise music, Henry Nelson is the father of that. And that is what really drives the services to the kinds of levels that you witness in House of God services today."[38]

Driving praise music was not Nelson's only contribution to the Keith Dominion steel guitar tradition. His voice-like renditions of hymns and gospel songs are legendary. Chuck Campbell recalled how congregants reacted to hymns poignantly rendered by Nelson: "I heard him playing this thing at a funeral, and people just started busting out crying. I mean it was just like somebody was singing it."[39]

Henry's son, Aubrey Ghent, grew to be a master lap-steel guitarist as well as an accomplished, fiery preacher. While Ghent's steel guitar playing reflects considerable influence from his father, he has found his own unique voice on the instrument and is considered one of the best six-string lap-steel guitarists to have served in the Keith Dominion. Occasionally father and son played together, usually for special events. On December 26, 1993, they joined forces for "Youth Day" at Mt. Canaan Keith Dominion church, just east of Ocala. This was a church Bishop W. L. Nelson helped build with his own hands, and the edifice Henry Nelson had attended as a boy. (Visiting Ocala sparked fond memories for Henry and he often spoke of moving from New York to live peacefully in his hometown.)

The capacity of Mt. Canaan was about 150, but routine Sunday services usually drew only a couple of dozen souls, maybe fewer. For this special service the day after Christmas, the building was packed to standing room only. There were guest speakers too, including Chief Overseer Bishop James C. Elliott, resplendent in his white vestments and *biretta,* a square hat topped by a tassel, similar to that worn by Roman Catholic clergy. I led a team from the Florida Folklife Program to document the service by multi-track audio recording and still photography.

Guest musicians were brought in to accompany the father and son steel guitar duo. Blind keyboardist and singer Francine Jones traveled from Plant City. The chief overseer's teenage son, Terrence Elliott, joined on electric bass. Slim and steel-eyed, twenty-two-year-old Tampa drummer Lejena Manning sported a high flat-top haircut in the style of singer and actress Grace Jones. Her black miniskirt caused a few of the more conservative congregants to raise their eyebrows.

When Elder Bessie Brinson belted out "Praise the Lord Everybody," the band exploded like some fire-breathing gospel train steaming for glory land. Nelson played a high lead that echoed Elder Brinson's voice while Ghent laid down punchy, syncopated riffs on the bass strings. After about three minutes of call-and-response exchanges between Elder Brinson and the congregation, the band cranked up the energy level and took over. By that point, holy dancing and spirit possession were occurring on a wholesale basis. I was bumped several times by dancers and shouters as I photographed. A team of male ushers joined hands to form a human barricade to prevent dancers from careening into the band. Because the ushers could not tend to the number of congregants experiencing spirit possession and the resultant involuntary body movements, other congregants pitched in to prevent those so possessed from colliding with people and furniture. The energy continued to build as Nelson gave his son a turn at the lead. Feeling the spiritual fire, Elder Ghent picked blazing improvisations for some three minutes as Nelson's steel grunted and groaned bass lines. At the climax of his solo, Ghent broke into a few bars of syncopated phrases consisting of a succession of staccato notes of the same pitch followed by a leap to a higher, longer note, a sound known in the vernacular as "chicken pickin'." On his return to take the lead, Nelson pulled out all the stops. He wrung a howling, wild vibrato from his ancient Fender, which he alternated with screaming octaves and dissonant chords. Underneath Nelson's final solo, his son played frams in a Bo Diddley rhythm. Heard out of context, Nelson's playing at this point did not sound like what most people would call music. But as functional Keith Dominion praise music played to a packed house, it was highly effective.

These first eight minutes set the tone for five hours of fiery Holiness-Pentecostal worship that day. It would be the only professionally recorded sample of Nelson and Ghent playing together in a Keith Dominion service.

Aubrey Ghent was the first Keith Dominion steel guitarist to appear on the folk festival circuit, and his early performances at festivals mark the beginning of exposure of the music to the secular public. On May 29, 1994, he performed at the forty-second annual Florida Folk Festival in White Springs. He was accompanied by his wife Lorie, a capable singer, Pensacola keyboardist Darryl Brundidge, and drummer Timothy Williams, who had packed the Mt. Canaan church drums into his car and hauled them to the festival. Ghent's group was surprisingly well received by the Florida Folk Festival audience, which is probably 99 percent white and favors acoustic singer-songwriters. Sensing the audience's musical preferences, Ghent's group was rather reserved in its delivery.

After hearing a sample of Ghent's playing that Mike Stapleton and I had recorded on our visit to his home on November 7, 1992, Joe Wilson, director of the National Council for the Traditional Arts (NCTA), booked him for the National Folk Festival in Chattanooga, Tennessee, in October 1993. Ghent's trio included Darryl Brundidge, who handled the double-decker keyboard synthesizer, and drummer Harold Crenshaw of Atlanta. They had the good fortune to be preceded on stage by a high-energy performance by a male step team from the historically black Morehouse College of Atlanta. African American step-dancing, also known as "stepping" or "soulstepping," involves using the whole body as a percussion instrument and is usually performed by groups in arrangements that resemble military formations. The Morehouse steppers gave an electrifying performance that left the largely African American audience charged and craving more excitement.

Ghent and company set up quickly and immediately launched into Oris Mays's classic novelty gospel song "Don't Let the Devil Ride," which in musical terms is a slow blues shuffle. The sound of Ghent's searing steel guitar was instantly compelling. Here was the sound of electric "slide" guitar with a gospel voice. His technical command of the instrument was astounding, his vibrato divinely lush. His soaring phrases were rich with melismas and voice-like slurs as passionate and inventive as those belted out by the best gospel vocalists. Ghent's singing was remarkable as well. The audience—black and white—went wild. Ghent had previously performed on major black gospel programs, where he appeared with such stars as Albertina Walker and Shirley Caesar, but his performances at the Florida Folk Festival and the National Folk Festival marked the first appearances of a Keith Dominion steel guitarist before the general public in recent times, and the first ever at folk festivals. The cat was out of the bag.

Among those who witnessed Ghent's landmark performances at the 1993 National Folk Festival in Chattanooga was folklorist Nick Spitzer, host of the prestigious Folk Masters concert series at the Barns of Wolf Trap in Vienna, Virginia. After Ghent's first set, Spitzer invited him and Henry Nelson (without having heard the latter) to perform at the Folk Masters Good Friday gospel concert April 1, 1994. The program also featured Madison's Lively Stones, a large brass band from the United House of Prayer for All People, from the capital city. Nelson had been aware of the House of Prayer brass bands for some time and was eager to meet the Lively Stones.

The United House of Prayer for All People was founded in the 1920s by Afro-Portuguese immigrant Marcelino Manuel de Graça, who was known as Daddy Grace. Daddy Grace's appearance was remarkable; he grew long, curved fingernails, wore his curly hair long, and dressed in robes. In his churches, he established brass bands that were modeled in part on early jazz bands. Upon his death in 1960, he was succeeded by Daddy McCullough, who was in turn succeeded by Daddy Madison, the current leader and the band's namesake. As in the Keith Dominion, House of Prayer congregations practice ecstatic Holiness-Pentecostal worship that includes dancing and "shouting" to loud music. The trombone is the lead instrument in contemporary House of Prayer bands. The bands usually total more than a dozen instruments, with trombones generally outnumbering all the others combined.

When members of the Lively Stones heard Nelson and Ghent playing during the pre-concert sound check, they rushed over to see who was making such a joyful noise and what sort of instrument they were speaking through. The Keith Dominion steel guitarists and the House of Prayer trombonists quickly formed a bond of mutual admiration. The concert was a memorable presentation that marked the first time the two vibrant African American sacred music traditions were presented on the same bill. Sadly, it would be the only performance before the general public by the father-and-son steel guitar duo.

In 1994, Nelson began a serious physical decline, as described in this excerpt from the memorial booklet distributed at his funeral:

> Henry's physical body began to slow down in April 1994. He was afflicted with a stroke that brought his traveling and playing to a standstill. His family and church family encouraged him to come out to the Lord's house and the Lord would anoint him to play again. In May 1995, he began to have excessive nosebleeds and his nose bled for 14 hours. In August 1997, he was hospitalized for chest pains and he had to be tied down. Elder Janet Hampton and Elder Elaine Blue came to have prayer and talked with him. They noticed that he was not responding. He slipped away at that moment. He was revived and taken to ICU diagnosed with pneumonia, a kidney and urine infection and meningitis of the brain. The family was called and told that his body was in shock and the final state would be his departure from this life. The family

refused to sign any papers. His pastor, General Elder Ernestine Funches, and son-in-law, Dea. Ronnie Washington, entered the room. They had prayer and talked with the Lord. As they began to pray and lay hands, his body shook and he said, "Jesus!" The next day he was sitting up in bed, talking, eating and joking like he had never been sick a day in his life. Once again the fervent effectual prayer of a righteous man availed much.[40]

Nelson continued to suffer a series of strokes in the years that followed, and on April 8, 2001, passed away. There were two homegoing services for him: one at the spacious New Greater Bethel Ministries in Queens Village, New York, on April 14, and the other a week later on April 21 at Ocala Keith Dominion Number Two, Mt. Canaan.

In Queens Village, there was a quiet wake the night before the "homegoing" service. Nelson lay in state dressed in a white suit, his large, thick hands folded peacefully. On his thumb and two fingers (albeit on the wrong hand) were fitted the picks that identified him as a steel guitarist. Off to one side, Aubrey Ghent finessed hymns on his lap-steel, his instrument speaking soaring melismas and soulful moans as poignant as any ever uttered by a human voice.

Ghent was also the principal steel guitarist at the homegoing service in Queens. For much of the service he was joined by his protégé and Nelson's godson, Darryl Blue of Ft. Lauderdale, Florida. The family and clergy dressed in white—from necktie to shoes, from hat to high heels—the color reserved for the most auspicious occasions. Included among the dozen honorary pallbearers were steel guitarists Maurice "Ted" Beard Jr., Calvin Cooke, Chuck and Darick Campbell, and Lonnie "Big Ben" Bennett.

In the Keith Dominion, the ceremonial gathering that marks mortal death is referred to as a homegoing service, not a funeral. In addition to the prayer, eulogy, and song common to death ritual services in other churches, there is a considerable amount of praise or "shout" music, which inspires many to become filled with the Holy Spirit and give the Lord a dance. At Henry Nelson's homegoing there was much dancing, shouting, and infusion with the Holy Ghost, especially among the family. Three women dressed in white nurse uniforms kept busy caring for those so filled with the Spirit and overcome with grief that they lost physical control of their movements. Periodically, the various speakers would remind the congregation that they were not there to lament Nelson's death, but to celebrate his departure from this world of toil and trouble to be in everlasting peace with the Lord.

Nelson's longtime friend, Bishop Henry Dillard, state bishop of North and South Carolina and one of three chief helpers under the chief overseer, delivered the eulogy. During his presentation he shared an anecdote that gave testimony to Nelson's reputation as a sharp dresser. Bishop Dillard related how he and Deacon Nelson traveled to a distant church where they were greeted by hosts who had not met either man before; they knew only that the bishop and deacon would be traveling together. When the pair arrived, the hosts took one look at the nattily dressed Nelson and assumed he was the bishop. Much to their embarrassment, Dillard politely explained in his soft-spoken South Carolina accent that he, not Nelson, was indeed the bishop.

The final viewing was a highly emotional experience for most of the homegoing participants. Many wept and wailed uncontrollably as they looked at Nelson's cold body and touched, kissed, or spoke to him one final time. Immobilized by grief, Johnnie Mae, his wife of thirty-nine years, had to be carried away from the casket. Antjuan Edwards, Nelson's grand-nephew from Ocala, collapsed at the casket.

Although Henry Nelson's time on earth has passed, his legacy as a major contributor to the Keith Dominion steel guitar tradition lives on. Willie Eason probably did more to popularize the instrument among Keith Dominion musicians and congregations than any other early steel guitarist, but Henry Nelson was profoundly influential—perhaps more so than any other—in shaping the steel guitar music heard in Keith Dominion churches today. On any Sunday, his syncopated frams, trademark praise-music riffs, manner of playing hymns, and approach to accompanying soloists and choirs are heard in dozens of churches throughout the geographic range of the Keith Dominion.

8 The Jewell Dominion

As in the Keith Dominion, the electric steel guitar is the dominant instrument in the Jewell Dominion. One of the most significant differences between the two traditions is that in the Jewell Dominion one individual shaped the steel guitar style and repertoire far more than any other: Bishop Lorenzo Harrison. By contrast, the Keith Dominion tradition was shaped by several individuals of varying levels of musical influence.

For decades, the Jewell Dominion leadership was dominated by one family. Chief Overseer Mattie Lue Jewell led the Jewell Dominion from 1937 until her death in 1991, a reign of more than half a century. Upon Chief Jewell's death, her great-granddaughter, Bishop Naomi Manning, was appointed chief overseer and led the organization until her death in 2003. Leadership of the church by the Jewell family ceased when Bishop Faye Moore of Mt. Clemons, Michigan, became the chief overseer in 2005.

The Jewell family dynasty shaped the church's steel guitar tradition. When Bishop Lorenzo Harrison married Chief Jewell's adopted granddaughter, Nettie Mae, in 1942, he became the organization's sole national-level steel guitarist. Harrison's steel guitar style totally dominated the music at Jewell Dominion regional and national assemblies from the early 1940s until his death in 1986, a period of more than four decades. As a result of Harrison's dominance, the Jewell Dominion steel guitar tradition—as well as rhythm guitar and drum accompaniment, and even the manner of dancing—is conventionalized to a much greater extent than the music of the Keith Dominion. As Chuck Campbell quipped, "Harrison's playing wasn't the style, it was the law."[1]

Although there are a few Jewell Dominion steel guitarists, such as Sonny Treadway and Tubby Golden, for example, whose playing does not closely resemble Harrison's, the vast majority play very much like Harrison and draw from a repertoire of Harrison's compositions and licks that have been transmitted aurally from one generation to the next, from one steel guitarist to another. The overwhelming majority of Jewell Dominion steel guitarists play the same configuration of instrument as Harrison: a single eight-string neck tuned, from low to high, E-B-E-B-E-G♯-B-E, and employ a wah pedal as a tone (timbre) control.[2] Many have composed new tunes that sound so similar to what Harrison played that only someone thoroughly familiar with Harrison's repertoire could discern with certainty that he did not compose them. Ronnie Mozee of Indianapolis, who serves as the Jewell Dominion national-level steel guitarist, learned the Harrison style directly from the master himself and plays very much in the manner of his mentor. The uniformity of technique and repertoire among Jewell Dominion steel guitarists distinguishes them from their Keith Dominion counterparts. In comparison, Keith Dominion steel guitarists may often play phrases or licks by Henry Nelson, Calvin Cooke, Glenn Lee, or Chuck Campbell, for example, but are generally quite individualistic in their playing and take pride in that individuality.

The manner of dancing is also conventionalized in the Jewell Dominion. On those rather rare occasions when Jewell Dominion members attend a Keith Dominion event, such as the centennial celebration at the Keith Dominion headquarters church in Nashville in 2003, members of the Jewell Dominion are readily identified by their distinctive manner of dancing during praise or "shout" sessions. Jewell Dominion dance is thoroughly discussed and compared to Keith Dominion dance later in this chapter.

Bishop Mattie Lue Jewell stands out as one of the most interesting and colorful persons in the "sacred steel" milieu, so much so that it is difficult to separate fact from fiction. Many remember her as the biggest woman they had ever seen. She towered at six feet-two inches, weighed three hundred pounds, was filled with Pentecostal fire, and ruled with strict authority. But she had a big heart, especially when it came to young people.

When Mother Tate married her third and final husband, Robert Tate, in 1914, she became stepmother to his six children, including Mattie Lue, an exceptionally tall and large-boned eighteen-year-old. Under the tutelage of her stepmother, Mattie Lue became deeply religious and immersed herself in the activities of the church. In 1919, Mattie Lue married Bishop Bruce L. McLeod, one of Mother Tate's chief helpers. Bishop McLeod was born in Macon, Georgia. He evangelized extensively in Florida and helped establish several churches in the Sunshine State. McLeod is said to have helped many church members who lived in the South relocate to the North, often packing large families into his own automobile. Once they were relocated, he helped the new arrivals find homes and employment.[3]

When Bishop McLeod died in 1936, Mattie Lue succeeded him as chief overseer. On November 2, 1937, she married William B. Jewell, a successful businessman who served as treasurer of the Pilot Mutual Life Insurance Company of Cleveland, Ohio, and was a stockholder in the Southern Potato Chip Company. He fully supported his wife's church activities and became involved himself. He served as a general trustee and comptroller and was appointed senior bishop. William Jewell applied his business expertise to help the church become financially sound and stable.[4]

Fred Neal (1922–91) was one of the first in the Jewell Dominion to play the electric steel guitar. Neal was born in Guys, Tennessee, about eleven miles north of Corinth, Mississippi, and raised in Mississippi. Sometime in the mid- or late-1930s he bought an electric lap-steel guitar and amplifier and began to play it for worship services at the Jewell Dominion church in Corinth. According to his son Lemuel, who is a deacon in the Jewell Dominion church in Los Angeles, "Bishop Jewell came through Corinth, Mississippi—and my dad may have been seventeen [1939] at the time, something like that—and saw him playing at the church at that time and asked his mother if he could travel with her, and that's how it got started."[5] Lemuel Neal further related that while traveling with Bishop Jewell, Lorenzo Harrison met Fred Neal at the Jewell Dominion church in Cleveland, Ohio, in about 1941. Shortly after Lorenzo Harrison met Fred Neal, Harrison became Bishop Jewell's exclusive steel guitarist and Neal ceased to travel with her. Neal was then assigned to Bishop Arthur Washington Taylor, who was responsible for the Jewell Dominion churches in Florida and Alabama, and continued to travel with him until 1947.[6] Fred Neal's limited range of travel meant that he was little seen or heard by the musicians in northern cities, such as Detroit, after 1941. When he ceased to travel with Bishop Taylor in 1947, he returned to Mississippi to play. He later moved to Nashville, then settled in Los Angeles in 1953.[7]

As Chief Jewell evangelized throughout the eastern United States, from Florida to Michigan, she established part-time residences in a few strategic locations. In Ocala, Florida, she established a church and residence on Silver Springs Boulevard within a few blocks of the House of God, Keith Dominion church and the full-time residence of its pastor, Bishop W. L. Nelson. By 1941, she had informally adopted her granddaughter, Nettie Mae Campbell (1929–). Young Nettie Mae was attractive, slim and lithe, an exceptionally good dancer, and had a talent for music. Chief Jewell used Nettie Mae's dance skills to attract young people to her church. Music was provided by Fred Neal on electric lap-steel guitar and by rhythm guitarist Franklin "Harvey" Jones (1922–).[8]

One of the young people attracted to the church was Lorenzo Harrison, who was born on February 11, 1925. In 1941, his family was living in western Ocala, the same African American neighborhood where Chief Jewell and Bishop Nelson had each established a residence and a church. Young Harrison was attracted to the environment at the Jewell Dominion services—especially the music and dance—and smitten by Nettie Mae. Although Lorenzo Harrison's family was affiliated with the Keith Dominion, he joined the Jewell Dominion in Ocala on February 2, 1941, just nine days before his sixteenth birthday.[9] In addition to falling for young Nettie Mae, Harrison was also a budding musician. Attracted by the possibility of having a musician as a son-in-law, Chief Jewell arranged for Nettie Mae and Lorenzo to get married. The Marion County courthouse was just a few blocks from their western Ocala neighborhood, but they chose to journey some thirty five miles to the Alachua County courthouse in Gainesville on September 7, 1942, to obtain a marriage license. Apparently the Alachua County laws with regard to minimum age for marriage must have been more lenient than those of Marion County at that time. Nettie Mae was two months shy of her thirteenth birthday. Their union would be the most important matrimonial bond in shaping the steel guitar music of the Jewell Dominion.

In a 2004 interview, Nettie Mae Harrison recalled the circumstances of her marriage to Lorenzo:

> Yeah, he fell in love with me. Then he wanted to follow Bishop Jewell. Yes, you know it was like a little, I don't know, I would call it a little "pre-proposal." He was putting his bid in. He told my grandmother, he said, "I know now she's too young, but when she gets old enough can I marry her, please?" And of course [my grandmother] got excited and jumped the gun: "Marry her now."
>
> She always got her desires and what she wanted, now that was for sure . . . she was the director, the dictator, the controller, she was all of that. Yes sir. Everything revolved around her, that's how it went. She was the captain or she'd sink that ship. That's the way she ruled. . . . She was a powerful woman in her day. You've got to give it to her. She was a powerful woman in her day.[10]

Nettie Mae had taken a few lessons on the electric steel guitar from a Hawaiian man, whose name she cannot recall, who taught her in her home when she was ten or eleven. In turn, she helped Harrison get started on the Hawaiian steel guitar.

> Now I started taking Hawaiian [guitar] lessons from a Hawaiian musician. I was living in Cleveland at the time, and I was just a kid, going to school. I knew how to play like the Hawaiian songs, the music.
>
> Well, Bishop Jewell was my grandmother, and I traveled with her. I played the piano. I played the xylophone. I played the drums. I played the guitar. In fact, I taught Harrison how to strum on the [Hawaiian steel] guitar. The cutest thing, he used to—I used to be so angered by him—he always wanted me to show him how to play while I was pregnant, and I didn't feel like play-ing the guitar or listening to anybody learning. And he would get upset and he would tell [my grandmother], "Will you make her show me how to play the guitar? Will you make her play with me?" I either had to play the piano along with him or show him how to strum it.[11]

It is likely that the first electric steel guitarist young Lorenzo Harrison heard was either Willie Eason or his older brother Troman. Ocala was one of the Gospel Feast Party's first stops in the Sunshine State as they worked their way south. After leaving Lockley's entourage, Willie Eason continued to play and sing on street corners independently, and to a lesser extent, at church worship services and revivals. As an itinerant musician, Willie Eason used Ocala as his North Central Florida base in the winter, and married Bishop Nelson's daughter, Alyce, there in 1941. Nettie Mae remembers encountering Willie Eason sometime in the early 1940s, although Lorenzo Harrison, as an Ocala resident, may have seen and heard him earlier. The details of where and when she first met Eason are unclear, but he made a lasting impression. "We were all taken by him because he was amazing," she recalled. "After we heard Willie Eason playing, well, different ones started trying to play like Willie Eason."[12]

Eason's approach of using his steel guitar to imitate the singing voices heard in Keith and Jewell Dominion churches, as opposed to playing in the straightforward "Hawaiian" manner, caught on with church steel guitar-ists, including Harrison. While Harrison ultimately developed a manner of playing that differed considerably from Eason's, the core concept of imitating the vocal sounds heard in religious services is an essential ele-ment of his technique.

Shortly after Lorenzo and Nettie Mae were married, they left Ocala to travel with Chief Jewell as she evangelized and presided over larger church meetings such as revivals, state assemblies, and the annual General Assembly. Her musical entourage included Lorenzo Harrison on steel guitar, rhythm guitarist Harvey Jones, and drummer Corroneva Burns (1929–). Harrison had been playing steel for only about a year at the most, but worked incessantly to improve his skills. "He would play all the time," Nettie Mae remembered. "He was rehearsing and playing all day and all night. He became obsessed with the guitar, and he got very good . . . Harrison became so professional. He became so good at it. It just seemed like he was spiritually endowed. God just blessed this man. He became a legend. You talkin' about—listen, he was the greatest."[13]

Harrison, Burns, and Jones formed a musical triumvirate that reigned over Jewell Dominion assemblies from 1942 to 1957. The three musicians conventionalized the technique, rhythm, timbre, tempo, and canon of tunes that remain key characteristics of the Jewell Dominion sound today. One of the characteristics of Jewell Dominion music is the moderate tempo, usually considerably slower than most Keith Dominion praise music. Ask a Keith Dominion musician to talk about Jewell praise music and he will typically shake his head, maybe chuckle a little, and say something to the effect of, "I can't believe how slowly they play and how they dance. It's so different from they way we do it."

In addition to maintaining a moderate tempo, Jewell Dominion drummers are generally much more reserved than their Keith Dominion counterparts. Typically, within a few seconds after a Keith Dominion drummer begins to play a musical praise, he or she is playing at full volume and maintains peak dynamic level throughout the praise music segment, which may last about eight minutes.

Jewell Dominion drummers usually begin at a slow tempo, deliberately increase tempo as the energy builds, then return to a slower tempo to finish. They maintain a relaxed, swinging rhythm throughout. There is no explosion of cymbal crashes. Corroneva Burns set the tension of his drum heads and snares low, which helped reinforce the funky, relaxed feel. Today, his son, Laban, and a few other Jewell Dominion drummers, continue the practice, but many have opted for a tighter, brighter, modern snare drum sound. As in the Keith Dominion, in the course of praise music Jewell Dominion bands often stop playing for a period, which may last anywhere from several seconds to a minute or more before the music and dance are resumed and finished. In both dominions the periods during which the band is silent serve to heighten the intensity of the praise session. When the band begins to play again, the general energy level of both the musicians and the congregation usually increases. Lorenzo Harrison was known for his mastery at using changes in tempo and interludes without music to heighten the spiritual energy of a worship service.

Before Harvey Jones began to travel with Chief Jewell in 1942, he had never played an electric guitar. Electrically amplified guitars were a new technology and unfamiliar to many people, especially in the poor rural areas where many of the Jewell Dominion churches were located. Initially, Jones was afraid of the electric guitar Bishop Jewell provided him.

> Until I got with them I was playing just a box, just a regular [acoustic] guitar. But when I got with them I was afraid [the electric guitar] may shock me because I didn't know nothing about electricity. Being hooked up to that amplifier, I thought it may shock me. Everybody laughed at me because I was afraid of it. Say, this thing isn't going to shock me, is it? You know, like that. When I found out it wasn't going to hurt me, I got loose on that thing then. Bishop Jewell heard me, she asked Fred Neal . . . to see if he could get me to start traveling with her because she like the sound that I was putting out. I grabbed it. I was glad to get a chance to get some exposure. Well see, everybody was country people and they wasn't used to anything like that.[14]

Harvey Jones picked the guitar with a thumb pick and a single pick worn on his index finger. He developed a repertoire of walking bass boogies, rhythmic shuffles, and strums that served as a foundation upon which those who followed him built. Today, experienced Jewell Dominion rhythm guitarists are noted for having a large canon of boogies and shuffles from which they draw. Virtually all of them play with a thumb pick and one finger pick. Most play from first position in the keys of E, A, C, and G and use a capo to play in other keys. This approach contrasts sharply with the Keith Dominion backup guitar style, where a flat-pick is the norm and capos are rarely seen. At times, Jewell Dominion guitarists partially mute the bass strings and use the thumb to provide a bass line while picking a melodic line on the treble strings, or they may just strum chords rhythmically.

Chief Jewell and her entourage traveled tens of thousands of miles by automobile each year. Harvey Jones served as a chauffer, and Chief Jewell even outfitted him in a uniform. "See, my job was driving and playing. I was the chauffer. Yeah we'd do seventy thousand miles a year—seventy thousand miles in one year. And see, that was getting to my back. That's one of the reasons I stopped, because I thought it was messing with my kidneys, but come to find out it was arthritis in my back, it wasn't the kidneys. . . . I drove the bishop's [black Cadillac], then I drove—see we had two—I drove the Bishop's car, then when they got the second car they put me in the second car and then Harrison drove the bishop's car."[15]

Traveling throughout the South in the 1940s and 1950s was difficult. To deal with the lack of overnight accommodations for African Americans, Chief Jewell bought a house trailer, which Jones towed. He vividly recalled an incident in Florida, where cattlemen were not required by law to fence their ranches until 1949.[16]

> I ran over a cow, wait now, down in Florida, leaving Ocala, coming home, coming out of Florida. Do you know they had open lanes down there then? Cows eatin' alongside the highway. I was following a big truck and the cows were a ways up ahead like they was fixin' to cross the road. I said, "Please don't cross." I was pullin' a house trailer, about a twenty-eight-feet-long house trailer. I say, "If she try to cross I can't stop." That's the very thing she tried to do. So when I saw it trying to cross the road, I hit my brakes but I couldn't stop. That was about 1948, '49, somewhere along there . . . I killed the cow, the cow that I hit. . . . She could've wrecked my car, but I had a bumper guard on the front. It protected me from being tore up, from tearing the car up. I was going about fifty miles an hour when I hit her.[17]

Jones experienced a similar incident with hogs. "Also, I was going to California, pullin' the same house trailer and some hogs ran out in front of me," he recalled. "I hit the hog and it almost wrecked me."[18]

Lorenzo Harrison also played steel guitar and electric bass with the Jewell Gospel Singers, or Jewel Gospel Trio, as they were later known.[19] The group was formed when sisters Canzetta (1943–) and Maggie Staton (1938–) sang at the Jewell Dominion General Assembly at the headquarters church in Cleveland in 1951. The Staton sisters created a sensation and the congregation showered them with applause and shouted "amens." Enthused by the congregation's response, Chief Jewell asked their mother, who was struggling to raise her daughters after leaving her abusive alcoholic husband in Alabama, if the girls could come to Nashville to attend the Jewell Academy and Seminary and sing to raise money for the school. Reluctant to surrender her daughters to another, but recognizing that traveling with Chief Jewell would be an opportunity for them and would ease her economic burden, their mother granted permission for her daughters to go. In Nashville they were joined by Lorenzo and Nettie Mae's daughter, Naomi Harrison (1943–2003). Nettie Mae played the piano, sang, and provided vocal coaching. With the addition of Lorenzo Harrison on steel guitar and electric bass, Corroneva Burns on drums, and Harvey Jones playing rhythm guitar, they became one of the first female gospel vocal groups to include a full rhythm section. The girls, who ranged in age from eight to thirteen, were neatly attired in matching pinafore dresses and patent leather shoes. They had a soulful sound that, in combination with their full band, thrilled audiences wherever they performed. To add excitement to their performances they routinely switched soprano, contralto, and alto vocal parts.

In 1953, they made their first two records for Ed and Leo Mesner's Aladdin label in Los Angeles, California: "At the Cross" / "Rest, Rest, Rest" and "I Shall Know Him" / "Over There."[20] The recording of "At the Cross" provides a rare example of Lorenzo Harrison's steel guitar playing before he began to use the Morley Rotating Wah pedal that defined the sound he is remembered for, and the overwhelming majority of contemporary Jewell Dominion steel guitarists (as well as many in the Keith Dominion) attempt to replicate. Nettie Mae sang a strong but fairly straightforward lead on "At the Cross," which was taken at a rather slow tempo. The attack, tone, and musical approach delivered by Lorenzo Harrison for his short solo on that selection is so clarinet-like that one could easily mistake his steel guitar for the reed instrument. His sweet, relaxed execution differs drastically from the blues-flavored howling voice of his steel guitar playing of later years.

Using Chuck Campbell as an intermediary, I asked Ronnie Mozee, the individual probably most familiar with Harrison's music, to listen to Harrison's recordings of "At the Cross" and "Rest, Rest, Rest" on the Aladdin label. Campbell reported that Mozee was certain that what sounds like an electric bass on "Rest, Rest, Rest" is actually Harrison playing the bass strings on his steel guitar.[21] Harrison often tuned the seventh string of his eight-string steel to B below a standard guitar's low E, the eighth string to E an octave below the low E on a standard guitar, and was adept at playing the bass part on his steel. Maggie Staton recalled that Harrison usually preferred to play a bass part on the faster numbers such as "Rest, Rest, Rest."[22] The Aladdin records, which were also released on their subsidiary Score label, did not sell well and are quite rare today. Consequently, despite an exhaustive international search by collectors of gospel sound recordings, I have not been able locate a copy of "I Shall Know Him" / "Over There."

After recording for Aladdin, the girls returned to Nashville and maintained a full schedule of performances. Chief Jewell outfitted them with a tour bus equipped with all the amenities and hired a tutor to travel with them to ensure they kept up with their schoolwork. They soon added two more voices to the group: Sederia Boles and Shirley Boyd. In 1955, they signed a three-year contract with Ernie Young's Nashboro label and recorded as the Jewel (spelled with one "l") Gospel Trio. They cut ten sides for Nashboro, but none features the steel guitar of Lorenzo Harrison.[23] The session logs did not identify the individuals who provided accompaniment on piano, bass, drums, and guitar.[24] A group publicity graphic for the Jewell Gospel Trio (the double-l spelling suggests that the graphic may have been created by the performers, not Nashboro) shows Harrison playing what is clearly a Gibson EB electric bass. In the early and mid-1950s, electric bass guitars were a new technology; the Fender Precision Bass was introduced in 1951 and Gibson followed with the violin-shaped EB in 1953. As the Chief Overseer's son-in-law (and later a bishop and vice president), Harrison was able to afford the latest and best instruments and amplifiers. However, guitarist Harvey Jones remembers that for many (if not all) of the Nashboro sessions Harrison played the bass part on his steel guitar, not the Gibson electric bass.

The Jewel Gospel Trio consisted of five vocalists, guitar, piano, drums, and Lorenzo Harrison doubling on bass and steel guitar. They toured widely to perform at venues that ranged from ball parks, churches, and theaters to the Ryman Auditorium in Nashville, the Metropolitan Opera House in Philadelphia (a venue where Willie Eason produced many gospel concerts), the seven thousand-seat Columbia Coliseum in South Carolina, and the Apollo Theater in New York. They shared the bill with Paul Robeson, Sam Cooke and the Soul Stirrers, Mahalia Jackson, a young Aretha Franklin, the Staple Singers, the Davis Sisters, Professor Herman Stevens, the Swan Silvertones, the Swannee Quintet, the Sensational Nightingales, the Spiritualaires and the Famous Skylights, among others. In Florida they stayed at the Daytona Beach home of Mary McLeod Bethune, the great educator and founder of Bethune-Cookman College. They even toured the Philippines, where Chief Jewell had established a mission. In later years Canzetta Staton called the group "the Jackson Five of gospel."[25]

By about 1961, the group began to break up. The little girls had become young ladies who now faced the responsibilities of family, education, and career. Maggie Staton was awarded a scholarship at Tennessee State University in Nashville and went on to teach in the Tennessee public school system for twenty-five years, then retire to a suburb of Atlanta. Canzetta changed her name to Candi Staton and has enjoyed a successful singing career, first in rhythm and blues, and more recently, back in gospel. Naomi

Harrison Manning became leader of the Jewell Dominion when Chief Jewell died in 1992. Throughout her tenure as chief overseer, singing continued to be a significant facet of Bishop Manning's life; she wrote several original songs and often led congregations in song when she presided over various church meetings.

Besides bringing a life of adventure and a level of prestige and self-esteem to the members of the Jewell Gospel Singers, the extensive experience in public performance and recording surely had a lasting effect on Lorenzo Harrison's musicianship in church. Church musicians who have not had that experience are usually known for rather ragged starts and for playing music that is often not well planned. Those who have made amateur recordings of Harrison in church and have taken time to listen closely to them realize that he was very organized in his approach to playing for worship services; his music always had a beginning, a middle, and an end. He skillfully employed changes in tempo and dynamics to increase the drama of a praise session and help the congregation become infused with the Holy Ghost.

The music that Harrison played for the praise sessions in worship services often followed a three-chord (I-IV-V) structure commonly used in gospel songs. And, as gospel singers often do, he frequently added a "drive" section, in which the rhythm section stays in the tonic chord while the lead voice—in this case the steel guitar—engages in a series of repetitive, rhythmic improvisations that build to a crescendo. This approach contrasts markedly with the praise music played by Henry Nelson in the Keith Dominion, in which the band starts on the tonic chord and stays there for the duration while the steel guitarist engages in a series of deliberately repetitive, rhythmic improvisations. Nelson's praise music is essentially one long "drive."

Harrison's music, at least that of his later years, is also characterized by its strong blues and boogie-woogie flavors. The sources of Harrison's boogie-woogie remain somewhat of a mystery. Inquiries to his contemporaries have failed to provide any specific influences, perhaps because they are reluctant to reveal connections to secular music, particularly blues. Certainly as he traveled widely he would have been exposed to a number of musical influences in live performance, over radio broadcasts, and on recordings. Maggie Staton remembers that Harrison often listened to country music on the radio, too, but there is very little evidence of country music influence in his steel guitar playing. Today, his style of blues- and boogie-tinged music is totally accepted in the Jewell Dominion, but not in the Keith Dominion. When Keith Dominion musicians play in the Harrison style, the more conservative members of the congregations and clergy may object and pronounce it blues or rock and roll.

Psalms 149:3, "Let them praise his name in the dance," is cited by Pentecostals as a scriptural basis for dancing. Worship services in the Jewell Dominion and Keith Dominions are experienced physically as well as spiritually, and dancing is an important physical expression of praise for God. The typical modes of Jewell Dominion dance contrast sharply with those of Keith Dominion dancers and shouters, whose movements often seemed uncontrolled. Moved by fast tempo and driving rhythm, many Keith Dominion shouters engage in movements that can only be loosely categorized as dance.[26] While much of the difference in the dance style of the two dominions is related to tempo, the distinction seems to go beyond that. Nettie Mae Harrison emphatically asserted her belief in the superiority of the Jewell Dominion style: "In mama's church boy they didn't just jump around like you see people do, they actually danced. There was dancers that came out of that church to the Savoy [Ballroom] and different stages. The only thing, they didn't have partners; they were solo dancers. Oh honey, let me tell you, some of the dancingest people that you've ever seen came out of [my grandmother's] church. . . . I mean they didn't jump straight up and down or shuffle across the floor. I mean they *danced*."[27]

When Nettie Mae and Lorenzo Harrison, Harvey Jones, and Corroneva Burns began to travel with Chief Jewell in the early 1940s, the jitterbug and Lindy Hop dance fads of the secular world may have influenced the Jewell Dominion congregations. Nettie Mae Harrison often danced at Jewell Dominion services. She took great pride in her dance skills and considered dancing one of her strongest talents. (After she divorced Lorenzo Harrison and left the church in 1964, she worked as a dancer and barmaid at various New York night clubs.)[28] Mary Nelson Linzy's statement in chapter 6 that Nettie Mae and the other young people at Chief Jewell's church were "doing the natural born dance steps . . . like you go to a ballroom, and all of that" back in the early 1940s, suggests the influence of secular popular dance.

When Lorenzo Harrison was in southern Florida for the Jewell Dominion State Assembly he would always visit with his sister, Vera Lee, and her family in Richmond Heights, south of Miami. Alvin Lee (1966–) remembers that when he was just a boy his father, Keith Dominion minister Elder Robert E. Lee, took him and his brothers to the Jewell Dominion church in Deerfield Beach many times to hear his uncle, Bishop Harrison, play. Alvin

Lee had attended Keith Dominion services since he was a toddler and was accustomed to the Keith Dominion style of music and dance. His reaction to the music and dance he witnessed at the Jewell Dominion church in Deerfield Beach echoed the response of Mary Nelson Linzy, when she saw the "natural born dance steps" at Bishop Jewell's Ocala church some thirty-five years earlier. Alvin Lee vividly recalled:

> So my dad would take us to their assemblies, and at that time that's when Sonny Treadway was playing [rhythm guitar] with [Harrison], and they would be playing the slow boogie-woogie. . . . I remember one time seeing this guy, he was actually doing like a boogie-woogie dance, and would get his handkerchief, flip the handkerchief from out of his pocket, and do a turnaround and catch it in the middle of the church service. As a young kid that was like: Wow! I can't believe this, you know. You know, you're eight or nine and looking at this and it's like: Wow, they doing this in church?[29]

Years later, Alvin Lee witnessed even more Jewell Dominion dance when he watched videotapes of Jewell Dominion assemblies made by his brother Glenn as he traveled extensively in the 1990s to play steel guitar and keyboard synthesizer with their cousin, Chief Overseer Bishop Naomi Manning. "The amazing way that these guys shout, with their foot movement," Alvin recalled, "you would think they go to the 'school for the Jewell dancers.'" Glenn and Alvin tried to get the Jewell Dominion style of music and dance started at the Keith Dominion church in Perrine, where their father served as pastor. Glenn even demonstrated the Jewell manner of dancing to the congregation. "Glenn would come out in the middle of the floor. He would do all these little slow dances," Alvin recalled. "Glenn had the dance down." But his attempts to teach the Jewell Dominion dance to the Keith Dominion congregation largely failed. While a few of the congregants at the Perrine church caught on, most did not. Rather than dance in the slower, swinging Jewell manner, which fit the medium-tempo Jewell-style music the church band played for them, most stuck with their Keith Dominion style and danced in double-time.[30]

Jewell Dominion holy dancers generally move much more gracefully than their Keith Dominion counterparts. Often the first to hit the dance floor are males in their twenties or thirties, and male dancers are frequently the most numerous. While the gender bias of the congregation as a whole may commonly be five, ten, or even more, females per male, often at least half the dancers on the floor are males. Generally, the young men are among the most accomplished and flashiest dancers.

While there is considerable individual variation of movement among dancers, I will attempt to describe some characteristics common to the general manner of dancing by Jewell Dominion congregants. The body is bent forward at the waist at an angle of fifteen degrees or so. The arms are bent too, with the hands generally about chest high. Some dancers swing the arms from time to time, others make a sort of boxing motion, alternating left and right. For brief periods some dancers may place one hand in the small of the back or place one or both hands on the hips. On the backbeat the pelvis generally moves rather sharply to the rear. The younger and slimmer Jewell Dominion dancers often take lengthy strides of about twelve inches, or more; older, heavier dancers take shorter steps. Probably the most common step pattern is to shuffle the lead foot forward on the downbeat, then shuffle the lead foot back while kicking the other foot to the rear and upwards on the backbeat. To complete one 4/4 measure of music, the pattern is then repeated by leading on the other foot. Common variations in footwork include stepping one foot across the other, and taking strides in a pattern of slow, slow, quick, quick, quick, with the quick steps executed as a rhythmic triplet, which takes as much time as the two slower steps.

Vertical movement, like the footwork, is executed smoothly: up on beats one and three and down on two and four. Another common variation is to keep the feet very close to the floor. When the friction between the floor and sole of the shoes is light enough to permit such movements, some dance for extended periods without their feet ever leaving the floor, gliding in a manner that may remind one of James Brown.

Many Jewell Dominion dancers—especially the young males in good physical condition—travel across the floor for considerable distances as they dance, and often include full 360-degree turns, or even double turns (720 degrees) as they travel. The turns executed by male dancers may be accentuated by the flair of an unbuttoned sport coat. The young male dancers may be giving God praise, but their prowess and flamboyance on the dance floor also make statements about style, personal bearing, and masculinity. I have never observed, however, any sexually suggestive pelvic movements, such as bumps, grinds, or hip swaying, among Jewell or Keith Dominion dancers.

Congregants of all ages dance. I have seen children as young as four dance with a surprising degree of skill and grace. By the age of ten, some youngsters—boys more so than girls, it seems—are very accomplished. At the other extreme, it is not uncommon to see dancers well into their seventies. The oldest and heaviest generally dance with minimal, economical movements.

The relatively slower tempos played by Jewell Dominion musicians can also result in longer periods of dancing. "The Jewell Dominion they may dance for two hours," exclaimed Mike Wortham, Jewell Dominion steel guitarist from Mississippi. "You know, they'll shout and praise God for two hours."[31] While Wortham may exaggerate somewhat the length of time that Jewell Dominion congregants shout or dance, his point is well taken: dancers can endure longer periods of dance when the tempos are moderate, and Jewell Dominion services generally include numerous and lengthy periods of dancing.

When Lorenzo Harrison, Corroneva Burns, and Harvey Jones began to travel with Chief Jewell in 1942, Harrison was playing a six-string lap-steel, as instruments with more than six strings were not common at that time. By the mid-1940s, eight-string steel guitars with one, two, or three necks became common and were preferred by many professionals. Because the multi-neck instruments were too heavy to rest comfortably on the musician's lap, they were fitted with telescoping legs that enabled playing from a standing or sitting position.[32] From the beginning of Harrison's service as a Jewell Dominion musician, Chief Jewell made sure that he always had the best and latest equipment available. As a mature family man, and ultimately first vice president to Chief Jewell, he had ample resources at his disposal. At some point, probably soon after World War II, he began to play steel guitars with eight-string necks. He experimented with multi-neck guitars; a photo from the 1960s shows him with a triple-eight Gibson.

Eventually, Harrison settled on a single-neck instrument tuned to an open E major chord with a tonic note on the high first string. Steel guitarists, especially those who play instruments with more than six strings, often experiment with a variety of tunings, and Harrison was no exception. To the best of my knowledge, most of his tunings were based on an E-major chord, with the top string tuned to the same E as that of a standard guitar. Many of his tuning variations involved the two or three lowest strings, which he often tuned to pitches as much as an octave below the bottom E note of a standard guitar.[33] While the low-pitched bass strings of his tuning were quite unconventional by Hawaiian or country steel guitar standards, such tunings served Harrison well. He developed a technique of playing boogie-woogie walking bass lines on the low strings. He combined these bass parts with notes picked on the treble strings. For example, he would play a full twelve bars on the bass strings then return to the treble.

Sometimes he engaged in a call-and-response of phrases from one to four bars in length between the bass and treble strings. Often he began a praise tune by playing the bass part several times through.

In later years, Harrison began to use an effect pedal that would become a significant part of his steel guitar legacy: the Morley Rotating Wah. Nineteen inches in length, six inches high, six inches wide, and weighing nine pounds, the gleaming chrome behemoth is a visually impressive piece of gear. It was manufactured from 1973 to 1983. The source of its bulk is a rotating element, housed in a large box in front of the foot pedal, which provides a tremolo effect similar to the Leslie rotating speaker system used on the Hammond B-3 electric organ. Sonny Treadway said that he was the one who first showed Harrison the Morley Rotating Wah pedal.

> I introduced him to the Morley pedal when he come here [Deerfield Beach, Florida]. I was the first one to play it in the church. But [the congregation] didn't like it, so I took it back to the store and got my money [refunded]. So, when we had our assembly here, he came down and I told him about it because it does the same way we used to play the steel with our hands on the tone control. We used to wiggle it to make the "wah" sound, you know, as you play. You had to have a technique to do it, play with your fingers and have your palm kind of twisting the knob. So I explained to him they've got a pedal that does that same thing, you know, and it had the rotation on it, 'cause he liked the organ sound too. And I told him it sounds like an organ with the rotation. He said, "Where is it?" So I carried him to the music store and he bought his. I say, "Well, If you bought you one, I'm getting mine back." People didn't like it either at first, you know. They was talking about, I don't like the way that sounds. He didn't care if they didn't like it or not. "They'll get used to it."[34]

While Harrison did make use of the Morley's rotating element, it is his technique without the rotating element engaged, using the straight wah effect, that became widely popular among the Jewell Dominion steel guitarists playing today. The Morley's rotating element was unreliable, a fact that probably limited Harrison's regular use of that effect and a major reason why it is rarely used today. Most Morley Rotating Wah pedals today (they are all more than twenty years old) have a nonfunctional rotating element.

When using the straight wah effect, Harrison did not pump the pedal, a technique that gives the familiar, often overdone, "wah-wah" sound. Rather, he depressed the pedal part way, settling on a "sweet spot" that was not too muddy or overly bright, and often played for extended periods with very little pedal movement, essentially using the Morley for a tone, or timbre, control. Used in this manner, the Morley Rotating Wah distorts the instrument's sound and produces harmonic overtones that result in a timbre that cannot be exactly duplicated by any other effects pedal, or combination of effects. Other setups may come very close, but the Morley Rotating Wah sound is unique.

Harrison became adept at using the Morley Rotating Wah to produce a howling, growling, focused timbre that seemed to penetrate to the very core of the souls of worshippers and helped move them to feel the presence of the Holy Ghost. It became his musical signature, the trademark sound that many attempt to duplicate today. The Morley Rotating Wah is used today by Jewell Dominion national-level steel guitarists Ronnie Mozee, Reggie "Footie" Covington, a highly regarded steel guitarist from Philadelphia, and just about every other Jewell Dominion steel guitarist who can find one. Those who cannot find or afford a working Morley Rotating Wah use a modern wah pedal (often staying with the Morley brand) and dial in a little overdrive from their amplifier to achieve a close approximation of the classic Harrison sound. There are a few Jewell Dominion steel guitarists who do not use a wah pedal, or use one very infrequently—Sonny Treadway being among the most notable—but the sound of the Morley Rotating Wah is what nearly all Jewell Dominion steel guitarists strive to deliver and what the congregations expect to hear.

Nettie Mae left Lorenzo in 1964 and plunged headlong into the secular world. At that time they were living in Inglewood, New Jersey. "I left and went across the bridge to New York, and I didn't go back," she recalled. "Oh honey, in New York, I used to work in night clubs there and I could fill up a club in a minute just dancing. And I was a bar maid. I used to work at the Zanzibar on 145th, and I used to work at the L Bar up on Broadway."[35]

On January 23, 1981, Lorenzo Harrison married Freddie Mae Tucker, a Jewell Dominion bishop. In time he began a physical decline due largely to kidney failure. He traveled throughout the Jewell Dominion system in a large custom bus, the "Gospel Cruiser," which was equipped with a dialysis machine. As his physical condition deteriorated, younger musicians traveled with him to perform for church meetings large and small. Eventually he became so ill that he could no longer play. Sonny Treadway recalled: "When he took sick I had to go play kind of regular a little bit for him. Traveled around Dayton, and Florida, and Mississippi, and then back to Indianapolis. And then he died. I was there when he died, playing for him. Yeah, they called me when he got sick and I went up to help out, you know. He told me he couldn't play no more, couldn't even hold the bar no more. So, I just took over and started playing from then on. Then after he passed I came back home."[36]

Bishop Lorenzo Harrison died the day after Christmas 1986. His home-going, or funeral, at the Jewell Dominion headquarters church in Indianapolis was a grand affair. The ceremonies included a congregational rendition of his favorite song, "Jesus Will Make It All Right" and a eulogy by Bishop E. M. Jennings.[37] A shiny new custom-built steel guitar was buried with him at the renowned Crown Hill Cemetery. The 555-acre historical property is the burial site of many notables, including President Benjamin Harrison, eleven Indiana governors, thirteen Civil War Generals, and the infamous bank robber John Dillinger.

Indianapolis resident Ronnie Mozee, who had played backup guitar and steel guitar with Bishop Harrison in his later years, became Harrison's successor as "national" steel guitarist.

Lorenzo Harrison's impact on the music of Jewell Dominion steel guitarists cannot be overstated; he is highly venerated as a musician, senior bishop, and vice president to Chief Jewell. There is no equivalent among Keith Dominion steel guitarists. Robert Boles played the steel guitar for worship services for more than a decade, and today serves as assistant pastor at the Jewell Dominion church in Toccopola, near Oxford, Mississippi. Boles's memories of Bishop Lorenzo Harrison and his music echo the reverence for him shared by many Jewell Dominion congregants. "Now his music was so outstanding the majority of the time when we would travel to Indianapolis [for the General Assembly] and walk in the foyer and he'd be playing, it was just like a message was coming to you. . . . Of course, he had a lot of guys try to play his tune, but the tunes that he had it just seemed like it came straight down from the Lord. It was just amazing. It was just so unique and so clear, and even the guys that pantomimes [mimic] him, there was even still a difference."[38]

Calhoun City, Mississippi, steel guitarist Mike Wortham gave further testimony to the power of Harrison's musical abilities: "Even when he set down to tune his steel just before church, the anointing began to get in people. He would sit down and, you know [makes sounds of tuning up], . . . and people would get to *whoo!* Bishop, why he was so unique; he played from his heart. When you give a man your heart you give everything you got. And somebody gonna be touched."[39]

Lorenzo Harrison was much more than the national-level steel guitarist who played throughout the geographic range of the church for more than four decades; he was a member of the Jewell family, vice president, and a bishop. He was in charge of, and in control of, the musical praise portion of a worship service. "He really conducted the service, with that steel," asserted Alvin Lee.[40] Unlike the situation in Keith Dominion services, where a member of the congregation may start singing from the pews and the band is expected to follow, Harrison would not start playing until he was ready. "After the preacher," recalled Lee, "sometimes he would wait two or three minutes till he gets ready. Then he'll bust out something real slow. He would keep it going for twenty minutes. Then after that, if he felt like it, he would go on to another little jam." Harrison often started the music by playing the bass line for several bars. The rhythm guitarist would then join to solidly establish the "groove," or as the Keith and Jewell musicians more commonly say, the "pocket," after which Harrison would begin taking treble leads on the steel guitar. He was known for carefully controlling the music to make the most of a praise session. He varied the tempo from slow to medium to fast, then back to slow again. His rhythm guitarists drew from a rich canon of boogies, shuffles, and vamps to give compelling accompaniment that moved him to play most passionately. Sometimes Harrison and the band teased the congregation by repeatedly playing one or two bars, then stopping, a technique that served to increase anticipation and excitement among the congregants.

No other steel guitarist comes close to the level of veneration by musicians, congregants, and clergy that Harrison achieved. For example, at the Jewell Dominion church in Tupelo, Mississippi, photos of Bishop Jewell and Bishop Manning adorn the walls near the pulpit area and a photo of Harrison is placed near the band. In the Keith Dominion, a photo of a steel guitarist may rarely be found somewhere within the church building, perhaps in the lobby or foyer, but virtually never within the sanctuary itself.

In addition to establishing the convention for Jewell Dominion music, Harrison is largely responsible for securing the steel guitar's position at the top of the musical instrument hierarchy in the denomination. Harrison was Chief Jewell's son-in-law and traveled with her to play at virtually all the state assemblies and at every General Assembly from 1942 to 1986, a period of more than four decades. Troman and Willie Eason, Henry Nelson, and other early steel guitarists did not play for services on every day of the Keith Dominion General Assemblies in the 1940s, 1950s, or even the 1960s. Most years there were steel guitarists, but apparently some years there were not. Other years there may be a steel guitarist who played for two or three days of the ten-day event.[41] While the Keith Dominion steel guitarists were slowly establishing the status of the instrument in their church, Harrison had secured its position at the top of the musical instrument hierarchy in the early 1940s and maintained it until his death in 1986.

The music of the Keith and Jewell Dominion churches reflects the manner of worship and general nature of each organization. Although my attendance at Jewell Dominion church meetings has been limited to a handful of occasions, I have discussed aspects of Keith and Jewell Dominion worship with members of both churches. Some, including Ted Beard and Calvin Cooke, were raised in the Jewell Dominion and later joined the Keith Dominion. There seems to be a consensus that compared to the Keith Dominion, Jewell Dominion worship services are more reserved, the music is not as loud, and there is a greater emphasis on scriptural teachings. My limited personal experience confirms this point of view. It also seems that the relationship between Jewell Dominion steel guitarists and clergy may be less frequently antagonistic. That is, the Jewell musicians are less likely to attempt to dominate the worship service by playing with increasing loudness.

The degree of difference in musical aesthetics between conservative members of the Jewell Dominion and more liberal members of the Keith Dominion is illustrated by behavior observed at a concert performance by the Campbell Brothers band at the Second Baptist Church on Jackson Street, Oxford, Mississippi, on February 18, 2005. The concert was part of the Blues Today Symposium produced by *Living Blues* magazine, which is published by the Center for the Study of Southern Culture at the University of Mississippi. Robert Boles is assistant pastor and steel guitarist at the Jewell Dominion church in Toccopola, a few miles east of Oxford. Boles had previously been identified by *Living Blues* and Mississippi Arts Commission staff as a good contact for the Jewell Dominion musical tradition in northeastern Mississippi. He had been interviewed by *Living Blues* staff, facilitated photographic documentation at the Toccopola church by David Wharton of the Center for the Study of Southern Culture, and was documented by the state folklife program. When I interviewed Boles a few weeks prior to attending the Blues Today Symposium I requested permission to take documentary photos at the worship service at the Toccopola church on Sunday, following the Friday night concert. Boles expressed interest in my book project and worked through his pastor, Bishop Calvin Worthem, to support the taking of documentary photos. *Living Blues* staff and I invited Boles to attend the Campbell Brothers concert, but he stated that he could not firmly commit to attending because his presence may be required at the regular Friday night worship service at his church in Toccopola.

Robert Boles and his son Derrick, whom I guess to be about twenty, arrived at the concert just before the performance began, too late to be introduced to the band. Boles and I exchanged warm greetings at this first meeting in person, then took our seats for the concert. I sat in the first row, close to the band, and Boles sat far to the rear of the sanctuary, maybe a dozen rows back. Immediately after the Campbell Brothers' last number of their performance, I looked for Boles to introduce him to the band. But he was not to be found. He had left before the concert was over.

Author and music journalist Elijah Wald was a panelist at the Blues Today Symposium and accompanied me to attend worship services at the Toccopola church on Sunday. Bishop Worthem announced to the congregation that I was researching and documenting the musical tradition of the Keith and Jewell Dominions and writing a book on the subject, and warmly welcomed us to the church. He explained that I had done much of my work in the Keith Dominion and that today I would have an opportunity to see how the Jewell Dominion worship differs. Bishop Worthem added that he hoped Wald and I would appreciate the difference between Keith and Jewell Dominion worship services.

After church, Bishop Worthem treated Boles, Wald, and me to Sunday dinner at a restaurant in Oxford. When I asked Boles how he liked the Campbell Brothers concert he commented that it sounded like they put a lot of blues in it. He cited "Don't Let the Devil Ride" as a specific example (it has a twelve-bar structure and a shuffle rhythm). He also said their music was too loud. Boles and his son had left the Campbell Brothers concert because the music clashed with their aesthetics for sacred music. When I related my discussion with Boles to Chuck Campbell a few days later, Chuck remarked that he was surprised Boles would acknowledge that he and his brothers could play at all.

This incident illustrates the vast differences in musical aesthetics between the conservative membership of the Jewell Dominion, represented in this case by Boles, and the more liberal extreme of the Keith Dominion, represented by the Campbells. The most conservative Jewell Dominion musicians believe that Lorenzo Harrison's steel guitar technique and repertoire are the only way to play the instrument. According to Del Ray Grace (1960–), who played steel guitar in the Jewell Dominion from 1975 to 1995, the Mississippi congregations are among the most conservative in the denomination.[42]

Anecdotes that Elvis Presley visited the Mississippi State Assemblies in Tupelo circulate among Jewell Dominion congregants. For example, Gamaliel Penn, who is Nettie Mae Harrison's grandson, recalled that she, as well as Lorenzo Harrison and Chief Jewell, had told him young Elvis came to their tent services. Nettie Mae Harrison insisted she saw Elvis at the Tupelo assemblies on more than one occasion. "Well, I'll tell you who else was inspired by [Lorenzo] Harrison: Elvis Presley. Elvis Presley used to come to our meetings in Mississippi, in Tupelo, Mississippi. Once a year we'd have camp meetings, we would put up a great big tent. People would come from miles around in wagons, vans, cars. Droves of people. Oh, that was back in the '40's. Elvis Presley was just a little boy and that is where he got that wiggling in his leg from."[43]

Nettie Mae Harrison's claim that Elvis got "that wiggling in his leg" from the Jewell Dominion dancers may be conjecture; in *Last Train to Memphis,* Peter Guralnick established a convincing case that Jim "Big Chief" Wetherington of the Statesmen, a white gospel quartet, was the source of Elvis's wiggling legs.[44] It does seem likely, however, that young Elvis was drawn to the excitement of the Jewell Dominion tent services.

Elvis Presley was born on January 8, 1935, in Tupelo. By the time he started seventh grade in the fall of 1947, the Presley family had moved to 1010 North Green Street, just north of Simmons Street (later renamed Barnes Street).[45] It was their last residence in Tupelo; Vernon Presley moved his family to Memphis on November 5, 1948. The home they rented on Green Street was located on the border of respectable white and black neighborhoods. Although it was one of two or three houses designated "white" in the neighborhood, it was surrounded by African American homes, social clubs, schools, and churches.[46] The Jewell Dominion had a small church on the corner of Sims and Barnes Streets, less than a quarter mile east of the Presley residence. When the Jewell Dominion held its Mississippi State Assembly each September, a tent was erected on the property to the rear of the church to accommodate the large congregation that gathered for the event.[47] The tent services were loud and spirited, and the soulful cry of Lorenzo Harrison's steel guitar could be heard for blocks. There were two Jewell Dominion annual Mississippi State Assemblies down the street from Elvis's home during the year and a half the Presley family lived in the neighborhood. The unbridled passion of Pentecostal worship, inspired dancing, and the powerful voice of Lorenzo Harrison's steel would have been quite a draw to the boy who brought his guitar to school every day and loved nothing more than singing gospel music.

As stated earlier, the bulk of my field documentation and research has involved the Keith Dominion, and this book therefore emphasizes the history, culture, and music of that church. Although only about a fifth the size of the Keith Dominion, the Jewell Dominion has a rich steel guitar tradition. My rather brief treatment of the Jewell Dominion steel guitar tradition and tradition-bearers here is strictly a consequence of my limited knowledge and experience and in no way a negative value judgment of the power and beauty of the music or the richness of the culture. The Jewell Dominion steel guitar tradition continues in the playing of Ronnie Mozee, Sonny Treadway, Reginald "Footie" Covington, and dozens of musicians who play for worship services in churches found in sixteen states, and Nassau, Bahamas. A number of steel guitarists have left the Jewell Dominion to become affiliated with other churches. Among them is Del Ray Grace of Toledo, Ohio, who is producing recordings of his own Amazing Grace Praise Band and albums of vintage recordings of Lorenzo Harrison, Tubby Golden, Wayne White, and other Jewell Dominion master steel guitarists playing "live" at church meetings. The recordings, as well as condensed biographical information on musicians past and present, are available at his Web site, www.sacredstrings.com. Freddie Mae Harrison, Lorenzo Harrison's second wife and widow, is the source of most, if not all, of the vintage recordings. The Amazing Grace Praise Band also performs for concerts and church musical programs.

After dominance by one family for more than half a century, the Jewell Dominion has entered a new era of leadership, and as in the Keith Dominion, the change in leadership will certainly affect the music. Music rooted in the Jewell Dominion steel guitar tradition continues to evolve as musicians young and old play for worship services and larger church meetings, perform concerts, and make recordings. All owe a tremendous debt to Lorenzo Harrison.

Jewell Dominion musician Kim Love is visited in her home by Keith Dominion musicians, Philadelphia, 2000. *Left to right*: steel guitarist Acorne "Flip" Coffee Jr. and rhythm guitarist Shevinah Johnson, both of Philadelphia; and Rochester steel guitarist Chuck Campbell. Photo by the author.

Jamel Woffard (*left*), and his father, James, take turns playing steel and rhythm guitar for Jewell Dominion services. Tupelo, Mississippi, 2006. Photo by the author.

Revival at the Jewell Dominion church, Tupelo, Mississippi, 2006. Photo by the author.

Chief Jewell picked up Maurice Beard Sr. in Beaver Dam, Kentucky, in the heart of "Kentucky thumb-picking" country, and brought him (and an unknown banjoist) to Mt. Clemons, Michigan, ca. 1933–34. Courtesy Ted Beard.

Felton Williams in his home, Ecorse, Michigan, 2005. He excelled on standard guitar and steel guitar and mentored several Jewell Dominion musicians in the Detroit area. Photo by the author.

Bishop Ron Hall and his son, Marcus, play for services at Mount Carmel Full Gospel Assembly, Ecorse, Michigan, 2005. Photo by the author.

Maurice "Ted" Beard Jr. and the Beard Sisters, Detroit, 1960s. Janie played piano and sang with Catherine (*left*) and Alfreda (*right*). Courtesy Ted Beard.

Ted Beard, accompanied on electric bass by his son, Rico, at the first Sacred Steel Convention, Rollins College, Winter Park, Florida, 2000. Photo by the author.

Calvin Cooke at the first Sacred Steel Convention, accompanied by Detroit Jewell Dominion guitarist Jay Caver, Winter Park, Florida, 2000. Photo by the author.

Chuck Campbell gives Glenn Lee a few pointers at the Keith Dominion headquarters church, Nashville, 1996. Looking on (*left to right*): Campbell's son Malcom Robinson and brothers Eddie (barely visible behind Campbell's head), Enrico, and Dante Harmon. Photo by the author.

Early publicity photo of the Campbell Brothers (*left to right*): Chuck, pedal-steel; Phil, guitar; vocalist Katie Jackson; Carlton (Phil's son), drums; Darick, lap-steel. Gainesville, Florida, 1998. Photo by the author.

The Campbell Brothers, Phil (*left*) and Chuck, "wreck the house" at the second Sacred Steel Convention, Sanford, Florida, 2001. Robert Randolph is second from left at the edge of the stage, pointing. Photo by the author.

Glenn Lee plays for the Keith Dominion Florida East Coast State Assembly, Blanche Ely High School, Pompano Beach, Florida, 1992. He inherited the Morley Rotating Wah pedal from his uncle Lorenzo Harrison. Photo by the author.

Frank Owens plays for shouting congregants at the House of God No. 2, Ft. Pierce, Florida, 2002. He is among the many Florida pedal-steel guitarists inspired by Glenn Lee. Photo by the author.

Robert Randolph about a year before he began to play professionally, Keith Dominion headquarters church, Nashville, Tennessee, 1999. Photo by the author.

The Lee Boys play for a party to celebrate the release of their Arhoolie album, *Say Yes!* the Bamboo Room, Palm Beach Florida, 2005. *Left to right:* Roosevelt Collier, pedal-steel; Keith Lee, vocal; Derrick Lee, vocal. Photo by the author.

Motor City Steel

Detroit, Michigan, was a destination for many African Americans who migrated from the South during the first half of the twentieth century to work in the automobile industry. The Motor City was home to several of the best steel guitarists from the Jewell Dominion, some of whom later joined the Keith Dominion and played a significant role in shaping its musical tradition. This chapter focuses on three influential steel guitarists from the Detroit area: Felton Williams, Ted Beard, and Ronnie Hall. Calvin Cooke, a fourth Detroit steel guitarist, is also introduced here. Because Cooke traveled so widely, spreading musical innovations that had such lasting influence on so many steel guitarists, chapter 10 is devoted entirely to him. Williams, Beard, Hall, and Cooke were all influenced by Lorenzo Harrison, but went on to develop recognizable individual styles of playing that differed in varying degrees from Harrison's.

Felton Williams

Felton W. Williams Jr. was a seminal figure among Keith and Jewell Dominion steel guitarists in the Detroit area. He never traveled much to play for regional or national church events, so he is not well known beyond his home turf. ("I didn't get around much, though. That's why most people don't know me and I don't know them.")[1] Indeed, he heard of important East Coast steel guitarists, such as Willie Eason and Henry Nelson, but never met them or heard them play. Detroit-area steel guitarists respect Williams highly and are quick to acknowledge his influence. Ronnie Hall affectionately refers to him as "Uncle Felton."

Felton Williams Jr. was born on January 3, 1934, in Tupelo, Mississippi, to Felton and Katie Lee (née Ware) Williams, both ministers in the Jewell

Dominion. After his father died circa 1937, Felton's mother moved her five children to Mt. Clemens, Michigan (about twenty miles northeast of Detroit) in 1938, with the assistance of Bishop Jewell. "Mt. Clemens was the headquarters after her husband took over, Bishop McLeod," Williams recalled. "After my father died my mother sent all us children. [My mother] had come up earlier and she had sent for us and we came up in the car with Bishop Jewell, and Nettie Mae, and a whole lot of folks."[2]

Life was difficult for widow Katie Lee Williams and her five children. For years her meager income from domestic labor was supplemented by welfare payments. Bright and ambitious, Felton Jr. would eventually rise from poverty and become a valued employee at the Ford Motor Company.

The extended Williams family included many musicians, and Felton Sr. had played guitar for Jewell Dominion worship services back in Mississippi. The first steel guitarist that Felton Jr. remembers hearing was Fred Neal, the Jewell Dominion steel guitarist who preceded Lorenzo Harrison, when he played at the Mt. Clemens church sometime around 1942. Like many Jewell and Keith Dominion musicians, Williams is not trained in note reading or music theory, but plays "by ear." He recalls that Neal "had it tuned for the third string being the key string," which suggests the 1-3-5-1-3-5 (from bass to treble) major chord tuning that was commonly used in the early 1940s and known today as "Dobro tuning," or among Keith Dominion musicians as "Henry Nelson tuning."[3]

Williams's uncle, Bishop Mayes, was so inspired by Neal's playing that he bought an electric lap-steel. The bishop's son, Macluster, known as Mack, accompanied by his brothers, played the new steel guitar at the Mt. Clemens church. When Williams, who was only eight at the time, was given a turn at his uncle's steel, his musical talent was immediately evident. "Everybody was trying to play it and it just caught on with me," he remembered.[4] Back at home young Williams did not have his own steel guitar, so he pressed an old acoustic guitar into service. "I started on a regular Spanish guitar laid across the lap . . . and we played it with a can opener. That was our bar. The can opener was the bar and we put a clothespin under it to raise the strings up. Then we'd tune the strings open and play. That's the way we did it."[5]

By 1943, the Williams family had moved from Mt. Clemens to Detroit, where they attended the same Jewell Dominion church at Garfield and Rivard Streets as the Beard family. Among the musicians included in the talented Beard family were steel guitarist Ted (1935–) and his brother

Douglas, who picked the standard guitar. Learning to play was a laborious process for Beard; Felton Williams had more natural talent. "Felton Williams just picked it up and was playing," recalled Beard. "Oh, he was awesome. Yeah, he was really good."[6]

In 1947, Williams was given a six-string Epiphone electric lap-steel and amplifier for his thirteenth birthday and began to play the instrument regularly for worship services. After worshipping for a time at a church on Garfield Street, the Williams family joined the church on Brady Street, where Bishop Hankerson served as pastor. The family continued to attend Bishop Hankerson's church for several years and Felton served as the regular steel guitarist there.

In his early teens Williams traveled a bit to play for worship services at large church assemblies, which was about as itinerant as he would ever be during nearly four decades of service as a church musician. He recalled that ministers would take him to assemblies in Toledo, Cleveland, and Indianapolis, a range of about three hundred miles. In 1952, when he was eighteen, Williams traveled with his cousin Mack Mayes to Kansas City, Missouri, to help build a Jewell Dominion church. The two young men erected a tent on a hill, played gospel music, and solicited donations for building materials. "We went out there and built a church, and that's how we got the money. We'd just go out there on the street corner and pick up buckets [of money] and then go buy mortar and blocks and start building."[7] Over the years, he traveled to Nashville a few times to attend the Jewell Dominion General Assembly, but never played at the gathering.

In addition to the music he heard in church, Williams was influenced by country music artists and jazz saxophonists. During his teens he became competent on the standard, or Spanish-neck, guitar as well as the steel. Following the practice typical of Jewell Dominion guitarists, he played with a thumb pick and one finger pick. Williams says he often listened to jazz saxophonists he heard over radio broadcasts, but does not recall the names of any individual artists. He also frequently listened to the Grand Ole Opry on the radio and later watched *Hee Haw* on television. Although the steel guitarists he saw and heard on the Opry interested him, it was the artists who played the standard guitar that he was most strongly drawn to. "I love the Spanish guitar and I love Chet Atkins. . . . I heard [Merle Travis] first and then I started trying to emulate [Atkins] . . . on the steel. So, I had a kind of difficult thing. And then after Chet Atkins I heard Les Paul. I didn't know he was duplicating [overdubbing]. I was trying to do it all myself. So, I brought up a lot of new stuff that way. And I tried to do a lot of that on the steel. Mostly when I would riff it would be like a jazz sax man riffin'."[8]

Music was not the only area in which Williams was talented. "When I was in school I was really a science buff. . . . I made my first echo chamber. . . . I would solder old phonograph pickups on the end, each one on each end of a screen going to a spring."[9] He recalls that in the mid-1940s he electrified a cheap acoustic guitar by installing a pickup he had wound himself and connected to a radio he had converted into an amplifier. He landed a job with the Ford Motor Company in 1956 and worked through the apprenticeship program to become an electrician. Over the years, he worked at more than half a dozen different plants in the Ford complex and performed an array of tasks that ranged from building maintenance to machine repair to operating numerically controlled machines. After thirty-seven years with Ford he retired in 1994.

Williams applied his skills and creativity to his musical interests. He built four or five amplifiers, one of which he still uses today, and several steel guitars. Photos of a steel guitar with two eight-string necks he crafted in the early 1960s and a single ten-string neck instrument he made in the 1980s show handsome, functional instruments. (The body of Detroit-raised Floridian Sonny Treadway's homemade eight-string steel strongly resembles the latter.) Ever resourceful, Williams even wound his own pickups and fabricated the fretboards. "Only thing I had to buy was the tuning pegs. You know, you could pick those up anywhere."[10] Because he prefers to play from the "open" position (i.e., the key of E in E tuning), Felton made a sort of capo to enable him to play in other keys. "I play mostly out of the open. And I used to put a bar up under it to change the key. Keep it open but just move to a different key . . . like a capo. I did it on the steel. Yeah, I made one that wasn't too high that I could slide easily and just lock it in at the one, two, three, four, five fret, or somethin' like that."[11]

Included among the steel guitarists whom Williams says he influenced are Ted Beard, Ronnie Hall, Calvin Cooke, Tubby Golden, Henry Wayne White, Clifford Warren, Charles Flenory, Eric Russell, Sonny Treadway, and Robert Cook—all well respected by their peers. Several of these men also play standard guitar and credit Williams as an influence on that instrument as well. Jewell Dominion guitarist Jay Caver of Detroit, who was a member of Calvin Cooke's "Sacred Steel Ensemble" and the "Sacred Strings" group led by former Jewell Dominion steel guitarist Del Ray Grace, also cites Williams as an influence.

In later years, Williams became increasingly interested in teaching Bible studies and less interested in playing music. "As we get older, we have younger people coming up. So, I started slowing down and they started to pick up. It got to the point where my interest wasn't there anymore so I released myself from that."[12] In 1983, he left the Jewell Dominion over disagreements on scriptural interpretation and, with his brother-in-law, Clinton Kirkwood, started the Gospel Truth Tabernacle of God at 5169 Ogden Street in southwestern Detroit. His musical influence continues, as Bishop Kirkwood's son, Derrick, plays steel guitar there.

When I visited Williams at his neat, modest home in the Detroit suburb of Ecorse in August 2005, he played both the steel guitar and standard electric guitar. He explained that he rarely plays the steel guitar anymore, not even for personal enjoyment. Steel guitar technique is very much a matter of sensitive touch, and his neglect of the instrument was apparent as he played. But as he rendered several spirituals and older gospel standards on the standard guitar his nimble, syncopated finger-picking was a delight. Williams has no recordings of his music (or none that he was willing to share), but testimonies of his exceptional abilities as a steel guitarist when in his prime abound. For example, Harvey Jones recalled:

> You know, a lot of people could beat Harrison playing, but they didn't want to admit it. They didn't want to hurt his feelings. Felton could. Somebody had asked Felton for a number one day out there in Toledo, and he didn't have his [steel] guitar with him, so he used Harrison's guitar. And he took it and he made Harrison look so bad. When he give his guitar back to Harrison, Harrison wouldn't hardly play after that. Because see, he played so good until the people tried to give him a round of applause to come back and do another one, come back again. They didn't ever ask Harrison to come back again. See there? That sounds so good they want to hear some more of that. . . .
>
> Felton kinda knocked his ego down a little bit because he put a little more wind in the thing that he played than Harrison did. He'd take Harrison's song that he played and put more into it than what Harrison was putting in it. So [Harrison] didn't like that idea, you know.[13]

Talented steel and rhythm guitarist Ronnie Hall added further testimony: "His touch on a lap-steel is just—he can make that thing cry and bring you to tears. He was just that good. And my mother, bless her heart, when she was alive used to say, 'If you put Lorenzo and Felton in the same room, Felton would play rings around Lorenzo while he was running.' That's how my mother viewed it. He was that quick and fantastic, just tremendous. But he was very humble."[14]

Ronnie Hall

Although Ronnie Hall eventually dropped out of both the Keith and Jewell Dominions, he played a significant role in the formative years of several other steel guitarists from Detroit and contributed to establishing the presence of the steel guitar at the Keith Dominion General Assembly. Born October 9, 1943, in Detroit, Ronnie was the youngest of Phillip and Ruby Lee Hall's six children. The Halls had migrated north from western Georgia in the 1930s, first to Pittsburgh, Pennsylvania, then to Detroit, where Phillip got a job with the Ford Motor Company. The Halls were members of the Jewell Dominion. Ronnie Hall recalls that in 1953 his family left the Jewell Dominion and his mother became pastor of a small Keith Dominion congregation of ten or twelve members who worshiped at a storefront church at Madison and St. Albans Streets.

As a youngster growing up in the Jewell Dominion, Hall had heard Bishop Lorenzo Harrison play the steel guitar in Detroit. But the steel guitarist who was indirectly responsible for Hall taking up the instrument and who later became a lifelong musical influence was Felton Williams Jr. Williams had inspired Elder George White to purchase a lap-steel guitar. When George White could not get off from work to attend church one Sunday, his wife, Odessa, brought the instrument. Hall recalled seeing a lap-steel guitar for the first time when he was ten or twelve: "She sat there, and I never will forget that day 'cause she set it up and we were sittin' there looking at her and I'm sayin' to myself, 'What is that?' And then she sat down and she was playing this one-two-three [I-IV-V chord progression], just a rap [strum] kind of thing, across the strings. And the church went crazy! And so dad was there and he said, 'Now if this woman can do this, I can do this.' Her name was—well, she's still alive, bless her heart—Elder Odessa White."[15]

Inspired by White, Ronnie Hall's father bought an inexpensive lap-steel guitar from Montgomery Ward. Ronnie recalled: "I remember because it was a beautiful gold color, gold paint color, flashy gold, and it was a cheap one, but it was big-time for him. So, he brought it home and he started the process of trying to learn. Let me put that in a more clearer way: the *excruciating* process."[16]

Hall's father practiced the steel guitar daily and even got some pointers from experienced musicians, but he never achieved competency on the instrument.

I would come home from school and hide, 'cause I couldn't stand the noise. But he was trying to learn. And dad never really, of all his lifetime of trying to play, never seemed to get the idea or had the gift. And so, he thought he was pretty hot stuff there for a while. I mean, it went to his head, so to speak.

And I remember at one time during the time that Ted Beard and his brothers and his family came in the church, he invited Ted to come to the house, to our home, because Ted Beard's mother and father, and my mother and father, were friends in the Jewell Dominion. He came out to try and give dad some lessons. And I think Ted left in kind of a, "What's the use? He'll never get on to the thing."[17]

The Hall family lived four doors down from Felton Williams on Eighteenth Street in the Detroit suburb of Ecorse. The serendipitous close proximity of the Williams and Hall families helped foster the strong relationship between Felton Williams and Ronnie Hall.

Now how I got started at that point in time, I was a kid around these people playing: my father, Ted, Felton Williams. And Felton Williams used to have church in the basement [of his grandmother's home]. I would slip off sometimes on a Sunday evening when they would have "young people's service," so to speak. We would go down there and he would be playing his [steel] guitar to help the services in his home, in the basement. There was a church set up there. And I wasn't really interested in it until my dad bought the instrument.[18]

When his father was not home, Ronnie began to slip upstairs to try out his father's steel guitar. He quickly found that he had musical talent. When his father finally caught him and heard him play he realized his talented son could help serve as his accompanist. So he bought a standard electric guitar and young Ronnie began to learn to play a few chords on it:

I became the backup man for my dad, which was a nightmare, believe me. If you could have heard what I'm talking about, my dad was an embarrassment. And he had such a nerve that he didn't even care whose church it was. He didn't even care if he knew the people. He would drag that thing and drag me along with it into these various churches and play. You know, we used the term "Bogart" his way into these church services, set this thing up, and play for the church services, which sounded like somebody choking a cat. That's how bad it was. And I had to back him up on the Spanish guitar. For some reason, I developed a talent for picking on the Spanish. And I learned the chord patterns to the Hawaiian, or the lap-steel. So as time progressed, somewhere around 1955, and I was beginning to grow, that's how I got started.[19]

Hall's musicianship developed further when he became friends with two budding steel guitarists from the Jewell Dominion. The fact that Hall was from the Keith Dominion did not matter. The three teenagers were avidly interested in music and not concerned with church politics. Hall continued:

In 1957, I met another couple of young guys at one of the Jewell churches in Detroit, by the name of Sonny Treadway and Wayne White. Bishop Wayne White and I—he's a bishop now—we are still very close friends, and he still plays [steel] guitar just like I still play. In 1957, we visited their church on Joy Road. It was a converted bar that they had purchased and turned it into a church. And we visited that Sunday night and I was just astonished that somebody else could play besides Ted Beard and Felton Williams. Well, let me put it another way; Treadway was learning, just like I was learning. And Wayne was also learning, Bishop Wayne White. Treadway had a little . . . brown [Bronson lap-steel] that his dad had purchased in a pawn shop and given to him. And he was learning to play on that. And Bishop White was playing an old—just about every home had one—an archtop. At that time they used to call it "Japanese junk." I don't know what [brand] it was. He had one. And then he had another young fellow playing the drums to back him up by the name of Charles Rue [Hall's cousin]. I was inspired. I loved it. I used to beg my mom and dad. We'd get out of church on Sunday night, and our church wasn't that far from theirs, and I used to say, "Can we go by there? I'd like to get to know these guys."

Treadway had begun, and so I could play and he could play, and so we started. We struck up kind of a little group together. They used to come out to our house in Ecorse, Treadway and Wayne. We would all go upstairs to where the music room was and we'd stay up there most of the day playing guitar, way on up in the night. And my father would have to take them back home. . . . Treadway was gifted and my dad wanted to kind of pick up some of what we call "licks" on the guitar from him.

For a while there we used to travel together. I mean go to different states, go to Cleveland, and we even had an invitation to go over to Canada and play on a radio station over there for a church that was a Church of God in Christ. [Treadway and White] were still in the Jewell Dominion. I was in the Keith. But we struck up this you know, kid friendship. To us, you know, there wasn't such a thing as a Keith Dominion. We were thinking about guitar playing. And of course, our idols at that time were the three: it was Bishop Harrison, Felton Williams, and Ted Beard.[20]

In addition to providing musical inspiration to the young Detroit musicians, Williams also nurtured them. "We used to take up with him and he'd talk to myself and Wayne White and Sonny Treadway," Hall remembered fondly. "I mean he would talk to us like we were his sons."[21]

Lorenzo Harrison always had the latest and best equipment. Ronnie Hall was inspired by the sound of Harrison's Fender Deluxe 8 steel guitar and by the creativity Williams showed in making his own instrument and amplifiers.

> I went to Toledo. I heard Bishop Harrison play on a Fender 8-string guitar with three legs. And this guitar changed my entire life because it had a clarity about it. I mean, bell-like tones would come out from it. One of the times that we would go to Toledo—sometimes between the services, if we stayed the whole day on a Sunday, you know—we'd sneak back to the church, you know how kids will do, we'd go and investigate the music [instruments]. And he left it set up one day. And I went there and, you know, kind of hooked up and played a little bit before we got ran out. But I said, "Man, this thing is beautiful, just played so beautifully." But he had it covered, custom covered with a leather—some kind of leather thing, with his name engraved on it: "Bishop Lorenzo Harrison." . . . In fact, Calvin Cooke one time tried to do the same thing and messed his guitar up [laughs]. That was a mess. You should've seen that thing. . . . We all admired Harrison. At that time, I wanted that type of guitar. This was right around '59 to '62.[22]

In the summer of 1962, Ronnie traveled with his family to vacation in California. He hoped that his father would take him to the Fender factory in Fullerton to buy him a Deluxe 8 like Harrison's, but his dream did not materialize. Determined to have a guitar with the sound of Harrison's instrument, Ronnie bought a large California redwood board from which to make his own instrument:

> So I brought the board back from California. And when we got back home I went downstairs with some hand tools. Basically a flat blade screwdriver, a chisel and a hammer, and of course, a saw, and fashioned my own steel guitar, that had eight strings. I actually made the guitar. I couldn't get chrome legs like came with the Fender guitar, but I managed to get . . . from the lumberyard, these table legs. And I got four of them and put the brackets on underneath.
>
> The thing had dual pickups. The pickups I salvaged from old guitars. And actually, one of them was—remember the lady I told you that had the husband that wanted to play? We had her guitar and unbeknowing to them, I took the pickup out of that one. In a way of speaking, I stole it from them. But it was an abandoned guitar anyway. So I took that pickup, which was only a six-string, and it became what I call the bass position pickup, the one that is

furthest from the back bridge, and amplified the first six strings. And I took a second pickup which had the rest of the strings and put it near the bridge at the back. So, the one at the bridge had the first six strings and the one that had the bass, up further, was near the deck, or the fretboard, that I had hand painted. I had toggle switches I could switch back and forth. Yeah, man, I did it all "hand." I made the fretboard. Felton, he worked at Ford Motor Company, and he brought some scrap aluminum home. And I got enough to get a piece that was about an eighth of an inch thick, or less. And I took that and cut it with a pair of tin snips and painted it up.

I might say that the thing looked good. I played that thing from 1962 or –3 to 1973. That's true. Made a handmade case and everything for it. . . . I played it in Nashville [at the General Assembly].

After 1973 when I got the Fender, [the homemade steel guitar] went down the tubes. But I played that thing for the longest [time] in church. And it had a certain tone that—most of the guys in the community that were listening, Calvin and all of 'em—that's when it began to catch on.[23]

Hall eventually struck up a friendship with young Keith Dominion steel guitar sensation Calvin Cooke, who moved to Detroit in 1967. The pair seemed to have a special musical synergy. Many of those who heard them play during their heyday recall their music as some of the best ever played in the Keith Dominion.

Hall left the Keith Dominion around 1970. He became a minister, and in 1981, formed an independent church, the Mt. Caramel Full Gospel Assembly. On July 18, 1995, Hall was the victim of a terrible automobile accident that resulted in the loss of both legs. The accident served to heighten his religious faith and dedication to the ministry and he has learned to deal with his physical challenge. "But I haven't let that slow me down at all," he asserts. "I got prosthetic legs and I get up and do my thing."[24] Indeed, Hall seems to have twice the energy of most people. In 1997, the Mt. Caramel congregation moved to 4000 Fourteenth Street in Ecorse, where he serves as pastor and bishop. Although music is not his primary interest, Hall continues to play the steel guitar for the sake of his family.

I'm a minister first, a preacher first, and a guitar player second. Playing music is only one page in the book. Two of my sons play with me in church. Marcus Hall, he's one of two twin boys, he can play. He's like I am, he's multitalented. He can play the lap-steel, Hawaiian, the pedal, whatever. And he plays the Spanish behind me. And my son Michael, Michael Sean Hall, who is my drummer, is very gifted, but he only wants to play the drums as long as we're at service. He's not interested in traveling or anything. They've inherited my musical abilities, but my only reason for playing in church is not one of my desires, it's theirs. I really play because it keeps them at the church. Marcus is in his thirties now, and my son Michael is just turning twenty. He's getting ready to go to college. He's the baby boy in my family. So really, if dad doesn't play they don't want to be bothered with it. So dad has to play.[25]

Bishop Hall may see music as just one element of his ministry, but he recognizes the power of music and uses his musical talents to take his flock ever higher on their spiritual journey.

In service yesterday, a young lady came up to me, a little girl about eleven years of age. She had visited our church for the first time. And they had one of these, what we call "the-Lord-shows-up-and-shows-out" type of services yesterday. It was just—it was on fire. And the Lord allowed the old man to still have his touch on the [steel] guitar and everything was just "together." So, the little girl came up to me and she said, "Pastor?" I said, "Yeah." She said, "What is that?" I said, "What do you mean?" She said, "That." "Oh, that's a guitar." She said, "That's not a guitar!" I said, "Yes it is." She says, "Guitars don't cry like that." And I said, "This one does." And I said, "And it's called a lap-steel."

And then another minister who was visiting for the first time, one of the father-in-laws of one of my associate ministers, was there. But it's the first time he had ever heard it. And he said, "Bishop, I have never in my life ever heard anything like that." And he said, "I don't know. How come I've never heard of you?" And I said, "Doc, I'll tell you. There are hundreds of guitar players that play this thing. They're just in a different stream."[26]

Ted Beard

When Bishop Mattie Lue Jewell was evangelizing in Kentucky around 1933–34, the guitar playing of Maurice Beard, a young man from Beaver Dam, caught her ear. She invited him to join her and a banjo player, whose name is long forgotten, to travel to Detroit, Michigan, (or probably more precisely, Mt. Clemens), which served as one of her bases of operations at the time. In Detroit, Beard met Fannie Mae Asberry, who had arrived a few years earlier from Georgia with her mother and seven siblings.[27]

When Bishop Jewell and her evangelical team left Detroit, Beard stayed behind. He courted Fannie Mae Asberry and they were soon married. On June 15, 1935, she gave birth to her first child, a boy they named Maurice Jr. He was born in their home on Theodore Street, on the east side of town. As far back as he can remember, Maurice Jr. has been known as "Ted," but he really has no idea why. The Theodore Street address offers the only clue to his lifelong moniker. The Beards had eight children: two more boys and five girls.

Ted Beard is a soft-spoken, handsome, fair-skinned man who dresses nattily, but conservatively; his bearing is one of confidence and cordial authority. Although never the flashiest or fastest steel guitarist, he built a solid reputation during his heyday of the 1960s through the mid-1980s and remains highly respected as a talented, innovative instrumentalist and a dedicated teacher. Since about 1968, he has served as Coordinator of Music at the Keith Dominion General Assembly in Nashville, a position that only he has occupied since its creation by Chief Overseer Jenkins. His primary responsibilities as coordinator are to determine who is eligible to play at the General Assembly and schedule each musician for the ten-day event—not just the steel guitarists, but all the drummers, keyboardists, bassists, and others.

Ted Beard remembers his father's guitar playing as "like Chet Atkins."[28] The description certainly fits his place of origin; Beaver Dam is right in the heart of the birthplace of a distinctive regional guitar style known today as "Kentucky thumb-picking." The technique involves playing a bass line on the lower three or four strings, which are usually partially muted to give a percussive, thumping effect, while picking a syncopated melody on the top three or four strings. One of the most important people in the very early development of Kentucky thumb-picking style was Arnold Schultz, an African American. According to Kentucky folklorist William Lightfoot, many local informants place Shultz's February 1886 birth at "Taylor Mines, a defunct mining camp some two miles southwest of Beaver Dam."[29] Merle Travis, from Ebenezer in nearby Muhlenberg County, did so much to popularize the style that many people refer to it as "Travis picking." The style was popularized even further by Chet Atkins, who had learned much from the playing of Travis.

The extent of the direct influence by Maurice Beard Sr. on other guitarists is uncertain. He taught his son, Douglas (1937–60), who is remembered by many as an exceptionally talented guitarist. "He was real good. Matter of fact, he was the best one of us [Beard children]," recalled Ted.[30] (Douglas Beard died in an automobile accident in 1960.) It is interesting to note that the classic Jewell Dominion backup guitar style practiced today by musicians such as Ronnie Mozee and Jay Caver, for example, often includes variants of thumb-picking.

The first steel guitarist that Ted Beard ever saw was Fred Neal, when he played at the church on the corner of Garfield and Rivard:

> That had to be when I was somewhere between five and seven. With me being born in '35, that had to be in the early '40s. Fred Neal came into the church that we was having and he was carrying that little steel guitar, six-string, under his arm. And, you know, the first time I seen it I didn't know what he was going to do. And I think he must've had a little amp. And he came in and plugged it up. And it was for the service, and he started playing. . . . He probably came with Bishop Jewell at the time, but I'm not sure about that.[31]

Ted's father bought him a Gibson six-string lap-steel when he was twelve. His mother arranged for him to take a few lessons. Ted continued:

> When I first started playing the [steel] guitar . . . at twelve years old, you know, when I had my first guitar, my mother did send me downtown. I had a cousin to show me how to hold the bar. But my mother sent me downtown to a music store, and it was a famous music store in Detroit called Grinnell's. They taught different things and there was a guy there that did know how to play steel a little bit. I was able to get ten lessons from him, a dollar a lesson. After ten lessons, she told me she didn't have any more [money] and that I'd have to learn on my own.[32]

Ted played his new steel at the Jewell Dominion church at Garfield and Rivard, where his father served as associate minister.

> Me and my two brothers had a band in the church. I was on steel, Douglas was on lead [rhythm] guitar, and my youngest brother, Billie, was on drums. And at the same time the Williams brothers had them a band, with Felton Williams playing steel, and Shona Williams was the oldest one, he was playing lead. And then they had Lapious, he was the younger brother, that was playing drums.[33] And, you know, we all come out the same church. So it used to be quite a battle there, you know.
>
> We had something back then, we just didn't know it. . . . Ronnie Hall came along—he started playing guitar, lead guitar, along with me and my brothers. Then he developed into playing the steel, got his own style. We didn't realize how good we were then, especially this Felton. I didn't realize until later on, this Felton Williams, that guy—ooh, he was awesome. He carried his group. He was a good steel player. He was the best one at the time, and my brother, who was the lead player, was the best musician among us Beards. And the people kept wanting him as the steel player and my brother, the lead, to get together. But because we was part of a family group I don't know if they ever had a chance to get together, but people really wanted that. My brother was carrying me at the time. I was learning.[34]

Among the young musicians who played at Garfield and Rivard was Sonny Treadway. "Treadway was one of the young drummers," remembered Beard. "His mom and dad was right there at Garfield where we were, where the Williams were."[35] Treadway also played standard guitar and steel guitar. He recalled being abruptly drafted into service by Bishop Jewell:

> She stole me from my parents. She took me without my permission and told me and sent me to Nashville, Tennessee. And I didn't even know what was happening. I woke the next morning after we had a little assembly there, a meeting. I got home, my father told me he gave me away, so she had already made plans for me. When she first heard me play, she told my father, "I'm taking that boy. He's traveling with me." So that's what happened. It shocked me. I asked my parents why did they give me away? And they said, "Well, you'll be alright." So when I found out the next morning she called and talked to me. She said, "Pack your suitcase and get ready to go." I said, "Go where?" She said, "To Nashville, Tennessee." That was my first time leaving away from Michigan, too. It was a good experience leaving home.
>
> She was there in town because they had just closed the meeting down. She told me, "You don't have to worry about the money." She gave me the fare to go on the bus. That was my first time riding over five hundred miles away from home and being around different people and, you know, away from the family. It was a good experience. When I got there people was praising me and jumping for joy. She had told them what she had, said she had a great musicianer that could really play. So, they was excited to hear me.
>
> When I got there I had to play before I even knowed their names. They wanted to hear me so I kind of teased them a little bit. "I can't play." I said, "Aw, you won't hear nothing." So I started playing, then they started shouting and jumping all in the aisles. Oh, we got us a good player now! Then after that she came to Nashville and I started packing for the road. She told me to pack and get ready to go on the road.[36]

Treadway developed into one of the top musicians in the Jewell Dominion. He traveled with Bishop Lorenzo Harrison for three years to accompany him on standard guitar at large assemblies in several states, and was called into service again in Harrison's last days. In the 1960s he moved to Deerfield Beach, Florida, where he still plays lap-steel guitar at the Jewell Dominion church next door where his wife, Bishop Eunice Treadway, served as pastor until her death in 2009.

In 1955, strife arose among the Detroit-area Jewell Dominion congregations and several families left to join the Keith Dominion. (No one I have interviewed recalls the source of the strife.) Among those who moved from the Jewell Dominion to the Keith Dominion in 1955 were the Beard and Cooke families. Ronnie Hall's family had moved to the Keith Dominion too, probably a year or two earlier. Felton Williams's and Sonny Treadway's families remained in the Jewell Dominion.

The move by the Beard, Cooke, and Hall families to the Keith Dominion played a significant role in shaping its steel guitar music. The Detroit musicians had developed a musical style that differed considerably from the Henry Nelson one-chord drive style that dominated in Florida, South Carolina, downstate New York, and elsewhere in the East. By contrast, most of the praise music the Detroit musicians played had a distinct I-IV-V chord structure and, while rhythmic framming was heard, it was used considerably less than in the Nelson style. Beard and Cooke were known for inventing short melodies or riffs that served as "hooks" within their praise music in order to build excitement among the congregations during worship services. And Cooke had a dominant seventh note on the second string of his steel guitar, which gave his music a distinctive sound. Because Cooke and Beard were not framming as much as Nelson, their rhythm guitarists could be heard better, and because many of the rhythm players came from the Jewell Dominion too, they often played the walking bass lines, boogies, and shuffles associated with Jewell music.

Cooke and Beard employed "stop-time" effectively, a technique Nelson did not use. That is, in the middle of a heated praise music session they would give the rhythm section a cue to suddenly stop playing. The steel guitarist would continue to play unaccompanied, usually for two or four bars, sometimes longer. During the unaccompanied interlude the steel guitarist often introduced a new riff, or short melody line. When the rhythm section returned to play, the energy was elevated. The stop-time technique may be used several times within a single praise session. It was very effective in elevating the energy level of church services and became one of the hallmarks of the Detroit sound. The new riffs, also known as "tunes" or "jams," were learned by other steel guitarists, and the most effective jams spread quickly throughout the Keith Dominion's geographic range.

During Nelson's absence from about 1959 through 1972, Beard and Cooke were the dominant steel guitarists to play at the Keith Dominion General Assembly in Nashville, and in the latter part of this period they were often the *only* steel guitarists to play at the General Assembly. Their musical styles, including the sound of the ensembles that accompanied them, were firmly established on a national level during those fourteen years and had a lasting impact on the tradition.

In the 1960s, three of Ted Beard's sisters formed the Beard Sisters gospel group. Janie played the piano and sang with Alfreda and Catherine, and Ted played his Fender Stringmaster lap-steel with two eight-string necks. They performed regularly for early morning live radio broadcasts on WMBC 1400 AM, a pioneering Detroit-area black radio station. The Sunday morning programs at WMBC featured any number of local groups, as well as touring acts, that were trying to break into the Motor City gospel music scene. The Beard Sisters were on the air at 8:00 A.M., and after their broadcasts rushed to worship services at the House of God where their father served as pastor. They also performed for gospel music "programs" at churches throughout the Detroit area, but they never recorded. The Beard Sisters group disbanded in 1967 or 1968.

Transportation is a common theme in African American sermons and sacred music. The train—even though no longer the common mode of transportation it was before World War II—remains a popular symbol and musical theme in many black churches. Numerous steel guitarists in the Keith and Jewell Dominions have made train imitations an essential element of their musical canon and a component of their identity. Jewell Dominion steel guitarist Reginald "Footie" Covington of Philadelphia has "Footie's Gospel Train" professionally painted across the front of his instrument in four-inch letters. The electric steel guitar is well suited to imitate a train's sounds, and a musician with good technique can make any number of percussive chugging sounds and play a variety of chords or single notes for whistle effects. A foot-operated volume control pedal can be employed effectively for volume swells. In the Keith Dominion, Ted Beard has become renowned for his improvised compositions that imitate train sounds. "The first person I ever heard do it was Lorenzo Harrison," recalled Beard. "That was my hero. And he had a little train thing he would do. . . . Just about all of us in the [Keith Dominion] have a little train we do."[37]

At first Beard attempted to imitate Harrison's train sounds, but when his family left the Jewell Dominion to join the Keith Dominion in 1955, he was on his own. "And so, from then on I developed my own train. The way I used to do it, everybody used to like it. And then I would throw it sometime in the jubilee service when I was playin'. I would switch over and hit the train. And the people, they really liked it so I just kept developing it."[38] Eventually Beard incorporated a bit of preaching into his train numbers. The example on Arhoolie 472, *Sacred Steel Live!* which was recorded at the dedication services for the new House of God in Rush, New York, includes two minutes of Elder Beard's introductory preaching before his train chugs away from the platform and accelerates to full speed.

Following in the footsteps of his father, Beard was ordained as a minister and appointed pastor of the House of God in Flint in 1987, where he served until 1999. He was then appointed pastor of the church at 7529 Joy Road in Detroit, where he serves today.[39] Many Keith and Jewell Dominion steel guitarists who enter the ministry cease to play after serving a few years as pastor, but Elder Beard continues to play steel guitar well into his senior years.

When Beard became a regular steel guitarist at the annual General Assembly in Nashville he, along with Calvin Cooke, began to establish a reputation for his fresh musical ideas. "I was really like an innovator. Each year, during the time that me and Calvin was playin', each year in Nashville [church musicians] would come to see what I was playin' new. This was the thing, you know: What is Ted doing new?"[40]

Unlike some steel guitarists who closely guard their technique, tunings, and repertoire, Beard believes his musical talent is a gift to be shared. "The Lord would give me new tunes and things to play so that's how He let me know that He give me everything. Why should I hold on to something?"[41] Word that Beard was willing to take time to help aspiring steel guitarists learn the fundamentals of the instrument spread rapidly through the Keith Dominion. He gave impromptu lessons at the General Assembly, at church meetings around the country he traveled to, and back home in Detroit. Often a musician would spend a few days or a weekend at the Beard residence to study with him. Among them was Darick Campbell, now lap-steel artist with the Campbell Brothers band. "Darick was going with my daughter [Lisa] and he would come in from New York, but he spent more time with me than with her," Beard recalled.[42] If someone who needed steel guitar help could not meet with him in person, Beard gave instructions and advice over the telephone. Among his long-distance students was Robert Lee, whose son, Glenn, became an influential pedal-steel guitarist. "Glenn Lee's father, he was a great admirer of my playing. He would call me long distance [from Florida] and try to get things on the phone."[43]

The best known of Beard's students is young New Jersey steel guitar prodigy Robert Randolph, who went on to land a rock-star-magnitude recording contract with Warner Bros. and garner two Grammy nominations in 2004, another Grammy nomination in 2010, and was included in a various artist compilation album that won a Grammy in 2010. "His knowledge of music is just—woo, just amazing. I never helped anyone that was the type of a pupil that he was, that catch on as fast as he did. No one. And you know, there's some good guys out there. But his knowledge is just so—ah! He can just grasp it so fast, you know."[44] From 2003 to 2005, Beard, Cooke, and guitarists Jay Caver and Harvey Shaw held teaching sessions every Monday night at the House of God at 7529 Joy Road, where Beard serves as pastor. Since he retired from the U.S. Postal Service in 1995, Beard probably teaches more than ever. "I'm waiting for a guy now from South Carolina. He's waiting for the weather to get nice. He's in college right now, about twenty years old. He want to come up. He want me to . . . I don't know, it's something he can't quite grasp. His name is Richard Neal."[45]

The Detroit-area steel guitarists have made a lasting impact on the Keith Dominion steel guitar tradition. Felton Williams was a tremendous influence on Cooke, Beard, Hall, Sonny Treadway, and many more musicians in the region. Collectively, Beard and Cooke have had at least as much influence in shaping the Keith Dominion tradition as did Henry Nelson— probably much more than Nelson in some regions. The Detroit musicians would be a major influence on younger musicians that followed.

Calvin Cooke

Although he is not a large man, Calvin Cooke stands as a giant among contemporary Keith Dominion steel guitarists. His musical innovations in the form of inventive, exciting tunes, or "jams," which propelled congregations to ever higher levels of spiritual ecstasy, have been imitated by dozens of Keith Dominion steel guitarists. His unrivaled forty-seven-year tenure as a steel guitarist at the annual General Assembly has helped make him a venerated figure to thousands of congregants, spanning three generations.

Calvin Cooke was born January 11, 1944, in Cleveland, Ohio. He has three brothers and three sisters, all of whom are alive today. The Cooke family home was 8412 Linwood, near Huff Street, which he recalls as lined with barbeque restaurants and pawn shops. His mother, Elizabeth, was active in the Jewell Dominion, as was most of her extended family. She was a talented, passionate singer who was frequently featured as a soloist in church. The extended Cooke family was rich in musical talent; all of Calvin's brothers played instruments, his sisters sang, and several of his cousins and uncles were competent church musicians.

Calvin was raised by his stepfather, William Cooke, and never knew his biological father. William Cooke worked at the Republic Steel mill in Cleveland. It was hard, dangerous work, but it was steady, paid well, and he had the weekends off. He was not a member in any church, but sang at local gospel programs with a vocal quartet that also included his brother-in-law. Calvin cannot remember the name of the quartet, but recalls that they performed on gospel programs with well-known groups like the Soul Stirrers, in the era when Sam Cooke (no relation) sang lead in the group. William Cooke died of cancer in 1956, when Calvin was twelve. It was only then that Calvin's mother told him that he was his stepfather, not his biological father.

Calvin Cooke has fond memories of fishing with his brother Gary, his stepfather, and his uncle on the weekends. They called their favorite spot on the Lake Erie shore in downtown Cleveland "the rocks." They caught white bass, perch, pike, sheepshead, and shad. Following successful fishing trips, his mother's extended family visited to enjoy fellowship and mouthwatering fried fish and other food Mr. Cooke prepared on the brick grill that he had built in the backyard. Fishing has been a favorite leisure activity throughout Calvin's life and he remains an avid fisherman today. Since he has retired, he sometimes fishes several times a week.

Cooke's immediate family was among seven or eight families from the Ohio Jewell Dominion churches—about half the denomination's membership in that state—who left to join the Keith Dominion in 1955. Because several members of his mother's extended family stayed in the Jewell Dominion, he has maintained fairly close ties to that church. Elder Mae Hodge served as pastor at the local Keith Dominion church, which the kids called "down in the hole," because it was below street level on Euclid Street. Elder Hodge wanted someone to play instrumental music for worship services, to help "make a joyful noise" in praise of the Lord. She knew eleven-year-old Cooke was interested in music, and was alleged to have some ability, so she bought him his first guitar, a black standard, or "Spanish neck," electric instrument. Although he had learned a few chords from family members before he acquired his own instrument, his small hands made it difficult to reach far enough to form chords or play scales with any facility. "My fingers wouldn't fit the guitar," he recalls. "All I would do is turn it over and play it with a knife, with the back of a knife. And that's how I started."[1]

About the same time, Cooke's first cousin, Maynard Sopher, who was about a year or two older than Calvin, got an electric guitar. They teamed up to play in church; Cooke played knife-style steel as Sopher played bass lines and shuffles on the lower strings of his guitar. The two youngsters were the only musicians who played in the local Keith Dominion church at that time.

Cooke played the big, black electric guitar knife-style for about two years until his mother bought him a lap-steel. "I was about thirteen years old. She bought me a Rickenbacker lap guitar from the pawn shop. It was a black one with a silver covering [probably one of the renowned Bakelite plastic models, with chrome trim]."[2] Soon he was playing his Rickenbacker regularly for church services at the Euclid Street church. "Then after that she bought me a Fender eight-string."[3]

One of Cooke's earliest inspirations on the instrument was Bishop

Lorenzo Harrison. He first heard Harrison as a boy attending services in Jewell Dominion churches with his mother. Also, Cooke's cousin, Sonny Gaines, played standard guitar with Harrison. Because of his early bond with the members and clergy of the Jewell Dominion and the continued membership of his extended maternal family in the organization, Cooke often attended Jewell Dominion worship services and assemblies after joining the Keith Dominion, a practice he continued through much of his adult life. Lorenzo Harrison's musical influence began early in Cooke's life and remained strong until Harrison died in 1986.

Another early influence was Robert "Bobby' Tolliver (1928–), who lived in Dayton, Ohio, at the time. Cooke fondly remembers Tolliver helping him in the 1950s:

> He's the one who really encouraged me and gave me a chance when the church didn't want me to play, 'cause I played so bad. They couldn't stand to hear me play. One day they had an assembly and he said, "Well, I want you to play for this assembly, this night." The people was begging him not to let me play. He told 'em, "Well, he got to learn somehow." And he say, "Well, go on and play anyway." He had already prepped me to how the people was going to react. So after that, I started learning more and playing more and playing, playing until things gotten better and better and better. He spent a *lot* of time with me.
>
> He was a very personable guy, more like a father figure who talked to us, helped us, let us play. He was the top musician for the state of Ohio then.[4]

Tolliver's aunt, Bishop Bertha M. Massey (1897–2007), was in the congregation when Cooke played. When Cooke saw her in recent years he was reminded of the importance of the opportunities Tolliver provided him when he was a fledgling steel guitarist.

> Matter of fact, Bishop Massey is 106 [in 2003]. And every time I see her she always tells me how I used to play terrible, till they couldn't stand it. . . . And [today] when I get through [playing] and I go speak to her she says, "Calvin, I enjoyed you. I always remember when you couldn't play a lick. We'd have to close up our ears and tell Bobby, that's her nephew, 'Why did you let him play? *Why* did you let him play?' And he say, 'Well, aren't you glad we gave him a chance?'" I always remember that. Those things are good memories of where I come from and how people gave me a chance and stuck by me, didn't throw me away.[5]

In December 1958, Bishop Henry Harrison asked Cooke's mother to allow him to travel with him to play for the Christmas assembly in Columbus, Georgia, during the break from school. Mrs. Cooke obliged and her son began a tenure as steel guitarist at Keith Dominion assemblies that continued for nearly half a century.

Following the exodus of several Jewell Dominion families to the Keith Dominion, Henry Harrison became the state bishop for Keith Dominion churches in Ohio. Bishop Henry Harrison was a steel guitarist and brother of Lorenzo Harrison. Cooke teamed up with his cousin, guitarist Maynard Sopher, and the bishop's son, Starlin Harrison (1941–). Starlin and Cooke took turns playing standard guitar (Cooke's hands had grown by this time) and steel.

Bishop Henry Harrison was based in Knoxville, Tennessee, and was responsible for churches in Kentucky, Georgia, Alabama, and Tennessee as well as Ohio. On the way south to Georgia, they stopped in Kentucky coal country, an area they would visit many times over the years. Cooke remembered the mountain communities vividly.

> Hazard, Kentucky. I'll never forget it. Yeah, we went to Hazard, Kentucky, 'cause it was a very small place. And back then black and white was mixed together. They had a lot of mixed families back up in those hills. We stayed and met a lot of them, and we became personal friends because every time we went back there that's where we hung out, with them. I know a lot of families were mixed back in there.
>
> They had houses that was built on those mountains. It's a place where there's a lot of hills and mountains. And they had those houses where they had long sticks that held them up, up on those mountains. And we had to go along different paths to get to the different ones' houses. That was a lot of fun. Those were some of the best, beautiful people that we had. And we got to know different families personally, that would come in. And every year we'd go there, we head straight for their house. They had a little small [church] building. They all were elderly people, most of them, and they all came to the church when we were there. When they find out we were coming to town, mostly all the people would come down to hear us play.
>
> All those people were coal miner people, coal miners that worked in the coal mine. And Somerset, Kentucky, and all those places there, we toured there with Bishop Harrison because he was over that district.[6]

Calvin Cooke played at the Keith Dominion General Assembly for the first time in 1959. To play steel guitar at the General Assembly is an honor for any musician and a very special experience for a fifteen-year-old. Following their usual plan, Cooke and Starlin Harrison took turns playing steel and rhythm guitar. Cooke recalls that they were the only steel guitarists who played for the assembly that year.[7] Sopher played guitar as well. Cooke remembers that the Reverend Robertson of New York was one of several drummers who took turns. Bobbie Jean Moore played the organ and Alma Jean (Cooke does not recall her surname), played the piano.

In the Keith Dominion, a steel guitarist builds a regional and national reputation by playing for the various assemblies and large events. By playing at the General Assembly as a teenager and continuing to play annually at the church's grandest event, Cooke built a national reputation as a top steel guitarist by the time he was a young man. He says he played at the General Assembly every year from 1959 through 2005, longer than any other steel guitarist.[8] His longevity as a General Assembly musician is testimony to his ability to inspire a congregation with his steel guitar playing.

Throughout their school years Cooke, Sopher, and Starlin Harrison continued to travel with Bishop Harrison on weekends, during holiday breaks, and while on summer vacation. If Bishop Harrison was not in the area to pick them up, they took the Greyhound or Trailways bus to rendezvous with him. Traveling with Bishop Harrison, the boys were not permitted to listen to blues, rhythm and blues, or rock 'n' roll on the radio. They listened to the gospel programs broadcast over WLAC from Nashville and to country music broadcast over WWVA in Wheeling, West Virginia. Listening to the radio, Cooke developed an affinity for country music, which he maintains today. As is the case with many Keith Dominion steel guitarists, he has listened to hours of Grand Ole Opry radio broadcasts, and later *Hee Haw* television broadcasts, just to hear or see a few moments of country steel guitar. Cooke recalls that the Trailways buses were among the first to have personal radio headsets available for passengers. Riding the Trailways buses alone on long-distance trips to rendezvous with Bishop Henry Harrison, he was able to listen to blues, rhythm and blues, jazz—anything he chose—without sanctions by adults. Elements of all the worldly influences were infused, both consciously and unconsciously, into the music he played in church.[9]

Cooke was also influenced by two older cousins from the Jewell Dominion: Bobby and Tubby Golden of Cleveland, both deceased. "We would come in from off the road," he recalled, "And we would go over there and spend time with them on the weekends and stay up half the night and play and trade tunes. They played with us and helped me a lot, these particular guys."[10]

Henry Harrison was a carpenter by trade. In addition to his ministering, he also built and renovated churches within dioceses under his responsibility as well as in other areas, particularly Florida, where he had relatives in the clergy. He was assisted by a crew of local craftsmen and also put the three teenage musicians to work carrying bricks, making mortar, cleaning up, and performing other unskilled tasks. The musicians worked weekdays and played music for worship services and assemblies nights and weekends. Traveling with Harrison suited Cooke and he developed a strong bond with the bishop and his wife. "Actually, we wound up living with them because we loved being with them so much. After my [step-] father had died, [Bishop Henry Harrison] was actually my father. His wife treated me like I was the baby boy, and a lot of people thought I was actually his son. That's the way they treated us. I wind up leaving home, living with them, and staying with them, for a long while."[11]

Cooke, Sopher, and Starlin Harrison became the objects of much attention and admiration by their young peers. Church provides the opportunity to dress up and the young men enjoyed looking sharp. At one point they decided to dress up their instruments, too. Taking a cue from Lorenzo Harrison, who once had a steel guitar, including the fretboard, covered in leather,[12] Cooke glued a deer pelt over the entire body of his Fender Deluxe 8. Starlin Harrison similarly trimmed his in black-and-white cowhide. The instruments must have been a sight to behold.

The three teens also played for the chief overseer, Bishop Mary F. L. Keith. Bishop Keith was a spiritually powerful woman with penetrating, all-knowing eyes and a reputation for performing many miraculous healings. Cooke vividly recalled an interaction with her that not only changed his life, but also had lasting impact on the sound of Keith Dominion music.

> I was with Bishop Keith and a lot of times I would be hanging out. Being a teenager, we were into girls real tough then. By being in the church and traveling with her, [the girls] thought you were special. And we would rip and run. And [some of the adults] said, "Bishop Keith you ought to send them home." You know, them boys cutting up and this-and-that. She looked at us and said, "No, I ain't going to send them home. They're average, just like anybody else." We were in Barnesville, Georgia, playing for an assembly—it was hot—during the December assembly. She told us, she said, "Calvin, you get up and go in the back room." I thought I was going home. I was feelin' so bad, 'cause we was rippin' and runnin'. . . .
>
> She got me in the back and she prayed for my hands, her and Bishop Fletcher. When she got through praying for my hands, I didn't know what was going on. I thought she was sending me home so it was kind of bothering me. She got to prayin' and she went back out. Then she said, "Now you go on back out and play."

And I didn't understand that then. And when I went back out and played, it was like something I never heard before. I never heard such sweet music and I couldn't believe what was goin' on. After that, I played for this whole church and it look like my whole career in the church I've been a top musician for the past forty-five years, every since I've been here. It made me feel like Lorenzo, being a top musician. That had to be the year before [Bishop Keith] died. That had to be in 1960, or either '59.

When we played in Nashville [at the General Assembly] that next year it was like brand new music. Everything was totally different everywhere I played. Everywhere I played it was like a totally different thing. Then she taught me about fasting, dedicating myself to God, if I wanted to do this. And how the more I fasted, the more I dedicated myself to Him, the more He would use my music in healing, or doing whatever, different things, and aiding in the church service. A lot of people back then, because I patterned after Bishop Jewell [that is, Lorenzo Harrison's] style of music, they said I played blues and jazz and they didn't want me to play, a lot of the older ones. But a lot of youth that came up in my era would say, "Hey this is some different music," instead of hearing the old Hawaiian style. They started coming to the assemblies, they started coming to the General Assembly because the music was totally different, and was more popular. And she said, "No, I'm keeping these boys." And Bishop [Henry] Harrison enjoyed it. He loved it, even though he didn't play what we played.

I couldn't understand how people said we played blues until I started listening to that other music and understood what they meant. But from our hearts it wasn't blues. To us we were playing spiritual music according to the way that we play in church. Because we were connected from the Jewell [Dominion] a lot of people didn't know our history and that we were from there. But [the music] still helped the people to start coming in. And a lot of youth and a lot of grownups too who were against us, started saying, "Hey this music is totally different."[13]

This "totally different" music marks a change in what would become deemed as acceptable music for Keith Dominion worship services. The new music was a shift from a sweeter, more melodic sound to music strongly flavored by blues, rock, and boogie-woogie—the sort of music commonly played in Keith Dominion services today.

The era of Cooke's musical shift coincides with the period in mainstream culture when youth began to have a strong influence in cultural expression. Bishop Keith may have recognized that the new music attracted youth to the church and could play a role in keeping them in church. The blues- and boogie-woogie-flavored music of Jewell Dominion steel guitarist Lorenzo Harrison figured importantly in this shift. Today, driving, blues-tinged steel guitar music is a major factor in attracting young people (as well as some older folks) to the Keith Dominion. Cooke Continued:

> We would fast before we'd go play for a convention. I would always, before we'd go to Nashville, especially—well, not just Nashville, every assembly—we'd ask Bishop [Henry] Harrison and Bishop Keith to pray for us. And she would get our hands and she would pray for us, and anoint us with oil before we would play because we wanted to be dedicated to what we were doing. And we knew this was serious business, especially playing for Bishop Keith. This was *real* serious business. Then after due time people become to realize: hey, these guys are playing spiritually. . . .
>
> And still today—not as much, I can't do a lot of [fasting] today like I used to [since having a kidney transplant]—I still like to fast and have a special connection. Even if I go out and do a concert, I still like to go out and play so somebody would have a feeling of what we're doing, and have a special connection. So a lot of that is still a part of me. And I always refer back to Bishop Keith and Bishop [Henry] Harrison because they're the ones who had a very, very dominant effect on my life.[14]

Not surprisingly, playing for large assemblies for Bishop Harrison and Chief Overseer Bishop Keith while just a teenager went to Cooke's head. Keith Dominion congregations can be tough audiences. If the music fails to move them, they will let the musicians know, either by not reacting, or by direct verbal communication. After all, part of the process during worship services is shedding inhibitions. Cooke recalled a painful lesson:

> I got the "big head" one day. We had just played out of Georgia and we went to Alcore, Tennessee. And I just thought, I said, "Man, shoot. I already know in my head, these people gonna shout and cut up." I thought I was the baddest thing that ever lived 'cause of what people had been sayin', and I had just left [playing] with Bishop Keith. Bishop Harrison had this assembly goin' and I played. People just sit there and looked at me. And I said, "These people ain't shoutin'." Boy, and I got mad.
>
> A lady come up during the offering time, she said, "Calvin, I don't know why I'm saying this, but don't you ever get exalted. Don't you ever think you better than anybody else." And it look like the words that woman told me, I felt so bad. She said, "You not the only one that God give this gift to." She said, "I don't know why I'm sayin' this."
>
> I felt so bad I wanted to cry. And I held back them tears in front of that woman, because I didn't want that lady to see me cry. When she got through talking to me it was like she pricked my heart. And it looked like I couldn't play. And the service started back on after they raised the offering. After that, and that woman got through with me, it looked like she kept watching me

during the service. The Lord let me know: Don't you ever think you the only one who could do this. And I never felt that way again in life. I never did that again, because I learned a lesson. Because especially in the church, you think you can do because of what people tell you. Then I also find out those same people who would get you up, will be the same people who would throw you down, and throw you in the mud, and throw you out.[15]

Not too long after the change in Cooke's music that occurred after Bishop Keith prayed over him, he experienced a second major musical breakthrough: the dominant seventh tuning that would become a primary element of his musical signature. Having a minimal knowledge of music theory and harmony, Cooke conceives music and communicates about it in terms of sounds, not named notes. He remembered clearly how "his tuning" (tonic note on the first string, flatted seventh on the second string) came to him in a sort of aural vision while traveling with Bishop Henry Harrison in 1960 or 1961:

I was in Augusta, Georgia. We were there working on a church. I can't tell you exactly what year it was. I was playing the same tuning that Lorenzo Harrison played at the time [E major, with the tonic on the first string]. I woke up early in the morning and had a vision of how the guitar sounds, the tuning. Like, it was just as *clear*. And I got up that morning and I talked to Bishop [Henry] Harrison and told him about it. So he said, "Get the guitar and tune it up." So I tuned it, and that one particular string was high [that is, the "B" string was tuned to "D"]. He said, "I'll tell you what. You play it tonight and see what happens. If that tuning is for you and you know how to play it well, that's *your* tuning, for you to use." And that night we went to service and I told the guys I had a new tuning and they never heard it before. After I tuned it up and we played that night and the Lord really blessed the service, everybody begin to start talking about the new sound or the new tuning. They had never heard it before. And I been playing it every since.[16]

Traveling through the South opened Cooke's eyes to the world of racial discrimination. He and the boys were a little naïve, but his mother was aware of the perils that faced her son as he traveled south with Bishop Henry Harrison. Starlin Harrison recalled:

If you believe in God and you trust Him, He said He will never fail you. Back in those days, my daddy he had a van called a Corvair, a little van. I remember back during the days of the sit-ins and things, that Calvin's mother was afraid for us. And she said—and I always remember this 'til the day I die, Lord give me strength—she said she was worried about her son going down there in the South. But she said she saw in a dream that as we were traveling down through the South, that there was a white hand over the truck, the van we were driving. And God let her know that He was with them. She told that story and I never forgot that. And so, we had confidence before, we had even greater confidence after that.

All white people were not bad. We had some bad experiences, somewhat. You know, we'd buy gas and the guy wouldn't let us use the rest room. My sister, I remember she was with us, at the time she was attending Tennessee State. That was in 1955, I think it was. And we filled the gas tank up and we couldn't go and use the rest room. And my sister said [to the attendant], "Well, you better take this gas out of here then." My sister had a temper, man.[17]

Like Willie Eason, Henry Nelson, and countless others before them, Bishop Harrison and his young musicians drove the highways at a marathon pace as they traveled through the South, where overnight accommodations for blacks were very limited. "I did most the driving when I was with my father," recalled Starlin Harrison. "For me to get behind the wheel and stay seventeen, eighteen hours was no problem."[18]

Cooke continued to travel with Bishop Harrison through his high school years. After he graduated from Addison High School in Cleveland in 1962, he became a full-time church musician, living with the bishop and traveling with him to play for worship services and assemblies. Sopher and Starlin Harrison eventually were drafted, but Cooke was able to obtain a deferment from military service on the basis of his full-time occupation as a church musician.

Bishop Harrison's brother, Marshall, several sisters, and his mother all lived in Florida. Marshall Harrison lived in Richmond Heights, a suburb in the southwest section of the greater-Miami area, and served as presiding elder over several churches in the southeastern portion of the Sunshine State. For years, Bishop Harrison and his musicians spent each winter, from January until mid-April, in subtropical south Florida. They were usually based at Marshall Harrison's home in Richmond Heights, but ranged south into Perrine, Homestead, and Florida City and as far north as Palm Beach County. Since south Florida has the highest density of Keith Dominion churches in the nation, there was plenty of maintenance and renovation work for Bishop Harrison and his crew. They paced their work and worship services to allow ample time for visiting and relaxation. "Actually, it was like a vacation for me," Cooke recalled. "I fished a lot, stayed with different families. Like, I would go to Miami, go to Ft. Lauderdale and visit all the people there."[19]

The fishing in southern Florida was good in those days. Rather than the rocky Cleveland shore of Lake Erie, Cooke and his friends fished from the saltwater canals of Dade and Broward Counties, which teemed with delicious warm-water fish; mangrove snapper seemed to be endlessly abundant. There were seasonal runs of sea trout, Spanish mackerel, bluefish, and snook, too. One of the people Cooke and the Harrisons often fished with was Elder Robert E. Lee of Perrine, who was married to Bishop Harrison's stepsister, Vera Linton. (Robert Lee was a steel guitarist and father of Glenn Lee, Keith, Alvin, and Derrick Lee, who would join three of their nephews to form the Lee Boys band in the late 1990s.) Cooke fondly remembered many occasions when the fishing party returned to the Lee home for a feast of fresh fried fish, hushpuppies, and salad with the extended family.[20] South Dade County was known as the "Nation's Winter Vegetable Garden," so fresh produce was always plentiful for making salads to complement the day's catch.

Cooke grew quite fond of southern Florida; he had numerous friends there, thoroughly enjoyed the weather, and the fishing was terrific. He planned to move to Florida permanently, but as fate would have it, he settled in a much different place. Cooke recalled:

> In '67, I went to Detroit in October. They had just had a [Keith Dominion] convention then, and I went there for that. And after I came [to Detroit], actually I was moving to Florida. What happened, one of the guys, before I left, asked me on the street, would I take him to Chrysler? They were hiring. Would I take him over there and bring him back home, so he could see about getting a job? I took him over there and went in with him. They gave me a test paper. I took the test. I passed, he didn't. I haven't seen him no more since.
>
> I got the job, and I called my mother and told her what happened. She say, "Well I think you should take that job, because I don't think that would ever happen." Really, I didn't want the job, 'cause I wanted to move to Florida. Then what happened—the guys were saying if you asked for a janitor job, they'd tell you there wasn't no more, you could go. They wanted everybody for the [assembly] line. And I didn't want to work on the line. So when they called me in for an interview, they asked me what job I was interested in. I told them a janitor's job, 'cause I assumed they was going to let me go. They said, "We got one available, and you got it. Do you want it?" I said, "Yeah." I started working on October 16, 1967. Never forgot it.[21]

After going to work for Chrysler, Cooke continued to serve as a steel guitarist at local services and to travel to play for assemblies. Usually he would get back just in time to take a shower and grab a few hours of sleep before heading in to work at the Chrysler plant on Monday morning. On many occasions the trip home from a distant assembly was so long that he would be dropped off at the plant at daybreak, just before his shift started.

Back home in Detroit, Cooke enjoyed a rich musical life with several musicians in his same age group. He and Ronnie Hall worked particularly well together. Some consider the music played by Cooke and Hall to be the best church music they ever heard. Ronnie Hall recalled:

Calvin had moved to Detroit. We became very close friends. And I would be playin' at my church, and sometimes on Sunday night when they would shut down he would come over and, you know, be with us. In fact, after Calvin moved to Detroit and got kind of entrenched in Detroit, he was responsible for his brother and his cousin [Charles] Flenory and the rest of them wanting to move to Detroit. Detroit seemed to be the hot spot of all the guitar players.

[Calvin and I] had become fast friends and started hanging with each other. And I would from time to time back him up. And I used to tell him, I said, "Nobody can really backup a lap-steel player like another lap-steel player that can play Spanish guitar." I could anticipate what he would do on the Hawaiian before he would do it. And so, between the two of us we became quite a team with just playing. But I wasn't his, you know, what they call "standard backup man." I would play with him because I was better at playin' the Spanish than he was.

I can honestly say this without any reservation about Calvin Cooke—and I used to tell him this, back when we were very close and we used to hang out together and all of that—Calvin Cooke was one of the most creative [steel] guitar players I ever heard in my life. And I'm not saying that to just pat his back because he pats mine. I had more musicality in the sense of sensitivity to playing by the Spirit. Calvin plays by the Spirit and he was also creating the new tunes from his style of tuning with a lap-steel, not a pedal-steel. The pedal-steel came on later for him. To take that eight-string Fender and come up with as much as he did during the time that we used to play together, used to amaze me. . . . I show him the stuff that I used to come up with [on the rhythm guitar] and it would blend. So, I guess in that sense what he was say-ing about I being more than he ever was, was the fact that I had a sensitivity. I had an ear that could hear things that he couldn't, and chord patterns and various things. He would rely upon me, really, to set the pace for him with the Spanish before he would really start to cut up on the Hawaiian, or lap-steel. So we had, like I said, we had this spiritual connection that I didn't have to look at him to know what he was doing, or listen to him. I could sense it, put the right chords in the right place at the right time that would actually cause his music, what he was doing, to explode.

And he relied upon my sense of spirituality because I was closer I guess between the two—and I'm not poking who's more spiritual with the Lord or not—but he knew that I had a close walk with the Lord. I mean I would pray before I'd play and all kind of things like that. He'd look at me and say, "What are you doing?" I'd say, "I'm praying." "Oh," he'd say, "Oh, okay." He never made fun of it or anything. And the consequence of that would be a spiritual type of service, and not [merely] musical. . . . During those years I think he did some of his best playing.[22]

By the 1960s, the pedal-steel had become, with very few exceptions, the type of steel guitar preferred by musicians who played country music. The domination of pedal-steels in country music did not go unnoticed by the Keith Dominion musicians. After all, seeing and hearing country music on television and radio provided access to steel guitar music outside of church. Most of the musicians who made the annual pilgrimage to the General Assembly in Nashville also made it a point to visit the Sho-Bud steel guitar works and showroom, where the best pedal-steel guitars—and the musicians who played them—could be found. Ted Beard and Chuck Campbell acquired pedal-steel guitars in the early 1970s. Cooke soon hopped on the bandwagon and acquired his first—and only—pedal-steel.

I went to Cleveland, I believe it was the early part of '74, to see my mother. My cousin, Tubby [Golden], told me to go with him to a guitar shop. He saw one of the best steels he ever seen, 'cause we always playin' "lap" then. And he showed me this MSA. After he showed it to me I went back home and I was just telling my mother about it, that I was going to try to get it. And the guy said the guitar cost nine hundred dollars at the time. I come back from Nashville in June of '74. . . . My mother said, "Come home. I need to see you." When I got home she had already bought that guitar, her and my brother, Freddy, and gave me that guitar. And I've had it every since. That's been like twenty-nine years, almost thirty years. So I kept it, and that's the same guitar I've been playing for twenty-nine years.[23]

But Cooke did not know how to tune his new ten-string pedal steel or how to set up its five foot-pedals and three knee-levers. He sent for Chuck Campbell, the sixteen-year-old son of Bishop Charles E. Campbell of Rochester, New York. Campbell had acquired his first pedal-steel nearly two years earlier. He was fascinated by pedal-steel mechanisms and quickly earned a reputation among Keith Dominion steel guitarists as a person who thoroughly understood the mechanics of the instrument and knew how to adjust pedal-steels for optimum performance. He also had a solid understanding of music theory and harmony, and of course, Keith Dominion music, including Cooke's idiosyncratic style. Cooke recalled:

When I got [the pedal-steel guitar] I called Chuck. He had gotten one and I think Ted had gotten one the year before. So when my mother and my brother bought me that one, then Chuckie came up, I believe that same year and showed me how to play that guitar. Came up, spent a week with me and showed me what to do and how to tune it up, tune it in my tuning and how to change the pedals, what to do, and the different things on it. And that's how I started from there. . . . Then I started going back to church [in Detroit] and playing it every week and started developing the different sounds that I would want and started practicing at that.[24]

During the 1970s, Cooke continued to play for worship services at the Keith Dominion church at 2946 Mt. Elliott Street in Detroit, travel with Chief Overseer J. W. Jenkins on the weekends to play various assemblies, and play annually at the General Assembly in Nashville. Maynard Sopher and Starlin Harrison were drafted into military service in the late 1960s. Ronnie Hall and Ted Beard, both of the Detroit, Michigan, area began to play at the General Assembly in the early 1960s, but Hall ceased to participate around 1968. By the early 1970s, two other steel guitarists would join Cooke to share the steel guitar chores at the General Assembly: Henry Nelson of Queens, New York, returned to play at the 1973 General Assembly, and the following year Chuck Campbell, the musically adventurous teenage pedal-steel guitarist from Rochester, New York, broke into the ranks of the mature masters to play.[25]

Cooke is regarded as one of the most exciting steel guitarists to ever play for Keith Dominion worship services. He is renowned for creating a number of inventive praise music "jams," many of which he spontaneously improvised at the General Assembly. The General Assembly provides an opportunity for Keith Dominion musicians—including the dozens in the congregation who are not playing for the event—to hear the best musicians from throughout the geographic range of the church play their newest music. Playing exciting, inventive music year after year at the General Assembly earned Cooke the esteem of musicians throughout the Keith Dominion system. Cooke's new tunes and jams spread quickly among Keith Dominion musicians. In early years, musicians would rely on memory to capture Cooke's music. Later, they made audio and video recordings of his playing. Alvin Lee, who played bass at the General Assembly from the early 1980s through 1996, then switched to rhythm guitar, summed up Cooke's influence:

Both Calvin and Ted had a lot of good jams, but I think Calvin came out with the [greatest number] of identified jams throughout the Keith Dominion that everybody would get and go and take back home, you know. Every year we would look forward to just seeing what he had new. Sometimes it was just on the spur of the moment. We [the band] would come up with a hook and he would just do something and it would really catch.

Calvin has really been one of the biggest influences on the different known jams throughout the House of God. I think Calvin still has some of the most known praise jams throughout that we all use, all the sacred steel people use, in our playing today.[26]

Cooke played at the annual General Assembly every year from 1959 through 2005, five or six years more than Ted Beard, the steel guitarist who comes closest in years of service at the General Assembly.[27] During much of that time he traveled extensively throughout the country to play for some of the church's largest assemblies and special meetings. In nearly half a century of service to the Keith Dominion, Calvin Cooke has contributed immensely to shaping its steel guitar music. He remains a major influence as the tradition continues into the new millennium.

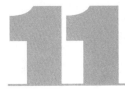

Shaping the Modern Sound

Pedal-Steel Guitar Innovators
Chuck Campbell and Glenn Lee

Two innovative pedal-steel players have figured importantly in ushering the Keith Dominion steel guitar tradition into the twenty-first century: Chuck Campbell and Glenn Lee. The groundbreaking music Campbell played at the General Assembly and at large church meetings throughout his father's dioceses in New York, Georgia, and North Florida profoundly affected musicians on a national level. Glenn Lee's influence was felt primarily in Florida, and his status there remains unrivaled. Unfortunately, he died in his prime at the turn of the new century. The playing of other inventive pedal-steel guitarists is admired by and sometimes imitated by their Keith Dominion peers—David Fonville of New Jersey and Lonnie Bennett of Rochester, New York, for example, are both fine musicians—but none has impacted the tradition as strongly as Campbell or Lee.

Charles Tyrone "Chuck" Campbell is the oldest son of Bishop Charles E. and Naomi Campbell. Being the son of a man involved so deeply in the Keith Dominion was, and remains, a major force in virtually every aspect of Chuck Campbell's life, including his musicianship. A review of Bishop Campbell's life provides insights into Chuck's development as a church musician and furnishes a frame of reference for those who see and hear him perform in secular venues.

Bishop Campbell's life is a story of a black male born in the South who rose from difficult circumstances to achieve a college education, become a successful professional, and attain the second highest rank in the Keith Dominion clergy. In 2004, on the occasion of his fiftieth anniversary of service in the ministry, he commissioned Keith Dominion member and close family friend, Verdis Robinson, to write his biography.[1] The following brief biographical sketch of Bishop Campbell, which draws from Robinson's opus, presents a condensed version of his life struggles and achievements.

Charles E. Campbell was born October 21, 1935, in Jacksonville, Florida, to Katie Wilkes, a fiery Baptist preacher, and deacon Andrew Campbell.

About a year after Charles was born, his mother contracted pneumonia and died. He and his sister Helen were adopted by their maternal aunt and uncle, the Reverend Bertha Blue and Deacon Andrew Blue, who had no children of their own. Bertha and Andrew Blue had purchased land in Pompano Beach a few years earlier and built a home, a small general store, and a Keith Dominion church, where Bertha Blue was pastor and Andrew served as chairman of the board of deacons. Charles and Helen were raised in a strict religious environment and attended church regularly.

The Blue family worked in the fields harvesting winter vegetables; Bishop Campbell recalled picking his first bushel when he was five. After completing the ninth grade in 1949, Charles dropped out of Blanche Ely High School to travel north "on the seasons" with his extended adoptive family to harvest crops. Wherever they stopped they would get permission from the farmer to hold religious services for the migrant workers. Often local ministers were invited to preach.

During one such "camp meeting" in 1952, in Taberg, New York, a rural area near Rome, Charles received the baptism of the Holy Ghost. When he returned to Pompano Beach he frequently began to preach spontaneously in church following periods of prayer during worship services. He even recalled preaching to the cashier at the local grocery store.

In the summer of 1953, he journeyed north again to follow the harvests. He preached at the services held at the migrant labor camps and worshipped at the Keith Dominion church in Utica, New York, on weekends. As he preached at the New York State Assembly in Utica, Chief Overseer Bishop Keith took notice. She saw great potential in young Campbell and requested that his aunt let him go to Tennessee with her, where he would attend high school and study at the Keith Bible Institute (KBI) in the evening. His aunt knew the value of the opportunity and graciously turned him over to Bishop Keith.

In Tennessee, Charles's high school studies included carpentry, and he applied those skills to help build dormitories on the KBI campus and erect churches in various locations as he traveled with Bishop Keith in the summer, serving as her chauffeur. In 1956, he graduated from high school and completed his ministerial training at KBI. He then moved to Rochester, New York, to be near his fiancée, Naomi Haygood, whom he had met while chauffeuring Bishop Keith, and they were married in November. In Rochester, the Reverend Charles Campbell served as an associate minister under Bishop S. J. Burke, first at a converted house on Rhine Street, then at a converted theater on Jefferson Avenue. In 1957, Naomi Campbell gave birth to Chuck.

Encouraged by Bishop Keith, the Reverend Campbell enrolled at the Tennessee Agricultural and Industrial College (later named Tennessee State University) adjacent to the Keith Dominion headquarters church in Nashville. His family joined him in Nashville during the academic year and they returned to Rochester for the summers, where he worked as a carpenter. In 1958, Bishop Keith appointed him pastor of the church at 2005 Heiman Street in Nashville and secretary of the General Assembly. In April, Naomi gave birth to their second son, Phillip. The Reverend Campbell received his Bachelor of Science degree, with a major in sociology, in June 1962, one month before Bishop Keith died. She had become a mother figure to him and her passing was a great personal loss. The Campbells moved to Rochester permanently shortly after her death. There, the Reverend Campbell established House of God Rochester Band No. 3 in September 1963, a congregation of eight adult members and seven children that worshipped at 381 Joseph Avenue in a former Jewish bakery.

Campbell found employment as a caseworker with the Monroe County Department of Social Services and quickly advanced to the position of service coordinator and supervisor. In 1964, race riots broke out on Joseph Avenue near the Keith Dominion church. Four were killed and some 350 wounded. Following the riots, Campbell became active in black community action organizations.

In 1966, Naomi Campbell gave birth to their third son, Darick. The following year the Reverend Campbell was awarded a scholarship to participate in a master of social work (MSW) degree program at the State University of New York in Buffalo, and he achieved his MSW degree in 1969. He was also promoted to presiding elder in 1969. In 1970, he led the ten adult members of his flock in Rochester to purchase the former Spence-Ripley Methodist Episcopal Church at 654 North Goodman Street for the sum of $80,000, and by 1978 they had paid off the mortgage. As Elder Campbell continued to gain stature among Keith Dominion clergy, he was assigned dioceses in Georgia, Florida, Alabama, and Texas. In 1983, he was appointed state bishop of New York and in 1987, appointed one of four chief helpers.

Chuck Campbell

Of all the musicians I have had the pleasure to work with and get to know, Chuck Campbell has probably been the most active in helping me document the Keith Dominion steel guitar tradition. Over the years we have had many thought-provoking conversations about the shaping of the music and, in addition to recounting many of his personal experiences, he has introduced me to many others whom I have documented. In 2002, he wrote down his personal history as a Keith Dominion steel guitarist, which he titled "Chuck's Sacred Pedal Steel His-story."[2] Throughout this chapter I quote extended excerpts from this autobiographical sketch. In addition to tracing his development as a steel guitarist, Chuck Campbell's narratives present valuable insights into relationships and negotiations of power and aesthetics among Keith Dominion musicians, clergy, and congregations.

Chuck Campbell was inspired to play the steel guitar when he heard the Reverend Luther Robinson play at the church on Joseph Avenue.[3] As is the case with many Keith Dominion musicians, Campbell played drums before the steel guitar. He recalled some early musical experiences:

Christmas of 1968, at the age of eleven, I received my first six-string Gibson lap steel. . . . It took somewhere around three months before I was able to play during church services, the first time being told to take it back home and practice.

In 1969, I attended my church's General Assembly for the first time since the death of the Bishop M. L. Keith in 1962. My father . . . was the General Assembly secretary and had just purchased a cassette recorder the previous year. His recordings of such great players as Calvin Cooke and Ronnie Hall inspired me to play the steel more than ever. These particular musicians seemed to be more accomplished than the local steel players I was accustomed to hearing. Examples include Bishop Henry Dillard, Elder Mack Dillard, Elder Luther Robinson, George Wright, and the Reverends Otis and Walter Blue, just to name a few.

My father, along with the Elder Luther Robinson, who at the time was a General Assembly drummer, gave me a chance at playing the drums the first night of the [General Assembly]. The steel player that night was the best I had ever heard. I felt so proud that I was able to be the drummer for the night as the church praised God to the likes of which I've never witnessed before. I remember leaning over to my father and saying that I didn't know that Calvin could play as good as we was playing. He responded saying that was not Calvin but Bishop Beard's son Ted, along with Larry Taylor on guitar and Harold Braddy on bass. They were the best guitar and bass combination I had ever heard. The reason we were all allowed to play that night and the next two following nights was because the main players, Calvin, Ronnie, and their crew, did not show up until the weekend.

During the next year our local church had several banquet fund raisers inviting the community in an effort to buy a new "best local church" in the organization. Calvin and his cousin, Charles Flenory, agreed to provide music for the banquets. A side product of this arrangement was that I would have a chance to study under Calvin and Charles as well as bonding with them. Charles ended up being the better mentor in teaching me the style.[4]

As a drummer in the 1970 General Assembly, Campbell had an opportunity to immerse himself in the steel guitar styles of Ted Beard and Calvin Cooke.

[At] the 1970 General Assembly I ended up becoming the main drummer, and the battle was on between Calvin and Ted as they alternated every other night. Ted and Calvin even backed each other up, with Calvin playing guitar and them both playing one-string bass.

The greatest thrill for me during the assembly was when Calvin requested me to play drums with him. Who was the best at that assembly? In my mind Calvin showed he was a monster with little or no backup. Ted, on the other hand, proved he would be a top player forever, while Calvin already had that status.[5]

Campbell traded his Gibson six-string for a cheap Japanese steel with two eight-string necks. He experimented with the tunings used by Beard, Cooke, and Hall. He soon learned, however, that being a successful Keith Dominion steel guitarist entailed more than mere musicianship.

I also found out how much I truly loved the instrument that summer. My church had a revival in which all the members were asked to compel their children to seek for the Holy Ghost. I wanted to play the music for the revival, so I told them how I felt after a night of being on my knees calling on Jesus. When asked "How do you feel and what is your determination?" I replied I didn't feel anything and I wouldn't be seeking anymore, at which I heard moans from the congregation. Everyone tried to talk me into getting my soul right first in order for me to be a great player through the power of God.

My father, being the pastor and also preaching and teaching to the members about having influence over your house, pulled out the ultimate punishment on me. No, not physical punishment, but he took my new double neck eight-string and put it in the closet with the understanding I could get it back as soon as I came to my senses. Two nights later I came to my right mind and was on my knees calling on Jesus with a mind to be ready when He comes. I didn't get converted just then but I found that playing my steel guitar would be one of the most important parts of my life.[6]

Campbell quickly became skilled enough to play the steel guitar for larger church meetings as well as for routine local services. As he traveled he learned of the respect that veteran musicians such as Henry Nelson and Calvin Cooke had earned among clergy and congregations.

> Downstate steel players played in what we termed the "old style," or a Henry Nelson style. At this time I didn't know Henry lived in New York City and played around town, but not at our churches. Henry Nelson stories were almost as "big" as the [Willie] Eason stories.
>
> Upstate assemblies would have Calvin or Ronnie Hall sometimes visit on the weekend of these five-day affairs. Since I was one of the first players to start really sounding like the "new style," in other words, like Calvin, or Detroit, I played until Detroit came to town. One particular convention I was playing on a Friday night and nobody was moving. Someone was setting up this lamb hide covered Fender steel behind me as I played. Next, I see Calvin behind me shaking hands with the ministers in the pulpit. I politely walked from my steel, through the front of the congregation, to a seat in the back and watched people fall out after the first note from Calvin. My family and friends told me to not be discouraged but keep working.[7]

Campbell also began to learn that certain steel guitarists are favored in particular territories, especially their home turf, and that rivalries could be intense.

> One revelation from visiting Bishop Thomas's Detroit assembly was that although Calvin and Ted lived in Detroit, they did not play at each other's assemblies, as they were under different bishops. Calvin was under Bishop Thomas and Ted was under his father, Bishop M. Beard. This was my first, or strongest, exposure to territories and rivalries. I would ask when was Ted going to play in the Detroit assembly and heard from different people that Ted can't play. "Why?" is what I would ask. I thought maybe he was working and couldn't get off. My rude awakening was when I heard them say, "No, you don't want to hear him. He is a horrible player and can't play. We don't want to hear him, and why would you?" My innocence about music was gone and I became aware that this type of attitude was always around me, and would be with me throughout my career as a musician.
>
> The same statement was made to me about Calvin at Beard's assembly. And some of the people from Ronnie Hall's church said the same thing about Calvin: that he can't play. Calvin's church said that Ronnie, when accompanying Calvin, was really just trying to mess Calvin up.[8]

He also witnessed how being able to afford a powerful amplifier could enable one musician to dominate others:

> I also remembered my cousin, the Reverend Otis Blue, because he had the resources to have a Dynacord power amp, Echoplex preamp, [a very loud]

2×12 JBL speaker cabinet amplifier, and an eight-string Fender Stringmaster. "Watch when I come in, setup. They all close up their boxes [instrument cases]. They can't do nothing with me. They can't play," is what he would say.

These judgments saying that they can't preach, play, teach, or sing is an attitude I finally started to understand and deal with at this time.[9]

At the 1971 General Assembly, Campbell learned still more about rivalry among steel guitarists. He also began to investigate how some of the older masters had earned such high regard as church musicians.

I additionally met Aubrey Ghent, as he was the big thing in the South and I was getting a solid rep in the North. He had a triple-neck Fender eight-string steel and played in the Henry Nelson "old style." I asked Aubrey who was the best out of Ted and Calvin, a topic of discussion for all General Assembly goers. He stunned me with the reply of, "Neither." "Okay, who is then?" I wondered. "Henry Nelson," he replied. This started my inquiring into Henry Nelson and Lorenzo Harrison, as other older players started giving me the same answers to the question of who's better between the two.[10]

Although Campbell was interested in learning more about Willie Eason, Henry Nelson, and Lorenzo Harrison, the music of Calvin Cooke appealed to him most at that time.

The next year I spent really learning more of the Calvin style: learning to re-tune on the fly, chime,[11] his fast picking style. My church felt I was good enough that they had no need to call Calvin or Detroit. The same thing happened in the state assemblies when I was playing the assemblies up- and downstate. At the same time I started getting calls to play other churches in the big state events such as anniversaries and banquets. I got my first paying event, an anniversary in Lockport, New York, for the Reverend M. Wilson. A lot of the gigs I got were gigs Calvin would get called to, and sometimes pastors would alternate between us from year to year.[12]

Sho-Bud brand steel guitars were some of the finest instruments made in the 1970s and were used by many of the top country music artists. Many Keith Dominion steel guitarists would visit the Sho-Bud steel guitar showroom when in Nashville for the General Assembly. Upon Campbell's first visits to Sho-Bud in 1971, he began to learn who the great country pedal-steel guitarists were, and that the Keith and Jewell Dominion steel guitarists whom he regarded so highly were of no consequence to Sho-Bud proprietor Shot Jackson. "Visiting Sho-Bud I asked about great players and was told about [country pedal-steel guitarists] Lloyd Green and Buddy Emmons.[13] I remember asking about Ted or Calvin, but no one at the store knew them. Shot Jackson did know Lorenzo [Harrison], as he ordered custom made eight-string, non-pedal steels, which he left at certain churches, as legend has it. 'But he can't play,' said Jackson. 'He only plays single notes in a straight tuning.'"[14]

Campbell became increasingly interested in pedal-steel guitars and the country musicians who played them. When he and his father visited Sho-Bud while in Nashville for the 1972 General Assembly, a musical demonstration by a country pedal-steel legend proved to be a defining moment for young Campbell.

> In the store was this guy moaning and cursing about "Give me Sho-Bud and not none of these other crappy steels." My father asked if he could play something. He tunes the pedals, which was music alone. He then takes a whiskey bottle in the left, or bar hand, and plays "What a Friend We Have in Jesus" while he's drinking from the bottle [without placing the bar on the strings]! The most beautiful rendition to this day of the song, as I have not recovered from that experience yet. He then plays using the bar—just pretty music. He encourages me to keep playing and then asks me to play. I try to play and can't hold the bar in his presence [because Chuck was so nervous]. My father is laughing at the fact that I am in awe and I know now that my father is always happy when a high standard is set that may take a lifetime for us to achieve. The person was Jimmy Day. From that day on I wanted to play pedal-steel guitar.[15]

Campbell first witnessed the power of Henry Nelson's "old-style" approach to the lap-steel guitar at the New Jersey State Assembly in Orange in 1972, and again at the General Assemblies beginning in 1973. Although he initially did not care for Nelson's style, he came to appreciate it, studied his general approach, tuning, and technique, and began to incorporate elements of Nelson's style into his playing. In 1973, he acquired a Fender Deluxe 8—the type of instrument played by Nelson and Cooke—and a powerful Fender Super Reverb amplifier from the Reverend Rhodes, a female pastor from Niagara Falls.

> Playing a single [neck] eight-string steel and playing so many styles, because Calvin, Ted and Henry had so many derivatives of their styles by other players that I learned different licks, riffs, turnarounds and tricks from, I was tuning and de-tuning constantly. I then reasoned that it was time for a pedal-steel, with which I could tune the different pedals to the tunings of different church players. I talked to my father about getting me a pedal-steel and what I planned to do with it, and I think we both had illusions of me eventually being able to play like "that guy" we saw in the Sho-Bud store. So we decided we would just look at double-neck ten-string models.[16]

But all the pedal-steel guitars they looked at were far too expensive. Finally, with the help of Chuck's grandparents and uncles, his father was able to purchase a beautiful Wright-Sierra with two ten-string necks mounted on Z-shaped legs. Campbell immediately began to investigate how he could adapt his new pedal-steel to best serve playing for Keith Dominion church meetings. It was an exciting process of discovery for him. He delighted in learning how the pitch-changing mechanism worked and trying his own innovative configurations.

> I found it as much fun changing [the setups of] pedals and knee levers as playing the steel. I left the E9th neck as is and tuned the bottom [inside] neck in a Calvin hybrid tuning: [high to low] E D B G♯ E B E E B E, with the two Es after the G♯ being the same. Sometimes I would de-tune the second unison E to a B♯. This tuning allowed me to go between Calvin, Ted, and Nelson tuning with pedal presses.
>
> One of my favorite chords, the suspended seventh [1-4-5 flat 7], was one I fell into from my first setup and is still included in my favorite progressions. Another favorite and a new deal, was being able to go from the I to the IV, or second change, as we called it, using pedals.
>
> As I played, many people who heard this new style with the pedals declared me ready to play the General Assembly.[17]

Campbell also started experimenting with various electronic effects. One of the first was the EBow, a J-shaped device held in the right hand that excites electric guitar strings by means of a magnetic field to generate and sustain a continuous tone with no decay in loudness. When using the EBow, Campbell regulates the loudness with the foot-operated volume control pedal to produce an eerie, voice-like sound very similar to that of a cello, violin, or Theremin (the electronic instrument used in several science-fiction films and the Beach Boys' "Good Vibrations"). His EBow technique is especially effective in slow-tempo hymns and gospel songs. A stunning example played during a worship service is "It Won't Be Very Long" on Arhoolie CD 461, *Pass Me Not: The Campbell Brothers featuring Katie Jackson.*

Campbell continued to improve his skills as a pedal-steel guitar player and technician, and his reputation spread quickly throughout the Keith Dominion. He soon developed a close relationship with Philadelphia steel guitarist Elder Acorne Coffee.

> Attending school in Nashville I began learning the E9th neck from books, the best being the "pedal-steel Bible" by Winnie Winston.[18] I learned right

hand blocking, some standard turnarounds and licks from that book. I also became great friends with and gained a mentor in Acorne Coffee, who came to Nashville for me to set up his pedal-steel, a Fender eight-string with five pedals. His steel was the first one set up with the more complex chord changes: minor seventh, major seventh, suspended seventh, and sixth. I'd just worked out converting the piano chords to our straight tunings. This also allowed playing the chord changes to contemporary gospel songs from Andraé Crouch, Edwin Hawkins, and James Cleveland, to name a few, instead of just melody fills. I've continued to develop in this vein, adding effects and chord setups on pedals.[19]

When Campbell's beautiful Wright-Sierra pedal-steel was stolen, Acorne Coffee graciously loaned him his Fender eight-string. Campbell later bought a twelve-string, single-neck MSA brand pedal steel fitted with seven pedals and five knee levers. He tuned it, from low to high: B-E-B-E-E-G♯-B-D-E-G♯-E-F♯. His tuning is essentially an eleven-string variant of Calvin Cooke's E7th tuning with a ninth (F♯) added on the top, or first, string. But while Cooke and Beard set up the pedals and knee levers of their pedal-steels rather simplistically, Campbell, with his thorough understanding of chord structure and the intricacies of the instrument's pitch-changing mechanism, took full advantage of the pedal-steel guitar's musical capabilities. Because he had spent some time studying the "E9th chromatic" tuning favored by country steel guitarists, he was able to apply the knowledge he had gained to his new tuning and pedal setup.

Some pedal-steel guitarists use the term *copedant* (from chord + pedal) to describe the combined tuning and pedal/knee lever configurations of their instruments. Campbell's copedant affords him several musical advantages. First, it enables him to play in the tunings used by Henry Nelson, Ted Beard, and Calvin Cooke. He is also able to play a broad palette of chords, including major sevenths, minor sevenths, suspended sevenths, ninths, sixths, and augmented and diminished chords. Campbell's copedant gives him the capability to achieve the classic Keith Dominion sounds as well as to play the chords necessary to accompany more harmonically complex arrangements associated with modern composer/arrangers. He may also play sophisticated original compositions and his own harmonically rich arrangements of gospel standards.

Campbell is an important influence on young Keith Dominion steel guitarists, the overwhelming majority of whom prefer the pedal-steel guitar and view the lap-steel guitar as merely an entry-level instrument. Many of the younger steel guitarists idolize and imitate Robert Randolph, who is discussed in the final chapter of this book, but much of Randolph's playing and his pedal-steel configuration are based on Chuck Campbell's pioneering work in integrating the instrument into the Keith Dominion musical tradition.

Campbell continued experimenting with a variety of electronic effects. In the 1990s, he often brought several effects pedals to church. "I made up a suitcase that had a phase shifter, a fuzz unit, flanger, compressor, and a guitar synthesizer," he recalled. "I tried to use all the effects in one service. Of course, that wasn't accepted in church because it got a little past the tradition."[20] Despite heavy criticism from clergy, congregants, and other musicians, some of his experimentation was eventually accepted. "One day I came into church and saw Henry Nelson with a phase shifter. That made me accept that what I was doing was not ridiculous."[21]

Campbell ultimately settled on a limited number of effects, which he uses rather moderately. He has a very keen interest in the music of Jewell Dominion master Lorenzo Harrison and has spent many hours listening to amateur recordings of him playing for worship services. The combination of effects he most often uses today reflects Harrison's influence. Although he varies his use of effects and continues to experiment, Campbell most frequently makes judicious use of a wah pedal to produced a focused, boxy timbre (as opposed to the overdone "wah-wah" sound so often identified with the device) combined with a relatively small amount of distortion or overdrive. The result is a penetrating tone with a biting edge. For some tunes, and often when playing chords to accompany brother Darick's leads on the lap-steel, he will play "clean," that is, sans effects, except for a little reverberation.

Campbell's commitment to the Keith Dominion and life as a clergy-man's son did not keep him totally isolated from blues and other forms of popular secular music. Jimi Hendrix and Stevie Ray Vaughn are among the secular electric guitarists whose playing he admired. Indeed, many of the younger Keith Dominion steel guitarists are avid fans of Vaughn's over-the-top style of blues guitar; it seems to fit the Pentecostal approach to music and worship of taking things to the limit, or escalating past what others might perceive as "normal" limits.

Among Keith Dominion steel guitarists, Chuck Campbell was a significant influence in pushing the church's praise music in the direction of contemporary hard rock and blues. Robert Randolph has taken the music even farther in that direction.

Chuck Campbell was one of four steel guitarists who dominated the music played at the annual General Assembly for more than two decades. He influenced dozens of musicians as he played his innovative pedal-steel guitar music before a national audience of thousands who gathered each June in Nashville for ten days of fiery Pentecostal praise and worship. As he and his brothers traveled to play for large church meetings at churches over which their father presided in New York, northern and western Florida, and Georgia, Chuck's musical innovations were absorbed by dozens more musicians on their home turf. Consequently, the pedal-steel guitar, and Campbell's approach to playing it, increasingly became the preference among many musicians, especially aspiring youngsters. He was a trendsetter, the musician many began to imitate. They placed cassette recorders close to the bandstand to record every lick he played, or captured his sound and his moves with video cameras, then played back the tapes at home and practiced for hours with them. They called him on the telephone for help with music and techniques they were unable to decipher on their own, and Campbell was a willing mentor who freely imparted his knowledge to all who thirsted for it.

Glenn Lee

The southeastern portion of Florida, known as the East Coast Diocese, has more than thirty Keith Dominion churches.[22] The Florida East Coast churches also have some of the largest congregations. From the late 1940s through 1958, the Florida East Coast steel guitar style was dominated by Henry Nelson. When Nelson moved to New York in 1958, Frank Blue of Ft. Lauderdale, who played in a style quite similar to Nelson's, was the most active steel guitarist in the East Coast churches. Blue recalled that there were others who played at local churches, but not necessarily with any regularity, and that he played most of the assemblies and other large church meetings.[23] By the 1970s, Nelson's teenage son, Aubrey Ghent, began to play for worship services and large church meetings. Although Ghent is a musician of exceptional artistry and has a unique voice on the instrument, in many ways his musical approach is an extension of his father's.

Sometime around 1970, after playing in the Church of God in Christ for about a decade or more, Nelson returned to Florida to play for the annual Florida East Coast state assembly, even though he still resided in New York. As the son of the late Bishop W. L. Nelson and the man who established the manner of playing the steel guitar that the Florida Keith

Dominion congregations had become accustomed to, Nelson was warmly embraced by the congregations when he returned to play for the Florida assemblies. Nelson's return reinforced the six-string lap-steel tuned 1-3-5-1-3-5 and played "Henry Nelson style" as the convention in Florida. Whether played by Nelson himself, or by Aubrey Ghent, Frank Blue, or any number of others, the style dominated in Florida Keith Dominion churches from the late 1940s through the 1970s.

In the 1980s, a young multi-instrumentalist from the Keith Dominion church in Perrine (about fifteen miles south of the Miami city limits) challenged the Nelson style. His innovative approach to playing pedal-steel guitar was a radical departure from Nelson's lap-steel technique and differed significantly from the music Chuck Campbell played on the pedal-steel.

Glenn Renard Lee (1968–2000) was one of eight children born to Vera and Robert E. Lee (1936–2000). Music was an important part of daily life to Robert and Vera Lee, and their extended families included many talented musicians. The Lees lived in Richmond Heights, a historically black suburban development in southwestern Miami-Dade County, a few miles northwest of Perrine. Robert Lee was born and raised in Pompano Beach and was related to the Blue family that included Bertha and Andrew Blue, the couple who raised Bishop Charles E. Campbell. Charles Campbell and Robert Lee were close friends; they both attended Ely High School and often worked together picking vegetables. Both worshiped at the Pompano Beach Keith Dominion Church, where the Reverend Bertha Blue served as pastor.

Glenn's mother, Vera Lee, was the sister of Jewell Dominion vice president and steel guitar legend, Bishop Lorenzo Harrison. Their brother, Marshall Harrison, a Keith Dominion minister, also lived in Richmond Heights and preceded Robert Lee as pastor of the Perrine House of God. Lorenzo Harrison visited his brother and sister whenever his travels brought him to southern Florida. Robert Lee was a great admirer of Lorenzo Harrison's music and, in addition to encouraging Harrison to give his sons musical pointers, he often took his boys to the Jewell Dominion church in Deerfield Beach when Harrison was in town to play for an assembly. Bishop Eunice Treadway was pastor at the Deerfield Beach Jewell Dominion church and her husband, Sonny, always played rhythm guitar for Harrison at these meetings. As a result of the family connection to Lorenzo Harrison, Glenn Lee and his siblings, although firmly ensconced in the Keith Dominion, were very strongly influenced by Harrison's classic Jewell Dominion style of music.

Robert Lee played the standard guitar and steel guitar in church and with an amateur gospel quartet that often rehearsed at his barber shop in Richmond Heights. While he was a competent musician, he never achieved the level of artistry to which he aspired. He wanted nothing more than to see some of his children become great musicians and enthusiastically encouraged all his progeny to play instruments, sing, and learn everything they could about music.

In addition to his father and Lorenzo Harrison, one of Glenn Lee's earliest influences was Willie Blue, whom the boys called "Uncle Blue." Also from Pompano Beach, Willie Blue was married to one of Robert Lee's maternal aunts. He developed a one-man-band gospel act and became a performer popular among blacks in southeastern Florida. Willie Blue had no formal musical training. He played the electric guitar in open-E tuning, operated a bass drum with a foot pedal, used a variety of early electronic rhythm machines, and was a strong and engaging singer. Glenn's brother Alvin remembers that one of Willie Blue's most popular songs was "If It Ain't Your Business, Leave It Alone." When Uncle Blue came to town he often spent a few days at the Lee family home. "My dad always took care of him, would bring him in, treat him like a king," recalled Alvin. "When he came we let him do a whole show at the church, raise him an offering, feed him."[24] He also would set up his one-man-band rig and play in Robert Lee's barbershop for tips. "You just don't see guys like him much anymore."[25]

Of Robert Lee's five sons, only Alvin and Glenn showed talent for playing musical instruments. Keith, the oldest, became a fiery devotion leader and a rough-voiced, all-out Pentecostal vocalist known for hair-raising screams and highly expressive body language. Derrick, the youngest brother, sings with a beautiful, soulfully smooth voice in a more contemporary, melismatic manner. Robert Lee was, to put it mildly, thrilled with the musical talents Glenn and Alvin showed from an early age. He bought them instruments, had Uncle Blue and Lorenzo Harrison provide musical instruction to them at every opportunity, and took them to the Jewell assemblies in Deerfield Beach to see and hear Harrison and Sonny Treadway in action.

In addition to ensuring that his sons were steeped in the musical traditions of the Keith and Jewell Dominions, Robert Lee was also determined that they would receive formal musical training in reading notation, theory, and harmony—training that neither Harrison nor Blue had. He paid for lessons for both Glenn and Alvin, first at Carroll Music, a store and studio a few miles north of Richmond Heights, then later at the Sunniland Music store on U.S. 1. Glenn studied standard guitar, Alvin the electric bass.

Glenn and Alvin were both fast learners; by the time Alvin was ten and Glenn was eight they were playing in church. Because of their strong family connection to Lorenzo Harrison, they first learned to play in the Jewell Dominion style. Glenn recalled, "Growing up in Keith Dominion, now down here, being in the Perrine church, I never really had to play the Henry Nelson type of music because Lorenzo's brother was so accustomed to us playing his style of music, which was my pastor, Marshall Harrison, which was Lorenzo's oldest brother."[26] Glenn's skill level developed very quickly and the congregations and clergy took notice. Before long he was playing for the largest Keith Dominion meetings in the state. "I started playing state assemblies when I was about twelve or thirteen. I was the youngest steel player ever to play down here in the state of Florida in an assembly meeting. Before me it was just Henry Nelson and his son, Aubrey Ghent, that played all the meetings."[27]

Prior to playing for the state assemblies, Glenn Lee had played in Lorenzo Harrison's loping boogie-woogie Jewell Dominion style. But the congregants who attended the state assemblies were accustomed to Henry Nelson's framming, one-chord-drive style of praise music, so he was advised to learn to play like Nelson. "But by me having to play the state assemblies—you know it was a unique style—my father and Lorenzo told me that because you are in the Keith Dominion you need to learn how to play like Nelson."[28]

While both Alvin and Glenn were very talented, it became obvious that Glenn was the quicker learner and had more intuitive musical sense. Robert Lee was a big fan of country music and encouraged his sons to listen to it, and to join him as he watched *Hee Haw* regularly on television. Glenn developed a keen interest in country music, especially the distinctive, twangy "Nashville" sound of the pedal-steel guitar played in the "E9th chromatic" tuning. Soon his father bought Glenn a pedal-steel guitar and sought a way for him to learn to play country music on it. Glenn recalled:

> I loved it, the way it sounded. I was a big fan of Willie Nelson. When I heard "On the Road Again" I was just . . . Dolly Parton, Hank Williams, I mean I just fell in love with that type of music. I loved the style of Henry Nelson playing on the six-string, but I was very limited because there is only so much that you can do with those little six-strings. . . . I liked that but I wanted more. When I was about thirteen or fourteen my father sent me to this school in Nashville. It was at the Grand Ole Opry; they had a program. I trained under this guy named Terry Crisp. And I met Buddy Emmons, and I had two classes with Buddy Emmons. They taught me about the E9th tuning and the C6th

tuning. It was a six-week course. My father flew me up there and I stayed with some relatives up there. . . . I got a certificate saying I completed this course. It was just a class showing you how to play country music, and I have grown very fond of that.[29]

Glenn Lee's study of country pedal-steel guitar in 1981 preceded public appearances by black "sacred steel" artists by more than a decade. At that time, a twelve-year-old black boy who played the steel guitar with some level of skill and was keenly interested in country music was quite an anomaly. Lee recalled that Emmons and Crisp were impressed. "They was amazed because of the fact I was—back then, being as young as I was, being interested in the pedal-steel guitar and being black—I was very unique. They was amazed at what I knew how to do already on the open E tuning."[30]

After Lee received his pedal-steel training, he began to apply his new skills in church:

When I came back from school, from Nashville—the Grand Ole Opry, studying with all them guys—what I brought back here, I stopped playing like Henry Nelson and I started playing country music in church. So if you can imagine from the Aubrey Ghent type stuff to kicking out pedal-guitar, people really didn't like it. What are you doing? You don't play like that down here. You got to be playing like Henry Nelson. What is this here? And I said, "Well, you know, you have to really kind of broaden-up. You have to kind of grow a little bit." I wasn't going to take away from Henry and them because they was doing a great work, but I felt, me being a younger person, it was time to move on. I wasn't satisfied being there. I was into the pedals.[31]

Lee took pride in bringing the country pedal-steel sound into the Keith Dominion. "I'm the first guy in the history of our church—now this was Calvin Cooke, Ted Beard, and Chuckie Campbell—they talked to me and they was telling me I'm the first guy that have ever played strictly E9th tuning and C6th."[32]

An essential difference between country pedal-steel technique and the approach used by most Keith Dominion steel guitarists lies in the use of the strum or "fram." Country music pedal-steel guitarists *never* strum the instrument, but most Keith Dominion steel guitarists incorporate rhythmic strums into their praise music. Henry Nelson used copious amounts of syncopated, percussive strums in his praise music. The predominance of rhythmic strumming in Keith Dominion praise music is rooted in practicality: most House of God congregations are small, and musicians may often be in short supply. It is not unusual for the steel guitarist to be the only instrumentalist present at a worship service, or more commonly, he may be accompanied by only a drummer. In such situations the steel guitarist provides much of the rhythmic impetus necessary to "move" the congregation by playing percussive, syncopated strums. Such situations were very common when Henry Nelson established his style of playing as he traveled with his father, Bishop W. L. Nelson, to play at churches throughout Florida and South Carolina. While congregations are generally more affluent today and instruments more plentiful than they were in Nelson's formative years, it is still not unusual for a steel guitarist to play with minimal accompaniment. Also, in smaller churches when there is a full band to accompany the steel guitarist, a good portion of the band members may be at a lower level of ability, which results in a rather weak rhythm section.

The situation in the Jewell Dominion differs. When Lorenzo Harrison developed the Jewell Dominion steel guitar style he was always accompanied by a competent guitarist and drummer. Consequently, he seldom strummed the steel guitar. Glenn Lee explained:

All of [the Keith Dominion steel guitarists] want to strum; that's very important to them. All of them want to strum. Why? Because you can get that excitement happening [taps his feet]. All of them want to strum. I didn't want to strum. Why? Because my uncle Lorenzo taught me that you've got to give a chance for the other music to be heard, for the other instruments to play their parts.

I wanted to play strictly country. I wanted to go all the way. I wouldn't strum at all. I'd pick out all my chords, just pick 'em out. And my uncle Lorenzo taught me this: he said you always want to allow room for your lead [rhythm] guitar. If you're strumming, what's the lead going to do? My focus has always been a full band. I've always had a full band, ever since a young age. Always. I've always had a lead [rhythm guitar], bass, drums, and myself. My uncle Lorenzo, he always taught me how to space that out and give everybody a chance.

Of course, I do play wild. You know, being in the Keith Dominion you have to be excited; you have to be an excited player. You can't be too laid back. You have to know how to give the punch and keep that excitement, and keep that adrenaline flowing. You have to be very energetic. That I do, and I have to give a lot of [credit for] that to Henry Nelson, again. You know, have all that energy, learning how to do all that stuff.[33]

Lee borrowed from several of his musical influences in the Keith and Jewell Dominions and country music and combined these elements with his own musical ideas to create a fresh, new sound.

What I did, I came up with my own unique style. . . . Now you have to remember that you had Henry Nelson, Calvin Cooke, Maurice Beard, and Chuckie Campbell. Chuckie played with a lot of pedals. You know how Henry played. Calvin played with a open-E with some pedals. Ted Beard played with some variation of a E-tuning, with a little pedals. I took all their styles, combined them into one style with my country stuff. So that give me my own unique style of playing. And the guys really like that. So, you know, everything I got, [the young steel guitarists in Florida] want to get. I got the MSA [brand pedal-steel], all of them want to get an MSA. I got the Emmons, they couldn't [afford] an Emmons.[34]

The Emmons Lee mentioned above was a crimson pedal-steel guitar with two ten-string necks: one tuned in C6th and the other in E9th chromatic—the standard setup for many country players. Emmons brand pedal-steel guitars were named for Nashville legend Buddy Emmons, whom some consider the most skilled and innovative pedal-steel guitarist ever. Emmons pedal-steel guitars are very expensive and highly regarded as fine instruments. The high cost of an Emmons double-neck pedal steel put it beyond the grasp of all but the most affluent Keith Dominion steel guitarists. Lee's Emmons became known as "Big Red."

As time passed it became increasingly obvious that Glenn Lee was tremendously talented. One of those who took notice was Bishop James C. Elliott, who in 1988 appointed Lee—just twenty years old at the time—head musician for the Florida East Coast Diocese, the largest diocese in the Keith Dominion system. In his service as head musician, Lee's influence on Keith Dominion steel guitarists continued to increase. As was the case with Chuck Campbell, Glenn Lee was tape recorded or videotaped by virtually every aspiring pedal-steel guitarist who saw him play. Because he lived and played in the geographic area with the largest concentration of steel guitarists, many were able to observe his playing repeatedly. Lee was a good teacher too, and gave many budding steel guitarists who lived within a few miles of him personal lessons. Those who lived farther away he helped by telephone. His steel guitar students included Ivis Hicks, Courtney Butler, Christopher Williams, Lee Arthur Pough, Kevin "Champ" Kimberlin, and the Reverend Mel Phillips. Lee took a special interest in helping his soft-spoken teenaged nephew, Roosevelt Collier. "Velt" learned his lessons well and a few years later became the sizzling pedal-steel guitarist in the Lee Boys band.

Steel guitar was only one of nine instruments that Glenn Lee played. He also played standard guitar, bass, drums, keyboards, saxophone, clarinet, harmonica, and accordion. He played the saxophone in the Richmond

Heights Middle School and Killian High School bands and was awarded a scholarship to study the instrument at the University of Miami. But Lee was diagnosed with cancer in his jaw during his senior year of high school, curtailed his saxophone playing, and never returned to the instrument. The tumor was removed surgically and he received radiation treatments and chemotherapy. Among those who prayed over him and counseled him during his illness was his uncle, Bishop Lorenzo Harrison, who was in serious physical decline himself.

Although Glenn Lee was tremendously influential in shaping the Keith Dominion steel guitar tradition in Florida, and to a somewhat lesser degree nationally, probably his strongest musical skills were as a player of keyboard instruments and as a music arranger for various vocal ensembles. As much as others admired and imitated his steel guitar playing, the time he spent as a keyboardist and arranger kept him from achieving steel guitar technique as sharp as it might have been if the instrument was his sole musical focus. And his choice of a pedal-steel guitar with two ten-string necks, each in a different tuning, fitted with seven pedals and five knee levers, rather than a simpler six- or eight-string lap-steel, made it much more difficult for him to play with total command. He recognized that in Florida, Aubrey Ghent had the most flawless technique among Keith Dominion steel guitarists. "Aubrey is, in my book, the cleanest player," Lee admitted without hesitation. "He's smooth, clean, swift, and everything, where I miss a lot. Playin' with ten strings compared to six, you just kind of miss a lot."[35]

In 1990, Keith Dominion Chief Overseer Bishop J. W. Jenkins died and Bishop James C. Elliott of Sarasota, Florida, was appointed the new chief overseer. Serving as chief musician for Florida under the chief overseer increased Lee's stature on the national and state level.

While many congregants at the Perrine Keith Dominion church were accustomed to hearing Lee play some percentage of Jewell-style music, that influence was not always appreciated when he played elsewhere in Florida, or at the General Assembly. "Now this is the funny thing," recalled Lee. "Even with the music they had the attitude, 'You stay your way. Don't bring that Jewell stuff over here, Glenn. We know you are Harrison's nephew and we know you know [Jewell music].' That was the case Ted [Beard] made, even before I got to Nashville."[36] Bishop Elliot, however, appreciated the variety of music Lee brought to church meetings. "But Elliott don't feel that way," recalled Lee. "He don't feel like that. He writes me notes at assemblies telling me to play Jewell Dominion. He wants to hear more of it.

So that broke a trend for me. That allowed me to go back to my original roots."[37]

Bishop Elliott was not the only national leader to recognize and employ Glenn Lee's talents. Bishop Naomi Manning, his uncle Lorenzo Harrison's daughter and chief overseer of the Jewell Dominion, appointed Lee minister of music and he traveled with her extensively to perform at larger church meetings held throughout the Jewell Dominion system.

By the time Glenn was in his early twenties, he was a full-time musician—one of the very few in the Keith or Jewell Dominion. As he worked to provide for his wife and children, he struggled with playing for Keith Dominion worship services, assemblies, and revivals for little or no pay. The Jewell Dominion paid him reasonably well—better than the Keith Dominion—but the work was not steady. Keith Dominion musicians are generally not paid for playing for local worship services and compensation for larger meetings, such as revivals and assemblies, is usually meager. Lee remarked: "For the assemblies I am the head musician, the top person, the head person in charge. . . . Now with Henry, one thing I can say—again, I don't get upset—when Henry come down they take care of Henry in a royal fashion. They pay his plane ticket, make sure he has a place to stay, and give him three or four hundred dollars. Whereas me, I'll be here the whole week with *all* my equipment and maybe get a hundred dollars, which is really a slap in the face. But, you know, you have to love it to do it."[38]

In 1990, Lee achieved a substantial degree of financial security when he was employed as organist for Bethel Missionary Full Gospel Baptist Church in Richmond Heights. "Bethel Baptist pays me four hundred dollars a week just to be the organist. So that's a job. I have a family. A lot of the people in the Keith Dominion don't know that I work for Bethel Baptist. . . . I told Bishop Elliott I have to pay my bills."[39] When things got especially tight he supplemented his income by substitute teaching or by driving a dump truck for his father, who owned a successful excavating and fill business. By 1994, he was making enough money through his music that he seldom had to perform other work. Over the years, the demand for his skills as a musician and arranger-conductor increased steadily and he achieved a degree of affluence. Bishop Malone, pastor at Bethel Baptist, valued Lee's musical talents and increased his compensation accordingly.

As young boys, Glenn Lee and his guitarist/bassist brother Alvin were also influenced by the innovative music of Chuck and Phil Campbell. Before they heard and saw them play at the General Assembly in Nashville, they were introduced to the Campbells' music by their friend, Perrine Keith

Dominion member, and tenor saxophone player, Winston Blunt. Alvin Lee recalled:

> [Blunt] went away and he went up actually to Detroit, and he was with Detroit, under Ted Beard and them's dioceses for a while. So, he used to always come back down and me and Glenn was little young boys seven and eight, seven and nine, whatever. He would always tell us, "Y'all got to hear the way them guys up north play, man. You know, they got a different sound." So he would always bring us tapes. And he would bring us tapes of Ted doing "The Train." And my dad really liked that. When me and Glenn actually started playing, [Blunt] brought a tape of Chuckie and Phil. Evidently they played an assembly up there somewhere up north. When me and Glenn heard this sound we were like, "Wow!" When we first heard that tape, we had to be eight and ten.
>
> But, we young guys, so we trying to catch the young flavor, or whatever. So man, we heard this sound of Chuck and them playing in this assembly and me and Glenn was just blown away. So we was like, "Blunt you got to give us that tape. You got to give us that tape." So he gave us two tapes and me and Glenn we just started studying it. We just started getting everything . . .
>
> Me and Glenn would always say, "We want to be like Chuck and Phil, Chuck and Phil." We were like two of their biggest fans. Come to find out they were like our big brothers because they family was close to ours. We always tell him, "Blunt, if it weren't for you we would probably still be in the whole Nelson mode." Me and Glenn was the rebels.[40]

In their quest for innovation, Glenn and Alvin drew from virtually every musical resource they encountered. In addition to country music, they also tapped into blues, rock, and diverse varieties of pop music, including at least one Broadway show tune. "I don't know if you ever heard this familiar song that a lot of the concert bands do called 'Fiddler on the Roof'?" asked Alvin as he hummed the first few bars of "If I Were a Rich Man." "We did a version of that [in church]. . . . It was just wild, just how we would open up our mind and go to different levels."[41]

Many who listen to "sacred steel" music—and especially, it seems, the music of Glenn Lee or the Lee Boys band—comment that they hear echoes of the slide-guitar playing of Duane Allman of the Allman Brothers band. I have discussed this at length with Alvin Lee and he has assured me that he and Glenn were unaware of the Allman Brothers when they were developing their musical style, and Duane Allman was definitely not a musical influence. Furthermore, in 1971, the year Duane Allman died suddenly in a motorcycle accident, Alvin was six and Glenn was four.

Conversely, many people wonder if Duane Allman was influenced by Keith Dominion steel guitarists. While that certainly is possible, given that he and his brother Gregg were born in Nashville and the band was formed while they lived in Florida, there is no evidence to suggest that he attended Keith Dominion worship services or even had knowledge of the Keith Dominion steel guitar tradition. Also, Duane Allman died more than twenty years before the music of the Keith and Jewell Dominions became known to the general public. In my opinion, the Allman Brothers–sacred steel connection that many people attempt to make is due to an inability to hear the distinctions between Duane Allman's slide work and the steel guitar playing of the Keith Dominion, and to a much lesser extent, Jewell Dominion, steel guitarists. Just as all Irish fiddling might sound the same to those unfamiliar with the finer points of the genre, those lacking a more thorough familiarity with slide guitar and steel guitar music might perceive all "slide" guitar, or steel guitar played in a rock/blues or "hard gospel" manner, to sound the same, or at least quite similar. Since Duane Allman was one of the first to popularize rock and blues played on the slide guitar, and is considered by many (rightfully or not) the paragon to which all slide guitar players are compared, he is the secular musician many people will connect with "sacred steel." Slide guitar prodigy Derek Trucks, son of original Allman Brothers drummer Butch Trucks (who is still with the group), and current member of the Allman Brothers band himself, offered his perspective: "Duane was very influenced by a lot of the blues slide players as well as the gospel, and the music that he grew up around. . . . You electrify the slide guitar and play some of those elements, you're going to hit on some of the same stuff." When asked if Duane Allman was aware of the Keith and Jewell Dominion steel guitarists, Trucks responded, "I would be surprised if he was. You never know. I mean those guys grew up in Florida. They played all kinds of spots, and they've been around. But I think that would have come up along the way. I don't think he had been turned on to it." When asked if he ever heard any of the original Allman Brothers band members mention Duane Allman's awareness of the Keith Dominion steel guitarists Trucks stated, "No. I'm sure that would have come up, because I have talked about the Campbells and Aubrey quite a bit on the [Allman Brothers] buses. And those guys have sat in—Chuck [Campbell] has sat in quite a few times with the Allman Brothers. So, it definitely would have come up by now, I imagine."[42]

In the summer of 2000, cancer was detected in Glenn Lee's liver and other vital organs. Once again, he underwent surgery, radiation treatments,

and chemotherapy. When Glenn's head was shaved for surgery and chemotherapy, his brothers and nephews all shaved their heads as a gesture of
solidarity. Chuck, Phil, and Darick Campbell flew down from Rochester to
visit and make music. It was a grand and bittersweet time; nothing could
have pleased Lee more than to jam with his "big brothers."

Glenn Lee died October 23, 2000, at age of thirty-two. His father had
passed away only eight months earlier. At the musical tribute at the Perrine
Keith Dominion church on the night of Friday, October 27, the church was
packed with nearly three hundred family members and friends. Among
those who played were Ronnie Mozee, national-level steel guitarist for
the Jewell Dominion and Bishop Manning's son, guitarist Gamaliel Penn,
both of whom traveled down from Indianapolis. Keith Lee led his sisters,
other family members, and friends in passionate vocal tributes. Roosevelt
Collier broke down as he played his uncle Glenn's well-worn Fender lap-
steel. Several men helped him up from the instrument as he wept and shook
uncontrollably with grief.

The homegoing service held for Glenn on Saturday, October 24, at Bethel
Baptist was attended by several hundred. Many of the attendees from
Keith Dominion congregations were surprised at the number of people
they did not recognize, testimony to Lee's widespread influence outside the
Keith Dominion. Representatives of several organizations, including Bethel
Baptist and the Miami-Dade County Commission, paid tribute to Glenn's
service to the community. Speakers from the Keith Dominion included
Bishop Campbell, Chief Overseer Bishop J. C. Elliott, and Presiding Elder
Charlene Jamison (who had been appointed pastor of the Perrine church
after Elder Robert Lee's death). Elder Tommy Phillips, pastor of the Keith
Dominion church in South Miami and member of the extended Lee family,
shouted, jumped, and dashed across the pulpit area as he delivered a fiery
Pentecostal eulogy.

Elegantly attired entirely in white, Keith and Derrick Lee each poignantly
sang songs in tribute to their late brother. Roosevelt Collier, likewise clad
in white from head to toe, coaxed cries and moans from his uncle's Fender
Deluxe 8 lap-steel, which bore the scars of hundreds of steamy worship
services stoked by Glenn and Alvin's music. When Chuck Campbell took
a turn at the old Fender he played some of the most moving music the
author has ever witnessed. He made the well-worn instrument growl like
a preacher consumed with Holy Ghost power and cry like a weeping,
wailing widow.

Four stretch-limousines followed the hearse that carried the body of Glenn Renard Lee on its last earthly journey. He was laid to rest at Graceland South Memorial Park in Richmond Heights.

Glenn Lee was tremendously influential among Keith Dominion musicians in Florida. Unlike Henry Nelson, who had established a distinctive style of playing the instrument and a relatively limited canon of tunes and licks, Lee was eclectic and expansive in his music. He borrowed heavily from many sources, including Chuck and Phil Campbell, Detroit masters Calvin Cooke and Ted Beard, Jewell Dominion legend Lorenzo Harrison, as well as country, rock, and blues. He respected Henry Nelson and his talented son Aubrey Ghent, and deferred to them in their presence, but was determined to bring a more modern, inclusive sound to Keith Dominion music. His accomplishments as a steel guitarist, composer, arranger, and choir director during his short life are staggering.

Glenn Lee's influence among Keith Dominion steel guitarists in Florida was summed up by a statement made by Henry Nelson's grand-nephew, steel guitarist Antjuan Edwards, of Ocala. In a conversation with Edwards in 2003, I asked him what he thought about New Jersey pedal-steel prodigy Robert Randolph and his recent commercial successes. By that time, Randolph had signed a recording contract with Warner Bros. for a rumored $1.5 million, appeared on network television several times, was performing at huge jam-band concerts and festivals, and was rising in public popularity at a meteoric pace. Edwards responded that he was impressed with Randolph's success, that in terms of ability and influence he was almost like another Glenn Lee.

Negotiating the New Millennium

The release of six hundred copies of the *Sacred Steel* cassette/booklet album by the Florida Folklife Program in late 1995 generated a wave of interest among the few people who obtained the albums. But it was the worldwide distribution of the CD version of the album, licensed by Arhoolie Records, that resulted in the initial wave of international enthusiasm for the compelling music. Since Chris Strachwitz founded the label in 1960, Arhoolie Records has released hundreds of albums in genres of regional and traditional music, including blues, Cajun, zydeco, norteño, and Tex-Mex, which were previously little known to many listeners. Among the artists Strachwitz introduced to fans of American roots music are zydeco great Clifton Chenier, blues legend Lightnin' Hopkins, Cajun masters Michael Doucet and Marc Savoy, and Tex-Mex accordionist extraordinaire Flaco Jimenez—all giants in their respective musical genres. By the late 1990s, however, it seemed to many, including Strachwitz himself, that the well was beginning to run dry. For the past several years, many of Arhoolie's releases had been repackaged material from earlier LPs or CDs, occasionally enhanced by the addition of previously unreleased tracks.

The January 21, 1997, release of Arhoolie CD 450, *Sacred Steel: Traditional Sacred African-American Steel Guitar Music in Florida,* was a watershed event in terms of bringing the music of the Keith and Jewell Dominions to the attention of the general public. The album was immediately heralded by fans of American roots music, critics, journalists, and scholars as a major vernacular music discovery of the late twentieth century. Unknown African American musicians played with passion, inventiveness, and virtuosity on lap- and pedal-steel guitars—instruments usually associated with country twang. The music was grounded in the familiar "hard" gospel tradition, but the soaring, howling, and screaming sound of the electric steel guitar provided a refreshing new musical experience.

This first recording presented a tradition of considerable depth. The Keith Dominion contingent included Willie Eason, who had been playing and singing for church meetings and street-corner music ministries for nearly six decades; his brother-in-law Henry Nelson, who influenced dozens of musicians in half a century of service to the church; and Nelson's son, Aubrey Ghent, a gifted musician and preacher born in 1958, who had already been playing for thirty years. Glenn Lee, the young multi-instrumentalist, nephew of Jewell Dominion steel guitar legend Lorenzo Harrison, and the only pedal-steel guitarist on the album, pushed the limits of tradition as he played a hybrid form of music that seemed to include a little bit of everything from country to classic gospel to rock. Jewell Dominion master Sonny Treadway played in a wonderfully idiosyncratic manner. The handful of artists included on Arhoolie CD450 represented the tip of the iceberg; there were perhaps three or four dozen "sacred steel" guitarists in Florida, and dozens more in other states.

In the fall of 1997, Strachwitz flew to Gainesville, Florida, to record three albums at Mirror Image Studios, for which I served as producer. The artists Strachwitz and I chose for the new albums were Sonny Treadway and Aubrey Ghent, both of whom had been featured on the first compilation, and the Campbell Brothers. All the members of Ghent's group were from southern Florida. Treadway, however, lacked talented local musicians, so we arranged for Ronnie Mozee to fly in from Indianapolis to finger-pick tasteful rhythm guitar on his Stratocaster. In addition to being the primary steel guitarist to play for Jewell Dominion national meetings, Mozee is one of their best rhythm guitarists.

The Campbell Brothers lineup featured pedal-steel guitar innovator Chuck Campbell; soulful lap-steel guitarist Darick Campbell; Phil Campbell, one of the finest rhythm guitarists in the Keith Dominion; Carlton, Phil's thirteen-year-old son on drums; and powerhouse vocalist Katie Jackson. The entire group was from outside Florida: Chuck, Phil, and Carlton were from Rochester, New York; Darick was from Macon, Georgia; and Katie Jackson hailed from Baltimore.

In typical Arhoolie fashion, the three albums were recorded in just two days and mixed in three. The Mirror Image sessions resulted in CD 461, *Pass Me Not*, by the Campbell brothers and Katie Jackson; Treadway's CD 462, *Jesus Will Fix It*, and CD463, *Can't Nobody Do Me Like Jesus*, by Aubrey Ghent and Friends. The Campbell and Treadway albums were released in October 1997, Ghent's album a month later.

Aubrey Ghent had created a sensation when he performed at the National Folk Festival in Chattanooga in October 1994, and when he and Henry Nelson played at the Folk Masters Good Friday gospel concert at the Barns of Wolftrap in 1995. Sonny Treadway had also made a few festival appearances. The Campbell Brothers, however, were the first sacred steel group to play for concerts and festivals, nationally and internationally, on a regular basis. Their career as a touring band was launched by their debut at the 1998 Folk Alliance conference.

The Folk Alliance is an organization of more than two thousand members worldwide that hosts an annual event that is one of the five largest music conferences in North America.[1] Chris Strachwitz had been honored with the Folk Alliance's Lifetime Achievement Award in February 1997. On the strength of their new Arhoolie release and the recommendation of Strachwitz, the Campbell Brothers were featured as special guests at the Folk Alliance conference in Memphis in February 1998. When they played for the banquet they brought the audience of about fifteen hundred musicians, booking agents, and arts presenters to its feet cheering wildly. Among the VIPs at the banquet was Memphis pioneering black deejay and recording artist Rufus Thomas, who has worked with some of the world's greatest rhythm and blues and gospel artists. While cheers from the predominantly white audience were thrilling, Thomas's no-nonsense compliments spoken to the Campbells when they exited the stage held special significance for the group. "The most memorable moment, of course, was . . . Rufus Thomas being in the audience and pretty much giving his approval of what we were doing, and saying that we were for real," recalled Chuck Campbell. "That was a real validation."[2]

A steady stream of invitations to perform for festivals and concerts followed their Folk Alliance debut. "When we first played out we were a little terrified as to what would be the reaction to the music since it was very close to what we played in church. We didn't know if secular audiences would get into it," remembered Chuck Campbell. "To our surprise it was a perfect fit, because the audiences we were playing to were mainly the folk audiences, and later on, the blues audiences. We were very shocked at the reaction that we were getting from the CD and the live performances. Certain numbers, like 'I've Got a Feeling' and 'Jump for Joy,' almost got the same reaction we get in church. So, it was very uplifting to us."[3]

Soon the Campbell Brothers were in great demand to perform at festivals, colleges, and other cultural venues, and on their way to solid careers as performers and recording artists. They very quickly mastered the art of public presentation and proved to be excellent ambassadors of the

Keith Dominion musical tradition. Their experience as Pentecostal church musicians had prepared them well for public performance; they were accustomed to speaking to an audience, they articulated their thoughts well and spoke from the heart, without hesitation or inhibition. Years of experience in taking cues from preachers and amateur singers resulted in an uncanny ability to keep the groove going while the steel guitarists and Katie Jackson—who is always a little unpredictable—improvised freely. After playing for years at churches with limited sound reinforcement systems, which were often in disrepair, walking onto a stage with a full PA—including monitor speakers, a feature virtually unheard of in most churches—and a technician to control it, was a dream. Chuck Campbell often remarked that any concert or festival gig was ten times easier than playing in church.

The press took notice of the compelling recordings and public performances, too. There were feature articles in *Guitar Player* (August 1996), *Living Blues* (September–October 1998), and other magazines with national distribution. *Newsweek* ran a short piece in the "Periscope" section of the July 15, 1996, issue and the *New York Times* published a feature article on the front page of the Sunday *Arts and Leisure* section on October 31, 1999. The early albums received critical acclaim and garnered awards: the Florida Folklife Program's *Sacred Steel* cassette album was designated as the 1995 "Disc of Destiny" in the January 1997, thirtieth- anniversary issue of *Guitar Player* magazine, and *Stereophile* magazine selected it as "Recording of the Month" for the February 1998 issue. In 1999, *Sacred Steel Live!* Arhoolie CD 472, was voted "Gospel Album of the Year" by the French Jazz Society.

The Campbell Brothers and Katie Jackson proved to be an exceptional group. In addition to being consummate musicians and articulate speakers on stage, they gave insightful interviews, were well organized, and were easy for presenters to work with. Consequently, their careers as performers developed very quickly and their date book stayed filled with just about all they could handle and still maintain their day jobs. Although Ghent and Treadway performed for a few concerts and festivals, the Campbell brothers and Katie Jackson remained the only sacred steel group that toured extensively through 1999. That changed in the spring of 2000.

Marcus Hardy, an aspiring young Keith Dominion steel guitarist from the bucolic northern Florida town of Crescent City, decided to produce a "Sacred Steel Convention," the first major gathering of Keith Dominion steel guitarists, to convene for two days of steel guitar showcases and workshops. Initially he envisioned it as a church-sponsored event, but when he presented the idea to the Keith Dominion national leadership and requested funding assistance his proposal was rejected. Determined to make his dream materialize, he found the answer in Matt Gorney, referred to him by Jim Markel, who was destined to become a significant force in the presentation of sacred steel music to the masses. Gorney worked with Rollins College radio station WPRK-FM, and a group of volunteers known as the Civic Minded Five, to promote and produce concerts. As a result of Gorney's efforts and plenty of support from the Civic Minded Five, the first Sacred Steel Convention was held on Friday March 31 and Saturday April 1, 2000, in the small but well-appointed Bush Auditorium on the stately campus of Rollins College in Winter Park, a charming city within the greater Orlando area that enjoys a reputation for supporting the arts.

Artists who participated in the first Sacred Steel Convention included legendary veterans Calvin Cooke, Aubrey Ghent, the Campbell Brothers, Willie Eason, and Ted Beard, as well as Rochester's Lonnie "Big Ben" Bennett and popular pedal-steel innovator Glenn Lee. Lesser-known and younger steel guitarists included Roosevelt Collier, Bryan "Josh" Taylor, Elton Noble, Dante Harmon, teenaged Chris Brinson of Leesburg, Jesse Green of Fort Pierce, and Robert Randolph, the flamboyant twenty-two-year-old son of a New Jersey Keith Dominion minister. Several of the young men surprised the older musicians and much of the audience with their high level of musicianship and the maturity of their playing.

Because the event was produced by and for the musicians and was not a church event, the Sacred Steel Convention offered a new experience for participants and audience alike. First, the *musicians* were in control, free from the restraints imposed by clergy and congregations. Second, although the nationally recognized senior musicians were given the prime spots for concert showcases on Saturday night, all the musicians were on more-or-less equal footing, free from the church politics that determine who plays and where and when they play. Younger musicians played on the same stage as the veterans, including the triumvirate of Chuck Campbell, Calvin Cooke, and Ted Beard, who had dominated the annual General Assembly in Nashville for nearly three decades.

The first Sacred Steel Convention was a magical event. Master of ceremony chores were shared by Elders Jerry Taylor (Josh's father) and Elton Noble. As preachers skilled at building the energy of a congregation, Elders Taylor and Noble kept the audience of about 150 entertained and excited.

Noble, a protégé of Aubrey Ghent, nearly burned the auditorium down with his wild praise music when he took a turn at his steel on Saturday afternoon. While veteran steel guitarists demonstrated the musical prowess that had earned them places in the church's musical history, several younger musicians gave impressive performances. Dante Harmon, raised in Ft. Lauderdale and recently relocated to Atlanta, played precise but freely improvised instrumentals that through his tasteful use of a wah pedal showed his debt to Lorenzo Harrison and the Jewell Dominion tradition. Miamian Josh Taylor massaged a battle-scarred old lap-steel with long, graceful fingers to sensitively render "Precious Lord Take My Hand" (which he dedicated to his late grandmother), then played with wild Pentecostal abandon to accompany his father's fiery singing of "God Is a Good God," demonstrating that the Taylor family's tradition of top musicianship would continue for another generation. Glenn Lee led the Lee Boys, a group that, with the exception of drummer Cecil Austin, was composed of brothers and nephews. Out front were two pedal-steel guitarists: Glenn and his teenage nephew, Emanuel Roosevelt "Velt" Collier. Glenn's original compositions featured arrangements for two pedal-steels and the passionate, raw singing of his oldest brother, Keith.

Among the younger musicians, Robert Randolph—flamboyant, sharply dressed, always upbeat, and known to many of his peers as a comedian and clown—gave the greatest display of pedal-steel pyrotechnics. On Saturday afternoon he presented a pedal-steel workshop in which he unabashedly stated his goal to become the world's fastest steel guitarist, regardless of musical genre. He demonstrated not only rapid-fire licks, but also a variety of gimmicks. He played harmonics using his lower lip, reached under the instrument to bring his bar hand over the top of the fretboard from the audience side, and using a small bar held in his right hand, executed "hammers" while he fretted notes conventionally with a bar in his left hand. For the evening concert he was all business. He dressed nattily in a dark pinstripe suit and two-tone shoes and sported a hip checkerboard-plaited coiffure. Two cousins accompanied him: vocalist and contemporary gospel recording artist Ricky Fowler and young drummer Marcus Randolph. Guitarist Harvey Shaw and Ted Beard's son, bassist Rico Beard, rounded out the band. Randolph demonstrated tremendous ability and a flair for performance. Calvin Cooke later observed, "He was so quick and so fast, and his showmanship surprised everybody. He became a superstar that night."[4]

Among those most impressed with Randolph's performance was Jim Markel, a young man from Wildwood, Florida, with a keen interest in sacred steel music. Markel planned to enter the music business, had the financial resources to get started, and for the past several months had been investigating various possibilities. Following Randolph's performance, Markel approached him with some ideas for developing his career as a performer and recording artist. About a month after the Sacred Steel Convention, they began to work together as manager and artist. Markel then invited New Jersey–based Gary Waldman, an experienced manager of recording artists and record producers, to join Randolph's management team. Shortly thereafter, Markel and Waldman arranged for Robert and his cousin, drummer Marcus Randolph, to make a demo recording at CTS Studios in Brooklyn. Two more members were added to the group to form Robert Randolph and the Family Band: bassist and falsetto singer Danyel Morgan, a longtime family friend whom both Robert and Marcus consider a "cousin," although he is not a blood relation, and organist John Ginty, an experienced white recording artist with a reputation for being able to cook tastefully on the Hammond B-3 in a variety of musical genres.

Robert Randolph and the Family Band began to gig regularly in New York City at venues such as the Bowery Ballroom, first as an opening act for John Medeski and the North Mississippi Allstars, and later as featured performers. Randolph's music and manner of performance was perfectly suited for the mostly white, twenty-something audiences. He took the exuberance of no-holds-barred Pentecostal praise music and added his own over-the-top moves to create performances that drove them wild. Unlike country musicians who sit nearly motionless at the pedal-steel, Randolph was constantly moving. He rocked and swayed, gestured with his hands to the audience, and often tilted the instrument forward, raising its rear legs several inches from the floor. He kicked his chair out of the way, played from a crouched position while dancing, and even abandoned the instrument altogether as he danced across the stage. He took the concept of the offertory march from church and called it simply "the march," created his own funky dance moves, and got audiences to dance with him. For a dramatic finish he often lay his custom built thirteen-string instrument face down on the stage. Although the group emphasized hot instrumental music, vocals were a big part of its repertoire. Randolph himself is a capable, albeit somewhat limited, singer who connected quickly with audiences. For several numbers in most sets, bassist Morgan belted out an eerie falsetto executed with an intensity that made the veins on his neck stand out. Careful to not alienate audiences by anything that might hint of proselytizing, lyrics focused on love and celebration, with little or no mention of Jesus or God.

The group did not dress like a traditional gospel ensemble; they simply donned their everyday hip, casual attire. Robert and his cousin Marcus often wore baseball or basketball team jerseys and baggy jeans. Morgan and Ginty dressed casually too, the bassist usually in sport shirts and the organist wearing the ubiquitous cotton ball cap. The ensemble looked more like a rap group than a band with deep gospel roots.

Sometime in 2000, Randolph had begun to wear derby hats. To the casual observer the derbies may seem like just another bit of show business, but in this case their significance is profound. He received his first derby from legendary country pedal-steel guitarist Buddy Emmons, who adopted a black derby as part of his persona years ago. Randolph recalled receiving a surprise package from Emmons one day: "He gave me a derby, sent it in the mail. He told me that I was the first person that he heard that could probably take the pedal steel guitar to a [mainstream] level. He said, 'Listen you don't even understand what's about to happen to you. Just do something different and in ten years you're going to understand what I just told you.'"[5]

By presenting Randolph with the derby and offering his words of encouragement, Emmons was passing the baton to the person whom he considered to have the opportunity and talent needed to take the instrument to the next level: mainstream popularity. Randolph took the baton and ran with it.

Robert Randolph and the Family Band quickly built a reputation among a loose confederation of jam-band fans known as the "New York City Freaks," who spread the news about the sensational new group through word of mouth, telephone, and the Internet. When the ensemble began to tour, they often found a couple of hundred fans, jazzed by the buzz spread by the Freaks, anxiously awaiting their performances at venues from Boston to Boulder, from Atlanta to Los Angeles.

Randolph joined John Medeski and the North Mississippi Allstars to record the July 31, 2001, release *The Word* for Ropeadope, a label distributed by Atlantic. Four of the ten selections presented on this all-instrumental album were from sources associated with the Keith Dominion: Glenn Lee's "Joyful Sounds" and "Call Him By His Name"; "Without God," a traditional number arranged by Randolph, which showcased his rapid-fire triplet picking; and "I'll Fly Away," a tune often included in offertory march medleys. The other selections on the album were drawn from the North Mississippi Allstars repertoire. *The Word* garnered good reviews and served to further Randolph's career, but did nothing to benefit the Family Band. Bigger things were not long in coming.

The highly effective management team of Markel and Waldman accelerated the rise in popularity of Robert Randolph and the Family Band to a meteoric pace. One of the group's milestone performance opportunities was opening for the Dave Matthews Band before a sellout audience of fifteen thousand screaming fans at Madison Square Garden on May 28, 2002. In the Keith Dominion, musicians look forward to playing at large church meetings such as state assemblies or the annual General Assembly because they know the energy level will be high. Their positive experience in playing for large congregations at special church meetings prepared Robert Randolph and the Family Band for playing on concert stages to large audiences. Rather than being intimidated by the huge crowd at Madison Square Garden, the band was energized. "From the first time they stepped onto a big stage, there wasn't any transition into like, 'Oh God, we're nervous,' or anything. They were pumped-up," observed Waldman. "The bigger the show, the better they are."[6] Four months later, Randolph signed a recording contract with Warner Bros.

Soon Randolph and the Family Band were at the prestigious Cello Studios in Hollywood, California, to record with renowned producer Jim Scott. The result was *Unclassified*, which was released August 5, 2003. The album title was most appropriate; the music was an amalgam of rock, funk, contemporary rhythm and blues, and gospel. With the full support of the Warner Bros. staff to promote the album and the accompanying video, media response was phenomenal. Randolph's stature as a popular music celebrity was further validated when in September 2003, *Rolling Stone* magazine named him as number 97 in its list of "The 100 Greatest Guitarists of All Time."[7]

While playing before an audience of fifteen thousand at Madison Square Garden was wonderful exposure for an emerging artist, Warner Bros. realized that national television audiences of five, six, or seven million were a key to mass popularity and large-volume record sales. David Letterman booked the group on the day of the album's release, which is almost unheard of in the recording industry. Within three months, Robert Randolph and the Family Band appeared on VH1, the *Tonight Show, Late Night with Conan O'Brien, Live with Regis and Kelly,* and were the subject of feature articles in *Esquire* and the *Los Angeles Times*.

Praise for the group and their new album continued to mount and *Unclassified* garnered two Grammy nominations: "Best Rock Gospel Album" and "Best Rock Instrumental Performance," for the track "Squeeze." But beyond receiving the Grammy nominations, an even bigger break was being chosen to perform at the televised Grammy ceremonies. "You can win fifty Grammys, but never play on the Grammys," observed Randolph.[8] For the televised Grammys show, the group gave a tight, electrifying performance in a special funk segment that included superstars Prince and George Clinton, among others.

As Randolph performs for concerts and national television he sometimes includes those who were among his most significant musical influences. Calvin Cooke, retired from Chrysler and working to develop his career as a performer and recording artist, has opened for or appeared with Randolph's group several times. When interviewed, Randolph is quick to give credit to Cooke, and always pays homage to Ted Beard, who took time to give him some one-on-one lessons early in his efforts to learn to play the instrument. When Randolph was featured on the PBS television program *Austin City Limits* on September 22, 2003, he was joined by Ted Beard, Calvin Cooke, and Aubrey Ghent for a sort of sacred steel extravaganza.[9] Randolph wants his audience to know that his music is rooted in the Keith Dominion tradition and that he has built on the foundation laid by senior musicians. "There's nothing better to me than when I hear somebody tell me, 'Man I kinda like what you do, but I sure love Calvin Cooke, or I sure love the Campbell Brothers, or I sure love Aubrey Ghent. I like that stuff a little better.' And I go, 'That's great man. You know, that's really cool.'"[10]

Randolph has enjoyed considerable success serving as an opening act for veteran rock stars, most notably on world tours with Eric Clapton and Carlos Santana. In addition to increased international exposure, Randolph's tours with stars of such renown and longevity bring a high level of credibility to his musical prowess and serve to validate him as an artist of the first magnitude. Indeed, Clapton has stated that only because he has reached a level of maturity is he not threatened by Randolph's ability.[11] Although sharing the stage and participating in recording projects with guitar greats such as Carlos Santana and Eric Clapton have been memorable experiences for Randolph, he asserts that playing for a spirited church service is the ultimate musical experience. "There's nothing, nothing—no Clapton playing, no being on tour with Santana—there is nothing better than playing in the great service at a House of God church. *Nothing.*"[12]

Despite his soaring popularity in the secular world, Randolph has never achieved what Keith Dominion steel guitarists consider the ultimate measure of success as a church musician: to play at the annual General Assembly in Nashville. Even before his entry into the world of public performance, he never was able to meet the criteria requisite for every musician who plays at the General Assembly. Once he assumed a heavy performance schedule it was literally impossible for him to participate in church activities on a regular basis, a fact that prohibited his eligibility to play at the General Assembly. The camaraderie of Keith Dominion musicians was, and still is, important to him. Despite his rapid rise to stardom, performances on national television, and a heavy touring schedule, he has repeatedly made it a point to drop by the General Assembly to visit with Keith Dominion musicians and friends.

Randolph's success has inspired countless youngsters within the Keith Dominion to take up the instrument and motivated some older steel guitarists to sharpen their skills. Just as some young African Americans shoot hoops with the hope of becoming the next Shaquille O'Neal, young Keith Dominion steel guitarists practice for hours on end in hopes of being the next Robert Randolph. Randolph recognizes, however, that the vast majority of the young steel guitarists who aspire to follow in his footsteps do not begin to grasp the amount of hard work, dedication, and good fortune it takes to achieve a level of success as a professional musician. Their delusion that merely being sacred steel musicians will magically open the doors to stardom upsets him. Randolph minces no words as he warns the starry-eyed youngsters, "I don't even know how I lucked up and got a major label deal to begin with. To think that that may happen to you, you know, you could probably make it to the NBA [National Basketball Association] faster than that."[13]

As interest in the steel guitar has increased, the music has spread to other African American churches. For example, Bryan "Josh" Taylor, one of the top young steel guitarists in Miami (who has since moved to Atlanta) found himself in great demand.

> I've played for National Church of God. I've played for Church of God in Christ, New Jerusalem, Primitive Baptist. I've played for Mt. Olive Baptist Church, New Covenant. . . . Just about every church that I have played, there has always been somebody in the congregation who knows somebody else and it just goes—it's a continuing thing. Like recently, I just did a women's conference in Savannah, Georgia, for the National Church of God, and from that they are inviting me to another conference in the Bahamas. . . . Pretty much, if you don't stop playing, the people will hurt themselves. Put it like that. They're just overjoyed. . . . The people's response is just amazing. Because for one, it's a sound that they have never heard before. And because of how it's played, it blows their minds pretty much. And I'm talking about I meet some of the big bishops and elders of all these big churches, and right now they will do almost anything to have a steel guitar played in their churches.[14]

As is the case with virtually all Holiness-Pentecostal churches, members of the Keith and Jewell Dominions recognize two spheres in which people lead their lives: the church and the "world." The latter refers to the secular world, which is viewed as a world of sin. To perform music outside the four walls of Keith Dominion churches is to tread on dangerous territory. The Decree Book does permit members to visit "places of amusement for sinners" to "preach the word of God openly and persuade sinners to come to Christ, and this shall be known and certified by reliable persons and dependable Saints."[15] As Keith Dominion musicians started to perform for mainstream audiences in 1994, they had to reckon with this Decree Book requirement. When the Campbell brothers began performing at festivals and concerts in 1998, they checked with their father, who was at that time New York state bishop and chief helper, for his approval and guidance. Today, the Campbell Brothers perform about two dozen times a year throughout the United States as well as in Europe, Africa, and most recently, Japan. In 2003, they played a few dates in New York area nightclubs. It is interesting to note that Katie Jackson, the elder of two vocalists who work with the band regularly, chose not to sing at the New York nightclubs. At which particular secular venues to perform remains a decision that must be made by each individual.

When they engage in public performances at festivals and concerts, Keith Dominion musical ensembles take a liberal interpretation of the Decree Book requirement to "preach the word of God openly and persuade sinners to come to Christ." I have observed several performances by Keith Dominion musical groups at festivals and concerts and cannot recall any proselytizing. If there is any "preaching" at all in such performances, it is usually heard in small doses, most often as an introduction to a song.

Chief Overseer Bishop J. C. Elliott held a rather progressive, if somewhat ambivalent, view of musicians performing at venues outside of church. His own son, James Denard Elliott, is a steel guitarist. When acting in my role as Outreach Coordinator for the Florida Folklife Program, I arranged for Denard Elliott and other Keith Dominion musicians from the Sarasota/Bradenton area to perform at the Taste of the Town food festival in Ft. Myers, and Bishop Elliott and Keith Dominion first lady Barbara Elliott attended. When Robert Randolph performed at the televised Grammys concert, he called Bishop Elliott and, according to Randolph's grandmother, the chief overseer was ecstatic and told the young musician how proud he was of his accomplishments. The telephones of Keith Dominion members across the country were abuzz with talk of Randolph's Grammy performance.[16]

On the other hand, Bishop Elliott did not permit sales of recordings by sacred steel artists at the General Assembly and other church meetings.

Although Bishop Campbell was one of four chief helpers who were all of equal rank, his actual level of political power within Keith Dominion clergy, in my opinion, appeared to be higher than that of his fellow chief helpers. He also seemed closer to Chief Overseer Elliott—or at least managed to make things go his way more often than the other chief helpers. The new church that Bishop Campbell built in the Rochester suburb of Rush, New York, gave striking testimony to his power at the time. Erected on a choice parcel of fifty-six acres in a smart suburban setting, the edifice included a five-hundred-seat sanctuary with two fifty-inch television monitors connected to a high-tech audiovisual system. In addition to the sanctuary, there was also a baptistery, a large fellowship hall with an ample kitchen, a reception office, a nurses' station, a library, and offices for Bishop and Deaconess Campbell. The educational wing included computer classrooms and provisions for vocational-skills training and audiovisual education.[17] People drove to Rush from as far as Ft. Lauderdale, Florida—and braved an upstate New York snowstorm—to attend the three days of worship services and events of the church dedication held March 13–15, 1998.

During the church dedication, the sanctuary was nearly filled to capacity, but the regular congregation was small, with a total membership of ninety-three.[18] When I attended a routine Sunday worship service on April 22, 2001, there were perhaps forty or fifty people in attendance; the sanctuary was less than ten percent full. If Bishop Campbell had a vision of "build it and they will come" it was not achieved.

Bishop Campbell and his sons, Chuck, Phil, and to a lesser degree, Darick, teamed up to be the driving force of large national Keith Dominion events and projects. At the turn of the twenty-first century, Phil and Chuck served as producers and project leaders to create the church's first CD album, *The Millennium Celebration Choir*, which was recorded live using the latest digital multi-track technology. Bishop Campbell shared executive producer credit with Bishop and Deaconess Elliott.

On September 18–21, 2003, the House of God celebrated its one-hundredth anniversary at the headquarters church in Nashville. The celebration consisted of multiple events that ranged from fiery worship services, to a somber memorial service at Mother Tate's gravesite, to a down-home reunion barbecue and a jubilant parade through several blocks of the neighborhood. Each of these events honored and celebrated aspects of House of God history. Bishop Campbell and his sons played key roles in the Centennial Celebration, the largest array of events and projects in the history of the Keith Dominion.

As Centennial Celebration chairperson, Bishop Campbell had overall responsibility for managing the centennial events and projects. Fellow chief helper (and former steel guitarist) Bishop Henry Dillard of Charleston, South Carolina, served as assistant chairperson. In his service as operations administrator for the centennial, Phil Campbell organized and managed eighteen subcommittees to accomplish the multifaceted events of the Centennial Celebration. Among the projects Phil Campbell coordinated were a professional broadcast-quality documentary video, an audio CD album, and a book that documented the church history from its founding in 1903. Although the documentary projects were completed, except for perhaps minor final editorial work, they have yet to be produced in final form and distributed to the membership.[19]

Just as the finishing touches were being put on the video, audio CD, and history book, and two weeks before the annual General Assembly, Bishop Elliott died. The official notice issued by the Keith Dominion stated that he died on May 26, 2004, following a brief illness, but he had apparently been in physical decline over an extended period of time. Bishop Elliott's death profoundly affected the distribution of power among the high-ranking clergy, which ultimately resulted in drastic changes in the environment in which Keith Dominion musicians—especially the steel guitarists—function. Bishop Campbell and his sons Chuck and Phil were among those most severely impacted by the power shift that followed Bishop Elliott's death.

On January 30, 2006, the House of God, Inc., Keith Dominion filed a suit in United States District Court in Nashville against Bishop Charles, Chuck, and Phillip Campbell. The Complaint listed seven "causes of action" related to expenditures associated with the Millennium and Centennial activities and projects: breach of contract by all three defendants and Bishop Campbell alone, conversion (of Keith Dominion funds), unjust enrichment, misrepresentation and fraud, negligent misrepresentation, and civil conspiracy. The church sought compensatory damages in an amount to be proven at trial, but not less than $275,000, plus interest and legal costs. In plain language, the suit alleged that the Campbells could not provide a detailed accounting, supported by receipts and canceled checks, for $275,000 of church funds given to them to pay costs associated with the Millennium and Centennial projects.[20]

The lawsuit was the culmination of disputes between Keith Dominion administrative staff and the Campbells that took place over a period of about two years. In a letter dated September 18, 2004, the interim chief overseer, Bishop Rebecca Fletcher, and the Supreme Executive Council notified Bishop Campbell that he was removed from all national committees of the church until the disputed matters were resolved. Four days later Bishop Rebecca Fletcher was ordained chief overseer. The complaint states that "on or about" February 9, 2005, Chief Overseer Bishop Fletcher wrote a letter to Keith Dominion bishops, elders, pastors, ministers, deacons, and lay members that articulated the charges that were brought against Bishop Campbell. The chief overseer and the Supreme Executive Council notified Bishop Campbell on June 24, 2005, that he was: "removed as a State Bishop of the House of God; that he was removed as a general, state, and local trustee of any property paid for or, in full or in part, by the House of God; that he was removed from every office held in any state of the House of God, including but not limited to Staff of Chief Helpers, Vice President and Board of Directors, Bishop of the State of New York, and Pastor of the House of God in Rush, New York; that he was silenced from any activities in the House of God; and that any previous licenses were revoked and annulled."[21] "They pulled his stripes and broke his sword," said Chuck Campbell of his father's drastically reduced status.[22] On a practical level, this means that Bishop Campbell is no longer the state bishop of New York, and no longer presides over any churches in other states. He does, however, still serve as pastor at the Keith Dominion church in Rush, New York, where he leads a congregation of twenty or thirty adults. When not traveling to play for public performances, Chuck, Phil, and their families and brother Darick attend services in Rush.[23]

After nearly two years of litigation, the lawsuit was dismissed without prejudice on March 13, 2008. In plain language, the Campbells were cleared of all allegations by the church.[24] However, all the sanctions imposed on Bishop Campbell by the Keith Dominion leadership remain in place.

In addition to Robert Randolph and the Family Band, the two busiest groups rooted in the Keith Dominion and performing publicly are the Campbell Brothers and the Lee Boys. The Campbell Brothers signed with Folklore Productions, one of the nation's oldest talent agencies to book traditional artists, and have maintained a performance schedule that strains the ability of the group members to hold full-time jobs, or in drummer Carlton's case, a full course load in electrical engineering studies. "Being full-time musicians and forsaking all and really going for the gusto is something we have tried to avoid," remarked Chuck Campbell. "We've tried to do it part time, to keep a semblance of what we had before this all started happening. We've known from church, and also from teaching in the Bible, that fame is fleeting, so we're always conscious of that, that it could be here today and gone tomorrow. It's a hard thing to do really, keep that balance and do enough to stay in the business, but also, keep your church, your family and your regular occupation together."[25]

The Campbells concentrate on "cultural" venues, such as college arts concerts and jazz and blues festivals. They have played all over the United States and nearly every country in western Europe. "Surprising to us, we have never had it where it wasn't accepted and not embraced, to the point where we have been back to most all of these places. We've made several trips and continue to do so," asserted Chuck Campbell.[26] They have also performed in Japan, and at the 2000 World Sacred Musical Festival in Fes, Morocco, where they shared the stage with black gospel musician and Black Entertainment Television host ("the longest running show on cable television") Dr. Bobby Jones.[27] "In Africa, playing the music in a Muslim country, and having it accepted there, and being with Bobby Jones, who is like the 'Ed Sullivan of gospel music,'" was an unforgettable experience for Chuck Campbell and the band.[28]

The Lee Boys, three brothers and their three nephews from the greater Miami area, also maintain a heavy touring schedule. Guitarist Alvin Lee and steel guitarist Roosevelt Collier are full-time musicians, while the other band members maintain full-time jobs in other fields of employment. The Lee Boys play for a variety of presentations, but seem especially popular with younger crowds (Roosevelt is a contemporary of Robert Randolph). Calvin Cooke and the Sacred Steel Ensemble also tour quite heavily, although as a man in his sixties who has had a kidney transplant, Cooke cannot maintain as demanding a tour schedule as the Campbell Brothers and Lee Boys. Cooke has performed many times with Robert Randolph, and continues to serve as an opening act for Randolph or as his co-performer. Aubrey Ghent performs for concerts and festivals too, and is probably the sacred steel artist most popular with mainstream black gospel fans.

Today, the term *sacred steel* is rather commonly used as a descriptor for a musical style. Even though there is considerable variation between the performance styles and repertoire among the sacred steel groups who perform publicly, they have enough in common to deliver what an audience expects from a sacred steel group: inventive, passionately played African American steel guitar, spirited gospel vocalists, and solid, funky rhythms. Consequently, some festivals regularly include one of the touring sacred steel groups on rotation. "One of them that comes to mind is the Pocono Blues Festival," stated Chuck Campbell. "It almost always has a sacred steel slot. The Winnipeg Folk Festival has a sacred steel slot that a lot of us rotate into."[29]

Sacred steel artists who perform for public concerts and festivals experience a variety of rewards that have been unavailable to them as church musicians. Many have shared concert stages with veteran gospel performers and recording artists such as the Blind Boys of Alabama, the Sensational Nightingales, Mavis Staples, and Al Green. Because blues and jazz fans constitute a good portion of the sacred steel audience, many of the artists have met such luminaries as B. B. King, Herbie Hancock, George Benson, and Wynton Marsalis. The Campbell Brothers have opened for B. B. King and played with the Allman Brothers, the latter "a match made in heaven," according to Chuck Campbell.[30] The sacred steel artists who perform publicly have been the subject of numerous press articles, primarily in blues magazines, but also in mainstream publications such as the *New York Times* and *Rolling Stone*. Over the years there have been several features about the music on National Public Radio's *All Things Considered*. They have met famous actors and Chuck Campbell appeared in the comedy film *Kingdom Come* (2001). Some have received significant awards. Chuck Campbell was awarded the 2004 National Heritage Fellowship, our nation's highest honor for a traditional artist, by the National Endowment for the Arts, and shared the awards concert stage with Dobro master Jerry Douglas, who also received the fellowship that year. Calvin Cooke received the 2007 Detroit Music Award for Outstanding Gospel Musician. The accolades and appreciation he has received in the public sector contrast sharply with Cooke's experience in church. As he contemplated his lifetime of service as a Keith Dominion steel guitarist Cooke asserted, "Next year, from 1958 to 2008, will be fifty years for me, and I've never received a plaque from the organization, never received an appreciation. Never received anything."[31]

The musicians enjoy being compensated fairly for their public performances. For a few, music is their full-time job. When they play for church meetings, Keith Dominion musicians virtually never receive enough compensation to offset the tithes required by the church. "We have to pay to play," stated Calvin Cooke. "And yet, they only give you such a small amount, like twenty dollars, fifteen dollars, eighteen dollars, twenty-eight dollars. It depends on how you play. But it still is a small amount compared to what they [the church leadership] get. So the musicians have never, really, in the House of God churches, really been treated fairly."[32] While they enjoy making money and playing at prestigious venues such as the Hollywood Bowl or the Kennedy Center, many musicians from the Keith Dominion tradition who perform publicly agree that sharing their music, winning the appreciation of new audiences, and making friends are the most rewarding aspects of public performance. "When we play out in public they treat us as though they never heard this before in their lives, and we are treated much differently [than in church]. We are very well-received everywhere we go by everybody at all the concerts we do," Cooke stated proudly. "It makes me really feel excellent. It makes me feel good, because they let me know that we're appreciated."[33]

In addition to accolades and public attention, sacred steel artists who perform publicly thoroughly enjoy traveling throughout North America, Europe, and less frequently, Asia and Africa. In their travels they have been exposed to a rich variety of music—from Cape Breton fiddling to Klezmer—that they probably would have never heard had they not journeyed far and wide to perform. It will be interesting to see what musical influences are incorporated into the playing of touring sacred steel artists and what musical collaborations they enter into with artists they meet as they continue traveling to perform.

The Campbell Brothers were not the only musicians affected by Bishop Rebecca Fletcher's appointment as chief overseer. Bishop Fletcher also placed restrictions on musicians who were performing publicly. Citing restrictions delineated in the Decree Book that were applied to Willie Eason in 1943, she made it clear that Keith Dominion musicians were not permitted to play outside the Keith Dominion—not even for another church.[34] Calvin Cooke, Aubrey Ghent, Robert Randolph, and, of course, the Campbells were banned from performing for church functions. Of the musicians who had performed on *Austin City Limits* with Robert Randolph in 2003, only Ted Beard was permitted to continue to play in church on the national level. Beard had made very few, if any, public appearances other than the *Austin City Limits* program, and remains the Keith Dominion's "National Music Department President," according to the church's Web site, www.hogc.org.

Calvin Cooke stated that he heard through other Keith Dominion members that he was no longer permitted to play for services, but was never officially notified. He further stated that he tried to contact Bishop Fletcher several times by telephone and email, but she never responded. Consequently, he was not allowed to play at the General Assembly beginning in 2006, thus ending his forty-seven-year tenure at the church's largest annual meeting.[35]

As was the case when Willie Eason played independently in the 1930s and 1940s—and probably even farther back than that—national church policy is not necessarily enforced at the local level. This may apply even more so today, as Bishop Fletcher's conservative policies are by no means universally popular among the congregations. Cooke, for example, still attends and plays music for Keith Dominion services in Pontiac, Michigan, as of September 2007. His lifetime bond to the church, however, is tenuous. "I'm still here by a thread," stated Cooke. "But I couldn't say how much longer."[36]

Lee Boys band members Alvin Lee and Roosevelt Collier had ceased to attend Keith Dominion services with any regularity sometime before Bishop Fletcher became chief overseer. Lee Boys vocalist Keith Lee, however, continues to be very active in the Perrine, Florida, Keith Dominion church, where he serves as a devotion leader. Keith Lee and Calvin Cooke are both deeply rooted in their local Keith Dominion church communities and their talents are valued contributions to local worship services.

Bishop Fletcher's conservative policies have profoundly affected the music at the General Assembly. With Calvin Cooke and Chuck Campbell out of the picture, the only remaining steel guitarist from the triumvirate that dominated for three decades is Ted Beard. Aubrey Ghent would have been a candidate to play at the General Assembly and other large meetings, but he has been performing publicly with some regularity and has left the Keith Dominion. Some musicians do not have 96 percent of their "reports" (church financial obligations) paid, or do not meet other administrative requirements for eligibility to play at the General Assembly. Consequently, with the exception of Ted Beard, all the steel guitarists who played at the 2007 General Assembly had little or no experience playing on the national level. This, of course, presents opportunities for new musicians to rise to national prominence.

The list of prohibitions contained in the Decree Book that Keith Dominion members must follow to live a life of Holiness has not been revised since it was first published in 1923. Most members seem to adhere strictly to dietary restrictions that forbid pork and grape juice, whether fermented or not (including salad dressings that contain vinegar).[37] Similarly, most comply with prohibitions against women wearing makeup, eschew profane language, alcohol, tobacco, and illicit drugs, and do not engage in social dancing. While many were raised not to attend movie theaters or sporting events, and some still do not, many, perhaps most, watch movies, sports, and the range of programming offered on television. Increasing numbers have computers with Internet access. It has been my observation that many, especially younger people, spend some time listening to popular secular music on the radio and watching performances by secular musicians on television. They certainly seem to be aware of the music of contemporary artists in virtually all genres of popular secular music, from rap to rhythm and blues, rock, and country. The prohibitions listed in the 1923 Decree Book seem deeply at odds with living in the "Information Age." It appears that many members of the Keith and Jewell Dominions are not in absolute compliance with the prohibitions listed in the Decree Book. However, to my knowledge, to date there has been no attempt to revise or reinterpret these prohibitions.

Marketing sacred steel music has always presented challenges. Record companies are most comfortable when an artist fits neatly into an established market category. Interestingly, sacred steel music has found its widest fan base among blues, rock, and jam-band enthusiasts. To date, the mainstream black gospel market has not responded that strongly to the music. In September 2007, Robert Randolph told me, "That's the one thing that's kinda been missing from this whole thing, this whole sacred steel thing. The one problem is that it has not translated over to the mainstream gospel world yet. . . . It really needs to be attached to the mainstream gospel side because that's where we're all from."[38] Randolph achieved a significant presence in the mainstream gospel market when he teamed with the Clark Sisters to record Stevie Wonder's "Higher Ground" on the EMI Gospel compilation album *Oh Happy Day* (October 2009). The song garnered a 2010 Grammy nomination for "Best R&B Performance by a Group or Duo with Vocals," and the album won the Grammy for "Best Traditional Gospel album."[39]

In addition to his efforts in the mainstream gospel, crossover pop, and jam-band arenas, Randolph continues to perform and record in a variety of expressions. He plays Bo Diddley in *"Who Do You Love?"* a film about Chess Records, released in April 2010.[40] He teamed with ten-time Grammy-winning producer T-Bone Burnett to record a new album, *We Walk This Road,* which acknowledges the roots of his music, and was released in June 2010.[41] Billed as "Sacred Steel featuring Robert Randolph," he will join a multitude of rock guitar stars for the 2010 tribute tour Experience Hendrix, which commemorates the fortieth anniversary of the death of Jimi Hendrix.[42]

While it is difficult to predict the future with regard to the steel guitar traditions of the Keith and Jewell Dominions, several factors will act to shape the music and the contexts in which it is played. For church meetings, the national leadership of both dominions will continue to be the greatest influence. My understanding is that there have been no significant changes concerning the music of the Jewell Dominion since Bishop Fay Moore became chief overseer in 2005, certainly nothing that compares to what is happening in the Keith Dominion. The conservative leadership of Keith Dominion Chief Overseer Bishop Rebecca Fletcher has affected its steel guitar tradition and the tradition-bearers profoundly. With virtually all of the top steel guitarists except Ted Beard banished from playing on the national level, the shaping of the music is in the hands of musicians who are generally younger and less experienced. Considering the conservative climate with regard to music at the General Assembly, it seems likely that whatever changes these musicians bring at the national level may happen very slowly under the administration of Chief Overseer Fletcher.

Some of the musicians I have been in contact with, including some who are still active in the church, tell me they hear that Keith Dominion membership has been in decline since the assumption of power by Bishop Fletcher's administration and the ouster of Bishop Campbell. Calvin Cooke told me he has heard that membership is down to about four thousand, but I have no means by which to test such rumors.[43] These rumors, however, make one wonder what the future of the Keith Dominion may be. Chief overseers are appointed for life, but it may be possible that if enough members are unhappy with the leadership that could change, either by decree or some sort of upheaval. It seems likely that some veteran steel guitarists will join other churches with less restrictive policies towards musicians performing outside of church. Such is the case with Aubrey Ghent, for example, who left the Keith Dominion to join the Church of God, Sanctified.

Up-and-coming steel guitarists may choose to join other churches, where their musical talents—and the passionate voice of the electric steel guitar—are refreshingly new to the congregations, and policies with regard to playing outside of church are more liberal. Some of the other churches may actually encourage musicians to become professional gospel artists. Of course, these musicians will be playing in an environment where the steel guitar is not necessarily the dominant musical instrument and in the absence of a steel guitar tradition of more than six decades with dozens of tradition-bearers.

Some steel guitarists with a background in either the Keith or Jewell Dominion traditions will doubtless continue attempts to expand the aesthetic boundaries of the music in the context of church meetings. Others will take the music—or variants of it—to the broader public, to play for mainstream gospel audiences as well as for folk, blues, and jazz festivals and black heritage events; jam-band concerts; various rock and popular music festivals; and cultural presentations, such as those produced by colleges and community performing arts centers.

Still other musicians from outside the church will bring some "sacred steel" into their musical mix, either by learning some elements of the music themselves or by inviting Keith and Jewell Dominion tradition-bearers to serve as guest artists for concerts and recording projects. Producers have already incorporated sacred steel music into television and film—among the most notable being the use of "I Feel Good" by the Campbell Brothers and Katie Jackson on the *Sopranos* television series soundtrack—and it seems likely that practice will continue.

Today, there are almost certainly more African Americans playing sacred music on the steel guitar than ever before. There seem to be enough talented musicians to provide some form of this passionate and compelling music for everyone. They range from those who function strictly in the church environment to those who bring their music to wider audiences in the secular world.

As is the case with all traditional art forms, the steel guitar traditions of the Keith and Jewell Dominions are not static, but dynamic; they are constantly changing and evolving. Today, the forces—both from within the sphere of the churches and from the external world—acting to shape these musical traditions seem more numerous than ever before. Time will reveal the nature of the changes yet to come, and the speed at which they occur. Whatever direction the music takes, it will be built on a foundation of one of America's richest, most distinctive, and most passionate musical traditions.

Notes

CHAPTER 1: Discovery

1. Aubrey Ghent interview, November 7, 1992.

CHAPTER 2: The Churches

1. The bulk of the information concerning church history in this chapter is based on two sources: *The House of God: A Centennial History of the House of God, Which is the Church of the Living God, the Pillar and Ground of the Truth, Without Controversy, Inc., Keith Dominion,* an unpublished manuscript written by Keith Dominion member Verdis Robinson; and *The Constitution, Government, and Third Revised Decree Book of The House of God, Which is the Church of the Living God, the Pillar and Ground of the Truth, Without Controversy, Inc., Keith Dominion.* The latter is the governing document for the Keith Dominion and will be referred to by its common name, the Decree Book. Much of the Decree Book was written by committee and contains unverified or unannotated accounts of events. However, those accounts are generally held by the membership to be true, and as such, reflect their beliefs.

2. Lewis, *Mary Lena Lewis Tate,* 5–6.

3. Ibid., 9.

4. Ibid., 6.

5. Decree Book, 92–95.

6. Ibid., 61–62.

7. At some point there was also a White Dominion. Information on the White Dominion is difficult to obtain and, since that organization did not have a steel guitar tradition, has not been sought.

8. Robinson, *House of God,* appendix E.

9. See http://www.cotlgnet.org/aboutus/history.php3, accessed August 4, 2004.

10. Gruhn and Carter, *Electric Guitars and Basses,* 10.

11. Bishop Campbell and chief helpers interview, September 14, 2002.

12. Ibid.

13. Ibid.

14. Ibid.

15. Bishop Elliott wrote a letter in support of the request from the Florida Folklife Program for a grant from the National Endowment for the Arts, Folk and Traditional Arts Program to partially fund the statewide survey and audiocassette and booklet album. A brief interview with Bishop Elliott is included in the Arhoolie Foundation's *Sacred Steel* documentary video.

16. Harvey Jones interview, September 25, 2003.

17. Mary Linzy interview, August 24, 2001.

18. Based on the number of churches in those dioceses today.

19. Calvin Cooke interview, August 4, 2003.

20. Ronnie Hall telephone conversation, May 17, 2006.

21. Ronnie Hall interview, September 1, 2003.

22. Ibid.

23. Ibid.

24. Ted Beard interview, August 18, 2003. Beard does not remember the exact year of his appointment as Coordinator of Music. In conversations with Chuck Campbell he recalled it as 1973, the year of Nelson's return to the General Assembly.

25. Ibid.

26. Campbell, "Chuck's Pedal-Steel His-story."

27. Ibid.

28. Ibid.

29. Counting from the player's left, the first two pedals are usually referred to as "a" and "b." Most pedal-steel guitars are set up so that depressing the "a" and "b" pedals simultaneously changes from the tonic major chord (I) to the subdominant (IV). This is usually the first pedal move a student of the instrument learns.

30. Chuck Campbell, "Chuck's Pedal-Steel His-story."

31. Gruhn and Carter, *Electric Guitars and Basses,* 32.

32. Per conversation with Chief Helper Bishop Charles E. Campbell, 2004. Apparently neither the Keith nor the Jewell Dominion places a priority on keeping accurate records of the number of members. When I began to document the Keith Dominion steel guitar tradition in 1992, I was unable to get a membership estimate except for an "educated guess" of ten thousand from some members. In 2004, church leadership began to use the figure of eight thousand consistently.

33. All data for the number and location of churches was taken from www.hogc.com, March 2, 2006. This data is constantly changing as church edifices are deleted or added. Moreover, at any given time there may be new churches

that have not been added to the Web site or deleted churches that have not been removed.

34. I have seen members from the Bahamas attend services at Keith and Jewell Dominion churches in southern Florida.

35. All data was taken from www.cotlgnet.org, March 3, 2006. As is the case with the Keith Dominion, the Jewell Dominion data is constantly changing.

36. Decree Book, p. 75.

37. Calvin Cooke interview, February 22, 2006.

CHAPTER 3: Church Meetings and the Steel Guitarist's Role in Them

1. It is my observation that of the four regular weekly meetings, the Sunday night service is the most likely to be canceled, or in some cases, not even scheduled on a regular basis. Because of the short interval between the end of the Sunday morning worship service, which could be 3:00 P.M. or later, and the evening service, which starts at 7:30, there may not be time to eat, rest a little, and start the evening service. This is especially true if the pastor lives some distance from the church and no one else is available, such as an assistant pastor, to conduct the service.

2. Much of the description of the Keith Dominion Sunday morning worship service is based on interviews with Elder Elton Noble, pastor of the Keith Dominion in West Palm Beach, Florida. There may be minor variations in the details of worship services conducted by other pastors.

3. Rosenbaum, *Shout Because You're Free,* 3, 167–72.

4. In the Arhoolie Foundation's *Sacred Steel* documentary video, Vera Lee states that shouting is done with the mouth while dancing is done with the feet.

5. Elton Noble interview, September 19, 2003.

6. Some steel guitarists tend to play most of the time in one key, usually the key of the chord to which the open (unfretted) strings of the steel guitar are tuned. Hearing music repeatedly played in one key, members of the congregation, even those with no formal musical knowledge and little natural ability, will have a tendency to sing in that key, or close to it.

7. Based on interviews with Sonny Treadway on December 18, 1993, and February 28, 2006, as well as personal observation.

8. The year of Bunk Johnson's birth has not been documented.

9. Hazeldine and Martyn, *Bunk Johnson: Song of the Wanderer.* Johnson mentions his lessons with Cutchey on p. 21 and whistles variations of the tune on track 1 of the enclosed audio CD. A search of records from New Orleans University, now contained in the Dillard University Archives, produced no documentation of Cutchey.

10. De Droit, *Complete Sets.*

11. Armstrong, *All-Time Greatest Hits*. The original recording was Decca 28803.

12. Frequently, a scriptural reading by someone appointed by the pastor may precede the scriptural reading and sermon by the pastor.

13. Henry Nelson. From the author's field notes taken at the Mt. Canaan Keith Dominion, near Silver Springs, Florida, December 26, 1993. Nelson tuned his steel to an open B-flat chord.

14. Bryan "Josh" Taylor interview, November 10, 2001.

15. Sonny Treadway interview, February 28, 2006.

16. Elton Noble interview, March 14, 2006.

17. Ibid.

18. Ibid.

19. Ibid.

20. Antjuan Edwards interview, December 15, 2003.

21. Hill, *New Encyclopedia of Southern Culture*, 132.

22. Elton Noble interview, March 14, 2006.

23. Acorne Coffee interview, July 17, 1999.

24. Bishop Charles E. Campbell, video interview from Arhoolie video, *Sacred Steel*.

CHAPTER 4: The Steel Guitar

1. Kanahele, *Hawaiian Music and Musicians*, 365–79.

2. Ibid.

3. Ibid., 290–92.

4. Hawaiian music, or even the "Hawaiian" sound, cannot be defined briefly. The characteristics identified here are among those most commonly associated with a popular conception of the sound of Hawaiian steel guitar.

5. Some musicians improvised slides or tone bars from found objects. For example, B. K. Turner, known as "Black Ace," played his guitar on his lap and stopped the strings with a small glass bottle.

6. Brozman, *National Resonator Instruments*, 24–26.

7. Goldmark, *Steel Guitar and Dobro Discography*, 157.

8. Brozman, *National Resonator Instruments*, 26.

9. Today the instruments used for Hawaiian-style playing are commonly referred to as "square neck" models, as their necks are of rectangular cross-section. The common shape for a fretted guitar neck is roughly half-oval in cross-section.

10. Ibid., 51–99.

11. Smith, *Rickenbacker Guitars*, 26–29.

12. The number of necks is limited by the distance a player can comfortably reach across.

13. Gruhn and Carter, *Electric Guitars and Basses,* 36. According to the liner notes by Rich Kienzle for MCA CD 088 112 442-2, *The Best of Webb Pierce,* "Slowly" spent seventeen weeks as the number one country music single in 1954.

14. Of course, a few country musicians continued to play steel guitars without pedals, most notably recording artist Jerry Byrd. But he eventually moved to Hawaii, where his instrument of choice was favored. (The pedal-steel guitar has never been popular among Hawaiian musicians.)

In recent years there has been a revival of interest in the electric lap-steel guitar, and today the instrument is heard in a variety of popular music genres, including country.

15. Gruhn and Carter, *Electric Guitars and Basses.* Gibson last made steel guitars in 1967 (p. 22), Valco/National in 1968 (p. 15), Rickenbacker in 1970 (p. 10), and Fender in 1980 (p. 32). Fender has introduced a new lap-steel guitar in recent years, but it has not been well received.

CHAPTER 5: The Eason Brothers

1. 1910 U.S. Census, Schley County, and 1920 U.S. Census, Schley County.

2. The number of Henry and Addie Eason's children is the result of deductions made from reviews of 1920 and 1930 U.S. Census records, Willie's birth certificate, interviews with Willie, and conversations with younger Eason family members. Anecdotes indicate that there may have been as many as eighteen children, but I found evidence of only fifteen.

3. 1900 U.S. Census, Camden County.

4. Register, *History of Schley County, Georgia,* 216–17.

5. Information is from Willie Eason's birth certificate. He was unnamed at the time the certificate was issued. The document states that he was the tenth child of Addie Eason, but only eight were living.

6. 1930 U.S. Census, Philadelphia.

7. Ella Mae Berry interview, August 16, 2001.

8. Birth and death dates for Jimmy Kahauolopua are from the 1920 U.S. Census, Honolulu, and the Social Security Death Index. The birth date for Jack Kahauolopua is from the 1920 U.S. Census. The date and place of his death are unknown.

9. Ralph Kolsiana interview, May 26, 1999. Lorene Ruymar wrote in *The Hawaiian Steel Guitar and its Great Hawaiian Musicians,* that the studio where Jimmy Kahauolopua taught was the Royal Hawaiian Studio of Music (57). Kolsiana clearly stated in his interview with the author that it was the Honolulu Conservatory of Music, and that name agrees with the "business name of present employer" stated on Kahauolopua's application for a Social Security account on

January 10, 1938. Kolsiana stated repeatedly that his teacher's surname was Kahanolopua (spelled with an "n"), which is consistent with the spelling that appears in *The Guitarist* magazine. It does not appear that Kahanolopua is a real Hawaiian surname; there are several listings for Kahauolopua in contemporary telephone directories, but none for Kahanolopua. Jimmy and Jack Kahauolopua's surname has been verified by telephone interviews with relatives in Hawaii.

10. Ralph Kolsiana interview, May 26, 1999.

11. Ruymar, *Hawaiian Steel Guitar,* 70.

12. Although I have not reviewed every copy of the *The Hawaiian Guitarist* and *The Guitarist* magazines, I do have all issues of *The Guitarist* for 1935 and have reviewed several later issues. Among the magazines I have reviewed, the last issue to include radio listings was the January 1935 issue of *The Guitarist.*

13. *The Hawaiian Guitarist,* February 1934, 7. The Honolulu Melody Boys were broadcast live in Philadelphia on Mondays from 2:00 to 2:15 P.M. over WLIT, Wednesdays from 6:30 to 6:45 P.M. over WHAT, Thursdays from 11:45 A.M. to 12:00 noon over WIP, Fridays from 6:00 to 6:15 P.M. over WHAT, and Saturdays from 11:30 to 11:45 P.M. over WPEN.

14. *The Guitarist,* February 1935, 23.

15. *The Guitarist,* April 1935, 13.

16. *The Guitarist,* November 1935, 9.

17. U.S. Social Security Act: "Application for Account Number."

18. Willie Eason interview, January 16, 1994.

19. "Old Virginia Moon," back cover.

20. Ella Mae Berry interview, August 16, 2001.

21. Willie Eason reiterated this story many times over the years. The 1930 U.S. Census lists Troman Eason's occupation as "washer" at a laundry.

22. Willie Eason interview, January 16, 1994.

23. Plummer's name is spelled phonetically here. To the best of my knowledge, there were no tenor electric Hawaiian guitars manufactured. The catalog of music folios produced by the Oahu Publishing Company included many selections that featured a tenor harmony part. Willie consistently referred to Plummer playing a tenor part and remembers his instrument as sounding "keener," that is, meaning either brighter in timbre or higher in pitch than Troman's. It seems almost certain that Plummer was merely playing a "tenor" part, that is, a harmony line above the melody, on a standard steel guitar.

24. New York, City of, "Death Certificate."

25. Ella Mae Berry interview, August 16, 2001.

26. Ibid. She is referring to reading tablature, not standard music notation.

27. Acorne Coffee interview, July 17, 1999.

28. Willie Eason interview, January 23, 1996.

29. Ibid.

30. Ibid.

31. Willie Eason interview, January 16, 1994.

CHAPTER 6: Little Willie and His Talking Guitar

1. Mary Linzy interview, August 24, 2001.

2. Philadelphia, School District of, "Certification of School Record."

3. Bishop Charles E. Campbell interview, March 15, 1998.

4. Willie Eason interview, January 16, 1994.

5. Tate, *Decree Book*, 107.

6. According to Alyce's sister, Mary Linzy, she also spelled her name "Alice," but most often with the "y."

7. On January 23, 2006, www.hogc.org listed forty-one churches in Florida, thirty-three in Georgia, and twenty-six in South Carolina. The number of churches is constantly changing as new churches are built, or purchased, and old churches are sold. In recent years there has been a movement to sell smaller churches and consolidate local congregations into a single larger building. In the 1990s, the number of churches in Florida was said to be fifty-three. South Carolina State Bishop Henry Dillard told me there were thirty churches in that state. In 2004, there were fifty-one Florida churches listed on www.hogc.org. Some congregations considered "missions" are not counted as churches. The figures listed on the Web site might not be current or accurate.

8. Mary Linzy interview, August 24, 2001.

9. Based on correspondence from David Evans in March 2007, Eason may have played in Atlanta with Blind Willie McTell in the 1950s. McTell had stated in an interview with Atlanta librarian Alma Johnson that he played gospel music with a "Little Willie" from Florida during that period.

10. "Service of Triumph Celebrating the Life of Reverend Willie Claude Eason." The date of Willie Eason's ordination to the ministry, as well as other historical information contained in the booklet, is unverified and some degree of inaccuracy is likely.

11. Jeannette Eason interview, January 24, 2006.

12. Mary Linzy interview, January 23, 2006.

13. Ella Mae Berry interview, August 16, 2001.

14. Ibid.

15. Ibid.

16. Ibid.

17. Although Eason's memory often could not be trusted, he seemed clear on the recollections of his earnings. The amounts recalled by Ella Mae Berry seem astronomical.

18. Willie Eason interview, January 16, 1994.

19. Willie and Jeannette Eason interview, April 19, 1996.

20. Logan and Winston, *American Dictionary of Negro Biography,* 173–74.

21. Willie and Jeannette Eason interview, April 19, 1996.

22. Willie and Jeannette Eason interview, August 30, 2001. Jeannette says they changed the name because Jeanette Harris, wife of Rebert Harris, leader of the Soul Stirrers, had a quartet by that name and objected.

23. Ibid.

24. Ibid.

25. Ibid.

26. Jeannette Eason interview, November 6, 2001.

27. Willie and Jeannette Eason interview, April 18, 1996.

28. Jeannette Eason interview, August 15, 2001.

29. Willie and Jeannette Eason interview, April 19, 1996.

30. Willie Eason interview, January 16, 1994.

31. Willie and Jeannette Eason interview, April 21, 1996.

32. Willie and Jeannette Eason interview, April 19, 1996.

33. Willie Eason interview, May 3, 1994.

34. Chuck Campbell interview, August 9, 2001.

35. Ibid.

36. While Eason's reputation was significant in the mid-Atlantic and southern states, he was not very well-known among the Detroit musicians and congregations. Apparently Michigan was not a state to which he traveled.

37. Chuck Campbell interview, August 9, 2001.

38. Ibid.

39. Hays and Laughton, *Gospel Records, 1943–1969.* Eason also recorded two songs for Regent that were not released: "Everybody Ought to Pray" and "Jesus Is My Only Friend."

40. Kennedy and McNutt, *Little Labels—Big Sound,* 65.

41. Roosevelt Eberhardt and Willie were very close friends and played music together for decades. Several senior bishops recalled that Eberhardt served as Bishop Lockley's chauffer.

42. Willie and Jeannette Eason interview, August 30, 2001.

43. Per email from Guido van Rijn, June 21, 2007.

44. Jeannette Eason interview, January 18, 2006.

45. Ibid.

46. Ibid.

47. Ibid.

48. Ibid.

49. Ibid.

50. Ibid.

51. Ibid.

52. Jeannette Eason interview, January 20, 2006.

53. Jeannette Eason interview, January 24, 2006.

54. Details of Willie Eason's fortieth anniversary celebration are from a ticket from the event owned by Jeannette Eason.

55. Jeannette Eason interview, January 20, 2006.

CHAPTER 7: Henry Nelson

1. The details of Henry Nelson's birth are from a certified copy of his birth certificate.

2. Mary Linzy interview, August 24, 2001.

3. The term "bush arbor" is prevalent among Keith Dominion communities, but "brush arbor" seems a more common general usage.

4. Mary Linzy interview, August 24, 2001.

5. Ibid.

6. Ibid.

7. Ibid.

8. Ibid.

9. Before the advent of the electric bass, it was a fairly common practice among Keith Dominion musicians to tune down the lower strings of a standard guitar or steel guitar and play a bass line on one or two strings.

10. Henry Nelson interview, November 26, 1993.

11. Mary Linzy interview, August 24, 2001.

12. Chuck and Phillip Campbell interview, March 15, 1998.

13. Henry Nelson interview, November 26, 1993

14. Henry Nelson interview, December 26, 1998.

15. Henry Nelson interview, November 26, 1993.

16. Ibid.

17. Mary Linzy interview, August 24, 2001.

18. Henry Nelson interview, December 26, 1998

19. Henry Nelson interview, November 26, 1993.

20. Corner Flat is not shown on Alabama maps. It is possible Nelson was speaking of Comer, Alabama.

21. Henry Nelson interview, November 26, 1993.

22. Ibid.

23. Johnnie Mae Nelson interview, January 26, 2006. When Johnnie Mae was born in Mississippi on August 20, 1943, her mother was fifteen. While still an infant, Johnnie Mae was sent to New York, where she was raised by her uncle, Charles H. Varnado, and aunt, Myrtis Mae Varnado, whom she refers to as her father and mother.

24. Ibid.

25. Henry Nelson interview, November 26, 1993.

26. "Home Going Service" (booklet). With reference to "blew his eyes out of his head," Nelson had normal vision after he recovered from the accident.

27. Johnnie Mae Nelson interview, January 26, 2006.

28. Ibid.

29. Campbell, "Chuck's Sacred Pedal Steel His-story."

30. Ibid.

31. Chuck and Phillip Campbell interview, March 15, 1998.

32. Johnnie Mae Nelson interview, January 26, 2006.

33. Chuck and Phillip Campbell interview, March 15, 1998.

34. James Hampton interview, July 18, 1999.

35. Anthony Fox interview, July 18, 1999.

36. Alvin Lee interview, October 25, 2003.

37. Elton Noble interview, September 19, 2003.

38. Chuck and Phillip Campbell interview, March 15, 1998.

39. Ibid.

40. "Home Going Service."

CHAPTER 8: The Jewell Dominion

1. Chuck Campbell interview, February 11, 1998.

2. Based on listening to recordings of Lorenzo Harrison playing for worship services and on conversations with Chuck Campbell. Harrison sometimes varied the tuning of the bass strings and may have on occasion tuned the whole instrument down a little, to an open D chord, for example. He also sometimes re-tuned the treble strings to include a sixth or dominant seventh. However, the eight-string E-major tuning was his basic tuning and is the one most commonly used by Jewell Dominion steel guitarists today.

3. "One Hundred Years of History."

4. Ibid.

5. Lemuel Neal interview, February 9, 2006.

6. Ibid.

7. Harvey Jones interview, September 25, 2003.

8. Nettie Mae Harrison interview, September 11, 2003.

9. "One Hundred Years of History."

10. Nettie Mae Harrison interview, September 11, 2003.

11. Ibid.

12. Ibid.

13. Ibid.

14. Harvey Jones interview, September 25, 2003.

15. Ibid.

16. Florida is one of the leading beef cattle producing states in the East.

17. Harvey Jones interview, September 25, 2003.

18. Ibid.

19. Unless otherwise noted, information in this section is drawn from Opal Louis Nations's article "The Jewell Gospel Singers," published in *Blues and Rhythm,* no. 126.

20. Hays and Laughton, *Gospel Records, 1943–1969.*

21. I have made repeated attempts to arrange an interview with Ronnie Mozee, but he has not returned my calls.

22. Maggie Staton interview, February 9, 2006.

23. There are three of the ten Nashboro sides that I have not heard: Nashboro 570, "I Looked Down the Line" / "Somebody's Knockin' at Your Door" and "Ease My Troublin'," from Nashboro 617. Maggie Staton recalled that Harrison did not play steel guitar on the Nashboro sessions, except possibly bass lines.

24. Hays and Laughton, *Gospel Records, 1943–1969.* The Jewell Gospel Singers and the Jewel Gospel Trio should not be confused with the Jewel (one "l") Gospel Singers that recorded prolifically for the Savoy label from 1963 to1968.

25. See http://www.soulwalking.co.uk/Candi%20Staton.html.

26. Segments of the Arhoolie Foundation's *Sacred Steel* video present some of the differences between Keith and Jewell Dominion dance. Although all the footage was taken at Keith Dominion services, the segment titled "While the Spirit Is Moving" demonstrates a rough approximation of typical Jewell Dominion dance. Of course, the Keith Dominion folks shown dancing are not as adept at the form as are experienced Jewell Dominion dancers. When compared to the shouting in the archival footage of Henry Nelson playing at the 1989 New York State Assembly in Utica, included in the *Sacred Steel* video, for example, the two styles of dance—if one can even categorize the movements of the Utica congregation as dance—are obvious.

27. Nettie Mae Harrison interview, September 11, 2003.

28. Ibid.

29. Alvin Lee interview, February 23, 2006.

30. Ibid.

31. Mike Wortham interview, February 11, 2006.

32. Today, steel guitarists in both dominions prefer instruments fitted with legs, and consider those not fitted with legs as entry-level instruments.

33. As indicated earlier, most of my knowledge of Harrison's tunings is based on discussions with Chuck Campbell. See note 2, above.

34. Sonny Treadway interview, February 28, 2006.

35. Nettie Mae Harrison interview, September 11, 2003. I have not verified the addresses or spellings for these bars.

36. Sonny Treadway interview, February 28, 2006.

37. "Service of Triumph and Victory of Bishop Lorenzo Harrison."

38. Robert Boles interview, February 1, 2005.

39. Mike Wortham interview, February 11, 2006.

40. Alvin Lee interview, February 23, 2006.

41. I have interviewed several senior musicians and members of the Keith Dominion clergy who have stated that there were many times when they attended the General Assembly and no steel guitarists played.

42. Del Ray Grace interview, June 2, 2005.

43. Nettie Mae Harrison interview, September 11, 2003.

44. Guralnick, *Last Train to Memphis,* 48, 78.

45. Peter Guralnick, personal correspondence, January 31, 2006.

46. Guralnick, *Last Train to Memphis,* 26–27.

47. On a visit to Tupelo on February 12, 2006, Bishop Calvin Worthem showed me where the church and tent had been located in the late 1940s.

CHAPTER 9: Motor City Steel

1. Felton Williams interview, August 28, 2003.

2. Ibid.

3. Ibid.

4. Ibid.

5. Ibid.

6. Ted Beard interview, August 18, 2003.

7. Felton Williams interview, August 28, 2003.

8. Ibid.

9. Ibid.

10. Ibid.

11. Ibid.

12. Felton Williams interview, January 17, 2006.

13. Harvey Jones interview, September 25, 2003.

14. Ronnie Hall interview, September 1, 2003.

15. Ibid.

16. Ibid.

17. Ibid.

18. Ibid.

19. Ibid.

20. Ibid.

21. Ibid.

22. Ibid.

23. Ibid.

24. Ibid.

25. Ibid.

26. Ibid.

27. Ted Beard interview, August 18, 2003. Beard was not certain of the spelling of his mother's maiden name, but thought it was spelled "Assberry." Because I cannot find that spelling in Internet telephone directories, I have taken the liberty of using "Asberry," a common spelling.

28. Ibid.

29. Allen and Schlereth, *Sense of Place,* 28.

30. Ted Beard interview, August 18, 2003.

31. Ibid.

32. Ibid.

33. Lapious is pronounced la-POH-shus. He is known informally as "Po."

34. Ted Beard interview, August 18, 2003.

35. Ted Beard interview, August 18, 2003.

36. Sonny Treadway interview, February 28, 2006.

37. Ted Beard interview, February 1, 2006.

38. Ibid. What Beard refers to as the "jubilee service," might be more commonly known among scholars of African American religion and sacred music as the "shout" portion of the worship service.

39. Ibid. The Beard family maintains a strong presence in the Keith Dominion. Two of Ted's sisters are pastors in Detroit: Elder Janie L. Beard serves at 9565 Iris Street, and Elder Jeanette Beard Lott, who shares the position of pastor with her husband, Bishop John Lott, at 8124 Burdeno Street.

40. Ibid.

41. Ibid.

42. Ibid.

43. Ibid.

44. Ted Beard interview, August 12, 2004.

45. Ibid.

CHAPTER 10: Calvin Cooke

1. Calvin Cooke interview, May 25, 1999.

2. Ibid.

3. Ibid.

4. Calvin Cooke interview, June 12, 2002.

5. Calvin Cooke interview, August 4, 2003. Tolliver is recognized by his contemporaries as the first to play pedal-steel guitar in Keith Dominion worship services, but he did not have a lasting impact on the popularity of the instrument in the church. He is presently retired in Orlando, Florida.

6. Calvin Cooke interview, June 12, 2002.

7. One cannot be absolutely sure of the accuracy of statements concerning

who played at the General Assembly until the roster of musicians was formally organized circa 1968.

8. Calvin Cooke interview, August 4, 2003. Cooke also stated that he may have missed one or two years due to illness. Ted Beard has played at the General Assembly from 1964 or 1965 to the present.

9. Bock, "Calvin Cooke," 24–31. In this article Cooke mentions later influences, from blues slide guitarist Elmore James to the band Yes.

10. Calvin Cooke interview, May 25, 1999.

11. Calvin Cooke interview, August 4, 2003.

12. Sonny Treadway interview, February 28, 2006. Sonny does not recall what became of Harrison's steel that was laced in leather "Mexican-style." He last saw Harrison play it in Nassau, Bahamas.

13. Calvin Cooke interview, August 4, 2003.

14. Ibid.

15. Ibid.

16. Calvin Cooke interview, May 25, 1999.

17. Starlin Harrison interview, July 20, 2001.

18. Ibid.

19. Calvin Cooke interview, May 25, 1999.

20. Ibid.

21. Calvin Cooke interview, June 12, 2002.

22. Ronnie Hall interview, September 1, 2003.

23. Calvin Cooke interview, June 12, 2002.

24. Ibid.

25. The dates of service by these steel guitarists at the General Assembly are based on interviews with them cited elsewhere in this book.

26. Alvin Lee interview, February 23, 2006.

27. Ted Beard interview, August 18, 2003. Beard recalled that he started playing at the General Assembly in 1964 or 1965. Also see note 8, above.

CHAPTER 11: Shaping the Modern Sound

1. Robinson, *Biography of Bishop Charles E. Campbell*.

2. Campbell, "Chuck's Sacred Pedal-Steel His-story."

3. The Reverend Luther Robinson is the father of Bishop Campbell's biographer, Verdis Robinson.

4. Campbell, "Chuck's Sacred Pedal-Steel His-story." Charles Flenory plays both steel guitar and "lead" guitar.

5. Ibid.

6. Ibid.

7. Ibid.

8. Ibid.

9. Ibid.

10. Ibid.

11. Among steel guitarists, "chime" means to play artificial harmonics.

12. Campbell, "Chuck's Sacred Pedal-Steel His-story."

13. Buddy Emmons and Lloyd Green, both born in 1937, are two of the most highly regarded country pedal-steel guitarists. Emmons is known for his highly technical playing and many consider him the world's foremost pedal-steel guitarist. He teamed with Harold "Shot" Jackson (1920–91) to form the Sho-Bud steel guitar company, which produced some of the finest early pedal-steel guitars. Green dominated Nashville recording sessions from about 1965 to 1989, appearing in approximately 25,000 songs, 116 of which were number one country hits. As youths, both Emmons and Green studied at Honolulu Conservatory of Music (Oahu) studios. Emmons, Green, and Jackson are all members of the Steel Guitar Hall of Fame.

14. Campbell, "Chuck's Sacred Pedal-Steel His-story."

15. Ibid. Jimmy Day (1934–99) was a legendary country pedal-steel guitarist known as "Mr. Country Soul." In the early 1950s, he backed up many country stars on the Louisiana Hayride. As a member of Ray Price's band, the Cherokee Cowboys, he contributed to several recordings, including the hit "Crazy Arms." He later worked with George Jones and Willie Nelson, among many others. In 1982 he was inducted into the Steel Guitar Hall of Fame.

16. Ibid.

17. Ibid.

18. Winston and Keith, *Pedal Steel Guitar*. One of the first publications to demystify the pedal-steel guitar.

19. Campbell, "Chuck's Sacred Pedal-Steel His-story."

20. Chuck Campbell interview, February 11, 1998.

21. Ibid.

22. The House of God, Keith Dominion Web site, www.hogc.org, listed thirty-one churches in the East Coast diocese on August 5, 2003. I was told that in the 1990s there were thirty-three. "East Coast" is a bit of a misnomer, as the diocese includes churches as far north and inland as Ocala, which lies in North Central Florida.

23. Frank Blue interview, August 14, 2007. The only steel guitarist of that era whose name Blue could recall was Quillan Mitchell (author's phonetic spelling). Calvin Cooke and Starlin Harrison also played in Florida, primarily during the winter months, while traveling with Bishop Henry Harrison.

24. Alvin Lee interview, July 11, 2006.

25. Ibid.

26. Glenn Lee interview, March 7, 1994.

27. Ibid.
28. Ibid.
29. Ibid.
30. Ibid.
31. Ibid.
32. Ibid.
33. Ibid.
34. Ibid.
35. Ibid.
36. Ibid.
37. Ibid.
38. Ibid.
39. Ibid.
40. Alvin Lee interview August 31, 2004.
41. Ibid.
42. Derek Trucks interview, August 29, 2006.

CHAPTER 12: Negotiating the New Millennium

1. Information from www.folk.org, accessed October 29, 2007.
2. Chuck Campbell interview, October 22, 2007.
3. Ibid.
4. *Press On* video.
5. Robert Randolph interview, August 31, 2007.
6. *Press On* video.
7. *Rolling Stone,* "The 100 Greatest Guitarists of All Time," http://www.rollingstone.com/news/story/5937559/the_100_greatest_guitarists_of_all_time/1, accessed January 21, 2010.
8. *Press on* video
9. The *Austin City Limits* Program has been rebroadcast many times.
10. Robert Randolph interview, August 31, 2007.
11. *Press On* video.
12. Robert Randolph interview, August 31, 2007.
13. Ibid.
14. Josh Taylor interview, October 5, 2003.
15. Tate, *Decree Book,* 61–62. In conversionist churches such as the Keith and Jewell Dominions, those who have been born again and received sanctification by the Holy Spirit are referred to as "saints."
16. *Press On* video.
17. Robinson, *Biography of Bishop Charles E. Campbell,* 94–95.
18. Ibid., 95.

19. Chuck Campbell has told me that a few copies of the media projects were produced for use as evidence in the lawsuit with the House of God, Keith Dominion.

20. Case 3:06-cv-00066, *House of God which is the Church of the Living God, Pillar and Ground of the Truth without controversy, Inc., (Keith Dominion) plaintiff v. Bishop Charles Campbell, Charles Campbell Jr., and Phillip Campbell, defendants.* United States District Court for the Middle District of Tennessee, Nashville Division, document 1, "Complaint."

21. Ibid.

22. Chuck Campbell interview, December 18, 2007.

23. Ibid.

24. United States District Court for the Middle District of Tennessee, "Memorandum," and "Order."

25. Chuck Campbell interview, October 22, 2007.

26. Ibid.

27. "The longest running show on cable TV," http://www.bobbyjonesgospel.com/, accessed October 24, 2007.

28. Chuck Campbell interview, October 22, 2007.

29. Ibid.

30. Ibid.

31. Calvin Cooke interview, September 5, 2007.

32. Ibid.

33. Ibid.

34. Ted Beard interview, September 6, 2007.

35. Calvin Cooke interview, September 5, 2007.

36. Ibid. Cooke moved to the Atlanta area in 2010.

37. In the 1939 revision to the Decree Book, Chief Overseer Bishop Keith's summary of the teachings of church founder Bishop M. L. Tate mentions: "we were taught not to eat swine flesh."

38. Robert Randolph interview, August 31, 2007.

39. See http://www.grammy.com/nominees, accessed January 21, 2010.

40. Jim Markel, telephone conversation and email, January 20, 2010. Robert Randolph appears at 2:10 in this trailer: http://www.youtube.com/watch?v=IbkvdVB8BkA, accessed January 21, 2010.

41. Jim Markel, telephone conversation and email, January 20, 2010, and http://www.billboard.com/news/robert-randolph-recording-with-t-bone-burnett-1003809566.story#/news/robert-randolph-recording-with-t-bone-burnett-1003809566.story, accessed January 20, 2010. Burnett's credits include the film soundtrack release, *O Brother, Where Art Thou? which sold more than eight million copies.* See www.tboneburnett.com for more information about him.

42. See http://www.experiencehendrixtour.com/, accessed January 22, 2010.

43. Calvin Cooke interview, September 5, 2007.

Bibliography

Allen, Barbara, and Thomas J. Schlereth. *Sense of Place: American Regional Cultures.* Lexington: University Press of Kentucky, 1990.

Anderson, John. "Steel's the Show." *Miami New Times,* June 3–9, 2004, 22–29.

Apel, Willi. *Harvard Dictionary of Music.* Cambridge: Harvard University Press, 1982.

Baer, Hans, and Merrill Singer. *African American Religion: Varieties of Protest and Accommodation,* 2d ed. Knoxville: University of Tennessee Press, 2002.

Baird, Robert. "Recording of the Month: Sacred Steel." *Stereophile,* February 1998, 177.

Basse, Craig. "Singer Was a Man of 'Sacred Steel.'" *St. Petersburg Times,* June 18, 2005.

Bock, Scott M. "Aubrey Ghent." *Living Blues,* no. 176, January–February 2005, 30–35

———. "Aubrey Ghent: Go Into All the World." *Juke Blues,* no. 57, 14–19.

———. "Calvin Cooke: I Was the Fastest." *Living Blues,* no. 184, May–June 2006, 24–31.

———. "Church on the Road: The Lee Boys." *Living Blues,* no. 190, June 2007, 24–31.

———. "A Conversation with the Campbell Brothers." *Living Blues, no. 176,* January–February 2005, 22–29.

Bourne, Peter. *Jimmy Carter: A Comprehensive Biography from Plains to Presidency.* New York: Scribner, 1997.

Boyer, Horace. *How Sweet the Sound: The Golden Age of Gospel.* Washington, D.C.: Elliott & Clark, 1995.

Brozman, Bob. *The History and Artistry of National Resonator Instruments.* Fullerton, Calif.: Centerstream, 1993.

Burckel, Christian E. *Who's Who in Colored America: A Biographical Dictionary of Notable Persons of Negro Descent in the United States.* New York: Christian E. Burckel, 1927.

Campbell, Charles T. "Chuck's Sacred Pedal Steel His-story." Brief autobiographical sketch, 2002. Unpublished manuscript in the author's collection.

Cha-Jua, Sundiata Keita. *America's First Black Town: Brooklyn, Illinois, 1830–1915.* Chicago: University of Illinois Press, 2002.

Collum, Danny Duncan. "Sacred Connections." *Sojourners,* September–October 2009, 52.

"Competent Instruction on the Guitar" (list of Oahu instructors). *The Guitarist,* January 1935, 12.

Darden, Robert. *People Get Ready: A New History of Black Gospel Music.* New York: Continuum, 2004.

"Did You Know That?" *The Guitarist,* January 1935, 16.

"Did You Know That?" *The Guitarist,* July 1935, 16.

"Discovering 'Sacred Steel.'" *Newsweek,* July 15, 1996, 8.

"Discs of Destiny: 30 Years of Breakthrough Albums." *Guitar Player,* 31.1, January 1997, 95–106.

DuPree, Sherry Sherrod. *African-American Good News (Gospel) Music.* Washington, D.C.: Middle Atlantic Regional Press, 1993.

———. *Biographical Dictionary of African-American Holiness-Pentecostals, 1880–1990.* Washington, D.C.: Middle Atlantic Regional Press, 1989.

———. "Father of the Hawaiian Steel Guitar Players: Rev. Willie Claude Eason." Tri-fold booklet. Gainesville, Florida, 1995.

Eason, Willie. "Willie Eason: Steel Guitar Artist of Phila., PA." Undated, ca. 1950, self- published booklet of lyrics to "Tell Me Why You Liked Roosevelt" (abbreviated version), "Blind Bartimaeus," "Does Jesus Care," "Didn't It Rain," "Standing on the Highway," and "Jezebel." From the collection of Chris Strachwitz.

Ellis, Andy. "Raw, Rockin', and Righteous: Robert Randolph Reinvents the Pedal Steel." *Guitar Player,* September 2004, 49–56.

Fassio, Edoardo. "Parla l'acciaio sacro." *Il Blues,* no. 68, September 1999, 12.

"Flash!" *The Guitarist,* January 1935, 19.

Fontenot, Robert. "Robert Randolph: The Second Coming of Sacred Steel?" *Blues Review,* February–March 2003, 8–15.

Fricke, David. "The New Guitar Gods: Derek Trucks." *Rolling Stone,* February 22, 2007, 42.

Friskics-Warren, Bill. "The Transcendent Sound of Sacred Steel Guitar." *Nashville Scene,* July 13, 2000, 22–28.

Fulks, Robbie. "Conscience of Steel: Lloyd Green's Search for the Soul in the String." *Journal of Country Music,* 24.3, 52–61.

Georgia State Board of Health. "Standard Certificate of Birth, Bureau of Vital Statistics." Eason, male child. Birth date June 26, 1921, Ellaville, Schley County.

Goldmark, Joe. *The International Steel Guitar and Dobro Discography,* 8th ed. San Francisco: Joe Goldmark, 1997.

Green, Tony. "Soul of Steel." *St. Petersburg Times,* April 21, 2002.

Gruhn, George, and Walter Carter. *Electric Guitars and Basses: A Pictorial History.* San Francisco: GPI Books, Miller-Freeman, 1994.

———. *Gruhn's Guide to Vintage Guitars.* San Francisco: GPI Books, Miller-Freeman, 1991.

Guralnick, Peter. *Last Train to Memphis: The Rise of Elvis Presley.* New York: Little Brown, 1994.

Harrington, Richard. "Robert Randolph, Man of Sacred Steel." *Washington Post,* December 13, 2002.

Harris, Michael W. *The Rise of Gospel Blues: The Music of Thomas Andrew Dorsey in the Urban Church.* New York: Oxford University Press, 1992.

"The Hawaiian Guitar on the Air." *Hawaiian Guitarist,* February 1934, 7.

Hays, Cedric J., and Robert Laughton. *Gospel Records, 1943–1969: A Black Music Discography.* Milford, N.H.: Big Nickel Publications, 1992.

Hazeldine, Mike, and Barry Martyn. *Bunk Johnson: Song of the Wanderer* (includes audio CD). New Orleans: Jazzology Press, 2000.

Heilbut, Anthony. *The Gospel Sound.* New York: Limelight Editions, 1989.

Hill, Samuel S., and Charles R. Wilson, eds. *The New Encyclopedia of Southern Culture, Volume 1: Religion.* Chapel Hill: University of North Carolina Press, 2006.

Himes, Goeffrey. "A Joyful Noise." *No Depression,* no. 24, November–December 1999, 70–81.

Hinson, Glenn. *Fire in My Bones.* Philadelphia: University of Pennsylvania Press, 2000.

"Homegoing Celebration for Rev. Glenn Renard Lee." Miami: Bethel Missionary Full Gospel Baptist Church, October 28, 2000.

"Home Going Service in Loving Memory of Deacon Henry R. Nelson." Queens Village, N.Y.: New Greater Bethel Ministries, April 14, 2001.

Hurston, Zora Neale. *The Sanctified Church.* Berkeley, Calif.: Turtle Island Publications, 1983.

"In the Public Eye," *The Guitarist,* January 1934, 6.

"In the Public Eye," *The Guitarist,* April 1935, 8.

Jarrett, Michael. "Aubrey Ghent: Steelin' in the Name of the Lord." *Pulse!* March 1998, 20.

Kanahele, George S., ed. *Hawaiian Music and Musicians: An Illustrated History.* Honolulu: University Press of Hawaii, 1979.

Katz, Larry. "Sacred Steel Guitar." *New Age,* January–February, 2000, 88–89.

Kennedy, Rick, and Randy McNutt. *Little Labels—Big Sound: Small Record Companies and the Rise of American Music.* Bloomington: Indiana University Press, 1999.

Ketchum, Jack. "Dante's Sacred Inferno." *Big City Rhythm & Blues,* 8.6, December 2002–January 2003, 36–37.

Koransky, Jason. "The Purpose behind Robert Randolph's New Gospel." *Downbeat,* October, 2002.

Korczynska, Jo Ann. "Elder Maurice 'Ted' Beard: Making a Joyful Noise." *Big City Rhythm & Blues,* 8.6, December 2002–January 2003, 20–21.

Lewis, Helen M., and H. Meharry Lewis. *The Beauty of Holiness: A Small Catechism of the Holiness Faith and Doctrine,* 2d ed. Nashville: New and Living Way, 1990.

Lewis, Meharry H. *Mary Lena Lewis Tate: "A Street Called Straight"—The Ten Most Dynamic and Productive Black Female Holiness Preachers of the Twentieth Century.* Nashville: New and Living Way, 2002.

Logan, R. W., and M. R. Winston, eds. *American Dictionary of Negro Biography.* New York: W. W. Norton, 1982.

Lornell, Kip. *Happy in the Service of the Lord: African-American Sacred Vocal Harmony Quartets in Memphis,* 2d ed. Knoxville: University Press of Tennessee, 1995.

Makin, Bob. "God-Sent Voodoo Chile." *Downbeat,* October 2001, 50.

Markel, Jim, and Jeff Truedell. "A Joyful Noise." *Orlando Weekly,* March 29–April 4, 2001, 20–22.

Marquis, Donald M. *In Search of Buddy Bolden: First Man of Jazz.* Baton Rouge: Louisiana State University Press, 1978.

Mazor, Barry. "Lee Boys: Next-Gen Sacred Steel." *No Depression,* no. 58, July–August, 2005, 26.

McGarvey, Seamus. "Candi Staton: I'm Gonna Hold On." *Juke Blues,* no. 2, Winter 2002–2003, 26–28.

———. "Sacred Steel: The Campbell Brothers." *Juke Blues,* no. 46, Spring 2000, 20–25.

"Memorial Service for Rev. Glenn Renard Lee." Perrine, Fla.: House of God, Keith Dominion, October 27, 2000.

"Memorial Service for the Home Going of Deacon Henry Randolph Nelson." Ocala: House of God, Keith Dominion, Ocala Band No. 2, Mt. Canaan, April 21, 2001.

Michner, Ed. "A Spiritual Tradition." *Gainesville Sun,* February 13, 1999.

Mitchell, Pat. "Robert Randolph and the Family Band." *Big City Rhythm & Blues,* 8.6, December 2002–January 2003, 19–20.

Moon, Tom. "A Gift from Above." *Esquire,* September 2001, 108–12.

Morris, Chris. "Just a Closer Walk: Lap Steel's Amazing Grace Notes." *LA Weekly,* January 16–22, 1998, 42.

Morthland, John. "Testifying to the Commercial Power of Sacred Steel." *New York Times,* October 31, 1999.

Nations, Opal Louis. "The Jewell Gospel Singers." *Blues & Rhythm,* no. 126, February 1998.

New York, City of. "Vital Records Certificate, Death Certificate No. 156–49–318676." Eason, Troman.

"Old Virginia Moon," diagram arrangement 42B. Cleveland: Oahu Publishing, 1931.

Oliver, Paul, Max Harrison, and W. Bolcom, eds. *The New Grove Gospel, Blues and Jazz*. New York: W. W. Norton, 1986.

"One Hundred Years of History," calendar. Indianapolis: Church of the Living God, Jewell Dominion, 2003.

Ott, Eloise R., and Louis H. Chazal. *Ocali Country: Kingdom of the Sun*. Ocala, Fla.: Marion Publishers, 1966.

"Paging Philadelphia." *The Guitarist*, July 1935, 35.

Payne, Wardell J., ed. *Directory of African American Religious Bodies*, 2d ed. Washington, D.C.: Howard University Press, 1995.

Philadelphia: Board of Education, September 2, 2004. "Certification of School Record" for William [*sic*] Claude Eason.

"Philadelphia Club and Student Activities." *The Guitarist*, November 1935, 9.

"Philadelphia Flash." *The Guitarist*, September 1936, 13.

Philadelphia, School District of. "Certification of School Record (Willie C. Eason)."

Piccoli, Sean. "Sacred Steel." *South Florida Sun-Sentinel*, January 12, 2003.

Powers, Ann. "Sacred Strings Wail Hallelujah in a Secular Setting." *New York Times*, August 13, 2001.

Rankin, Tom. *Sacred Space: Photographs from the Mississippi Delta*. Jackson: University Press of Mississippi, 1993.

Register, Pam, ed. *The History of Schley County, Georgia*. Ellaville, Ga.: Schley County Preservation Society, 1982.

Reich, Howard, and William Gaines. *Jelly's Blues: The Life, Music, and Redemption of Jelly Roll Morton*. Cambridge, Mass.: Da Capo Press, 2003.

Richardson, Michael. "Sacred Steel: The Campbell Brothers are Musical Ambassadors of the House of God." *Big City Rhythm & Blues*, 8.6, December 2002–January 2003, 14–15.

Ritz, David. *Divided Soul: The Life of Marvin Gaye*. New York: McGraw Hill, 1985.

Robinson, Dee, ed. *100 Years of History: 2003 Calendar*. Indianapolis: Church of the Living God, the Pillar and Ground of the Truth, Which He Purchased With His Own Blood, Inc., Jewell Dominion, 2003.

Robinson, Verdis L. *The Biography of Bishop Charles E. Campbell: A Charge I Have to Keep, I Have, A God to Glorify*. Rochester, N.Y.: Beta Publications, 2004.

———.*The House of God: A Centennial History of the House of God, Which is the Church of the Living God, the Pillar and Ground of the Truth, Without*

Controversy, Inc., Keith Dominion. Unpublished book manuscript, in the author's collection, 2004.

Rosenbaum, Art. *Shout Because You're Free: The African American Ring Shout Tradition in Coastal Georgia.* Athens: University Press of Georgia, 1998.

Rubin, Dave. "Men of Steel." *Guitar One,* January 2003, 107–10.

Ruymar, Lorene. *The Hawaiian Steel Guitar and Its Great Hawaiian Musicians.* Anaheim Hills, Calif.: Centerstream, 1996.

Schwerin, Jules. *Got To Tell It: Mahalia Jackson, Queen of Gospel.* New York: Oxford University Press, 1992.

Seedorff, George P. "By the Grace of God: Calvin Cooke Is Still Alive and Well in Detroit." *Big City Rhythm & Blues,* December 2004–January 2005, 20–22.

———. "Sliding on to Glory: Calvin Cooke Discovery Shakes UP the Blues World." *Big City Rhythm & Blues,* 8.6, December 2002–January 2003, 16–19.

"Service of Triumph and Victory of Bishop Lorenzo Harrison." Indianapolis: Church of the Living God, Jewell Dominion, 1986.

"Service of Triumph Celebrating the Life of Reverend Willie Claude Eason." St. Petersburg, Fla.: Norwood Baptist Church, 2005.

Shipton, Alyn. *A New History of Jazz.* New York: Continuum, 2001.

Sims, Walter Hines, ed. *Baptist Hymnal.* Nashville: Convention Press, 1956.

Smith, Richard S. *Rickenbacker Guitars.* Fullerton, Calif.: Centerstream, 1987.

Spitzer, Nick. *Folk Masters 1994: A Concert Program Book and Listener's Guide.* Vienna, Va.: Wolf Trap Foundation for the Performing Arts, 1994.

———. *Trombone Shout Bands: The Men and Their Music.* Booklet included with *Saint's Paradise,* SFW CD 40117. Washington, D.C.: Smithsonian Folkways, 1999.

Stiffel, Mary. "Philadelphia Philanderings." *The Guitarist,* April 1935, 13.

———. "Quaker State Interviews." *The Guitarist,* December 1935, 14.

———. "Sets a Fast Pace in the Staid Old Town of Philadelphia." *The Guitarist,* January 1935, 10.

———. "Two Students from Quakertown." *The Guitarist,* February 1935, 23.

Stone, Robert L. "American Roots Music Made Sacred." *Satellite,* 3.5, May 5, 2004, 8–9.

———. "Florida Folk Music." *Forum: The Magazine of the Florida Humanities Council,* Fall 2003, 18–21.

———. "Infused with Spirit: National Heritage Fellow Chuck Campbell." *Voices: Journal of New York Folklore,* 30:3–4, Fall–Winter 2004, 29–30.

———. "Make a Joyful Noise: A Brief History of the House of God and the Sacred Steel Tradition." *Living Blues,* no. 176, January–February 2005, 14–21.

———. "Sacred Steel and the Empire State." *Voices: Journal of New York Folklore,* vol. 28, Fall–Winter 2002, 3–4, 28–31.

———. "Sacred Steel: From Hula to Hallelujah." *Sing Out!* 48.1, Spring 2004, 50–57.

———. "Sacred Steel." *Forum: The Magazine of the Florida Humanities Council,* Winter 2004, 28–31.

———. "Sacred Steel Guitar." *Living Blues,* no. 141, September–October 1998, 36–43.

———. "Sacred Steel: Playing for the Holy Dance." *Guitar Player,* 30.8, August 1996, 33–36.

———. "Willie C. Eason." *Living Blues,* 36.5, September–October 2005, 87–88.

Strauss, Neil. "Making Spirits Rock from Church to Clubland: A Gospel Pedal Steel Guitarist Dives into Pop." *New York Times,* April 30, 2001.

Synan, Vinson. *The Century of the Holy Spirit: 100 Years of Pentecostal and Charismatic Renewal, 1901–2001,* ed. Vinson Synan. Nashville: Thomas Nelson, 2001.

Tate, Mary M. Lewis. *The Constitution, Government and General Decree Book of the Church of the Living God, the Pillar and Ground of Truth.* Nashville: self-published by the church, 1996.

Tennille, Andy. "Crossroads: Robert Randolph and the Sacred Steel Tradition." *Paste,* Issue 9, April–May, 2004, 39–41.

Tosches, Nick. *Unsung Heroes of Rock 'n' Roll: The Birth of Rock in the Wild Years before Elvis.* New York: Harmony Books, 1991.

U.S. Census, 1860. Slave Schedule, Appling County, Ga., 7.

U.S. Census, 1880. Population Schedule, Tattnall County, Ga., 23.

U.S. Census, 1900. Population Schedule, Camden County, Ga., sheet 2B.

U.S. Census, 1910. Population Schedule, Schley County, Ga., sheet 4B.

U.S. Census, 1920. Population Schedule, Honolulu, Hawaii, sheet 19A.

U.S. Census, 1920. Population Schedule, Schley County, Ga., sheet 5B.

U.S. Census, 1930. Population Schedule, Philadelphia, Pa., sheet 32A.

U.S. District Court for the Middle District of Tenn., Nashville Division, Case 3:06-cv-00066, documents 1, "Complaint"; 77, "Memorandum"; and 78, "Order."

U.S. Social Security Act: Application for Account Number. James K. Kahauolopua, January 10, 1938.

U.S. Social Security Death Index.

Van Rijn, Guido. *Roosevelt's Blues: African-American Blues and Gospel Songs on FDR.* Jackson: University Press of Mississippi, 1997.

Vito, Rick. "Aubrey Ghent: Master of the Sacred Steel Guitar." *Vintage Guitar,* December 2004, 24.

Volk, Andy. *Lap Steel Guitar.* Anaheim, Calif.: Centerstream, 2003.

Wald, Gayle F. *Shout, Sister, Shout!: The Untold Story of Rock-and-Roll Trailblazer Sister Rosetta Tharpe.* Boston: Beacon Street Press, 2007.

Weiss, Eric. "Derek Trucks: Strumming Joyful Noise." *Vintage Guitar,* October 2002, 86–91.

White, Forrest. *Fender: The Inside Story.* San Francisco: Miller-Freeman Books, 1994.

Winston, Winnie, and Bill Keith. *Pedal Steel Guitar.* New York: Oak Publications, 1975.

Wirtz, the Reverend Billy. "Sacred Steel Guitar Playing Is Bound to Stir Your Spirit." *Charlotte Observer,* February 26, 2006.

Woodbury, Pinkney, ed. *The Struggle for Survival: A Partial History of the Negroes of Marion County, Florida, 1865–1976.* Ocala: Black Historical Organization of Marion County, 1977.

Young, Alan. *Woke Me Up This Morning: Black Gospel Singers and the Gospel Life.* Jackson: University Press of Mississippi, 1997.

Zolten, Jerry. *Great God A'mighty! The Dixie Hummingbirds: Celebrating the Rise of Soul Gospel Music.* New York: Oxford University Press, 2003.

Interviews

Interviews were a major source of information for this book. Unless otherwise indicated, all interviews are by the author, were recorded on analog audiocassette tape, digital audio tape (DAT) cassettes, or digital minidiscs, and the recordings are in the author's possession. All telephone interviews were recorded on analog cassettes.

Allen, Bishop Kelly W. Nashville, Tenn., December 10, 2002.
Baldwin, Sam. Telephone interview. Palatka, Fla., September 6, 2001.
Beard, Maurice, Jr., "Ted." Nashville, Tenn., June 12, 1996.
———. Telephone interviews. August 18, 2003; August 12, 2004; February 1, 2006; September 6, 2007.
Bennett, Lonnie "Big Ben." Rush, N.Y., March 15, 1998.
Berry, Ella Mae. Telephone interviews. August 16, 2001; August 29, 2001.
Blue, Frank. Telephone interview. August 14, 2007.
Boles, Robert. Telephone interview. February 1, 2005.
Brinson, Chris. Leesburg, Fla., June 5, 2003.
Brown, Bishop Emmett. Nashville, Tenn., December 10, 2002.
Burke, Bishop Sylvester. Nashville, Tenn., December 10, 2002.
Burns, Corroneva. Telephone interview. September 14, 2004.
Bynum, Andrew, and Andrew Wortham. Calhoun City, Miss., February 11, 2006.
Campbell, Bishop. Charles E. Video interview. Rush, N.Y., March 15, 1998.
———. With Chief Helpers Henry Dillard and Rebecca Fletcher, interviewed by Chuck, Darick, and Phillip Campbell and the author. Nashville, Tenn., September 14, 2002.
———. Telephone interview. August 13, 2003.
Campbell, Charles T., "Chuck." Nashville, Tenn., June 13, 1996.
———. Telephone interviews. February 11, 1998; August 9, 2001; June 29, 2005; January 27, 2006; October 22, 2007; December 18, 2007.
Campbell, Chuck and Phillip. Video interview. Rush, N.Y., March 15, 1998

Coffee, Acorne. Telephone interviews. December 23, 1997; May 25, 1999; June 12, 2002; August 4, 2003; August 7, 2003; February 22, 2006; September 5, 2007.

———. Blythwood, S.C., July 17, 1999.

———. With Acorne, Jr., "Flip," Lonnie Bennett et al. Philadelphia, Pa., September 23, 2000.

Cooke, Calvin. Nashville, Tenn., June 13, 1996.

———. Telephone interviews. May 25, 1999; June 12, 2002; August 4, 2003; August 7, 2003; February 22, 2006; September 5, 2007.

DuPree, Sherry S. Gainesville, Fla., December 17, 2003.

Eason, Jeannette. Telephone interviews. August 15, 2001; November 6, 2001; January 18, 2006; January 20, 2006; January 24, 2006.

Eason, Jeannette and Willie. Gainesville, Fla., April 18, 2006.

———. In their van en route to Murfreesboro, Tenn., April 19, 1996.

———. En route to Gainesville, Fla., from Murfreesboro, Tenn., April 21, 1996.

———. St. Petersburg, Fla., August 30, 2001.

———. St. Petersburg, Fla., October 18, 2003.

Eason, Willie. St. Petersburg, Fla., January 16, 1994.

———. St. Petersburg, Fla., May 3, 1994.

———. St. Petersburg, Fla., January 23, 1996.

———. With Henry Nelson. Gainesville, Fla., December 22, 1998.

———. St. Petersburg, Fla., July 10, 2002.

———. St. Petersburg, Fla., January 16, 2003.

Edwards, Antjuan. Ocala, Fla., July 12, 1995.

———. Ocala, Fla., December 15, 2003.

Elliott, Bishop J. C. Nashville, Tenn., December 10, 2002.

Evans, Gilbert, Jr. Palatka, Fla., December 19, 2003.

Flenory, Charles. Memphis, Tenn., February 13, 1998.

Fox, Anthony. Henrietta, N.Y., March 14, 1998.

———. Charleston, S.C., July 18, 1999.

Ghent, Aubrey V. Ft. Pierce, Fla., November 7, 1992.

———. And Henry Nelson. Interview with Sherry S. DuPree, Herbert C. DuPree, and the author. Ocala, Fla., November 26, 1993.

Grace, Del Ray. Telephone interview. June 2, 2005.

Hall, Ronnie. Telephone interview. September 1, 2003.

Hampton, James H. Charleston, S.C., July 18, 1999.

———. Telephone interview. February 6, 2000.

Harmon, Eddie. Ft. Lauderdale, Fla., September 30, 2003.

Harrison, Nettie Mae. Telephone interview. September 11, 2003.

Harrison, Starlin. Telephone interview. July 20, 2001.

Hickman, DaShawn. Interview with Michael Knoll. Mt. Airy, N.C., November 20, 2005.

Jones, Harvey. Telephone interviews. September 25, 2003; March 27, 2006.

Jones, J. T. Ocala, Fla., December 27, 2003.

Kolsiana, Ralph. Telephone interview. May 26, 1999.

Jackson, Katie. Telephone interview. October 1, 2001.

Lang, Lisa. Miami, Fla., October 5, 2003.

Lee, Alvin. Orlando, Fla., October 25, 2003.

———. Telephone interviews. Orlando, Fla., August 31, 2004; February 23, 2006; July 11, 2006.

———. Orlando, Fla., October 14, 2005.

Lee, Glenn R. Perrine, Fla., March 7, 1994.

Lewis, Meharry H. Interview with Sherry S. and Herbert C. DuPree. Tuskegee, Ala., July 2, 1992. Recording not in the author's possession.

Linzy, Mary. Ocala, Fla., August 24, 2001.

———. Ocala, Fla., August 14, 2003.

———. Ocala, Fla., August 22, 2003.

———. Telephone interview. January 23, 2006.

Lott, Bishop John, Jr. Nashville, Tenn., December 10, 2002.

Lott, Jeanette Beard. Nashville, Tenn., December 11, 2002.

Love, Kim. Interview with the author, Chuck, Phil, and Darick Campbell, Acorne Coffee, Flip Coffee, and Lonnie Bennett. Philadelphia, Pa., September 23, 2005.

Neal, Lemuel. Telephone interview. February 9, 2006.

Nelson, Henry, with Aubrey Ghent. Interview by the author and Sherry S. and Herbert C. DuPree. Ocala, Fla., November 26, 1993.

———. With Willie Eason. Gainesville, Fla., December 22, 1998.

———. With his sisters, Audrey Pearl Gillum and Mary Linzy, Ocala, Fla., December 26, 1998.

Nelson, Johnnie Mae. Telephone interview. January 26, 2006.

Noble, Elton. Nashville, Tenn., September 19, 2003.

———. Telephone interviews. March 13, 2006; March 14, 2006.

Parkey, Pauline. Ocala, Fla., December 27, 2003.

Peebles, Maggie Staton. Telephone interview. February 9, 2006.

Penn, Gamaliel. September 6, 2001.

Randolph, Robert. Telephone interviews. May 25, 1999; August, 31, 2007.

Snelling, Bishop Dorothy. Nashville, Tenn., December 11, 2002.

Storey, Charlie. Telephone interview. August 22, 2001.

Summersett, James. Charleston, S.C., July 18, 1999.

Taylor, Bishop Semmie. Nashville, Tenn., December 11, 2002.

Taylor, Bryan "Josh," and Jerry. Telephone interviews. December 21, 2000; November 10, 2001.

———. Miami, Fla., October 5, 2003.

Tolliver, Robert "Bobby." Orlando, Fla., June 27, 2002.

Treadway, Sonny. Deerfield Beach, Fla., December 18, 1993.
———. Telephone interview. February 28, 2006.
Trucks, Derek. Telephone interview. August 29, 2006.
Tyack, Dan. Telephone interview. June 30, 2006.
Vickers, Cornelius "Juice." Largo, Fla., October 8, 2005.
Walker, Bishop Willie. Nashville, Tenn., December 11, 2002.
White, Bishop George A. Nashville, Tenn., December 10, 2002.
Williams, Felton, Jr. Telephone interviews. August 28, 2003; January 17, 2006.
Wortham, Mike, with Andrew Bynum. Calhoun City, Miss., February 11, 2006.
Worthem, Bishop Calvin. Telephone interview. February, 6, 2006.
Wright, Elester and Ophelia. Telephone interview. September 23, 2002.
Wright, George. Telephone interview. September 24, 2002.

Discography

Distribution sources for self-produced or independently produced recordings are listed where available, but may be dated. Information for 78 rpm recordings by Willie Eason and the Jewell Gospel Singers is from Hays and Laughton, *Gospel Records, 1943–1969*, with supplementary details on personnel by the author.

Amazing Grace Praise Band. *Glorious Triumph*. Amazing Grace Productions CD (no number), 2003. Distributed by www.sacredstrings.com. Produced by Del Ray Grace Sr., this album features musicians from the Jewell Dominion tradition. Steel guitarists include Del Ray Grace Sr., Yolando Ramsey, and Eric Russell.

———. *Let the Praise Begin*. Amazing Grace Productions CD (no number), 2005. Steel guitar by Del Ray Grace Sr.

Campbell Brothers, featuring Katie Jackson. *Pass Me Not*. Arhoolie Records CD 461, 1997. "I Feel Good" included on *The Sopranos: Peppers and Eggs*. Columbia CD C2K 85453, 2001.

———. *Sacred Steel on Tour*. Arhoolie Records CD 503, 2001.

———. *Sacred Steel for the Holidays*. Arhoolie Records CD 504, 2001.

———. *Can You Feel It?* Ropeadope CD 020286140221, 2005.

Campbell, Chuck. John Lilly: *Haunted Honky Tonk*. CD JL-2007, 2007. Chuck Campbell plays steel guitar accompaniment on "Friday, Sunday's Coming." Distributed by www.JohnLillyMusic.com.

Campbell, Darick (with Phillip Campbell). *Creole Bred*. Vanguard CD 79741-2, 2004. Darick

Campbell plays lap-steel on "Baby Please Don't Go," with vocals and accordion by Curley Taylor.

Cooke, Calvin. *Heaven*. Dare Records DR001, 2003.

Eason, Willie C. With his nephew, Leroy Eason (vocal), and Roosevelt Eberhardt (guitar), as the Gospel Trumpeters, probably King Recording Studios, Cincinnati, Ohio, June 1946. 78 rpm:

"Oh Lord What a Time!" parts 1 and 2, Queen/King 4130.

"Remember Me Lord"/"No More, No More," Queen/King 4131.

"Standing on the Highway"/"Does Jesus Care?" Queen/King 4145.

"I Thank You Lord"/"If I Could Hear My Mother Pray Again," Queen/King 4146.

———. With the Soul Stirrers, Chicago, Ill., June 2, 1947. 78 rpm:

"Why I Like Roosevelt," parts 1 and 2. Aladdin 2018, Imperial LM 94007 (LP).

"Pearl Harbor," parts 1 and 2. Aladdin 2025, Imperial LM94007 (LP).

———. As Brother Willie Eason, Atlanta, April 30, 1951. 78 rpm:

"There'll Be No Grumblers There." Regent 1043. Reissued on Gospel Heritage HT CD 09, 1992.

"Everybody Ought to Pray." Unissued.

"Jesus Is My Only Friend." Unissued.

"I Want to Live So God Can Use Me." Regent 1043. Reissued on Gospel Heritage HT CD 09, 1992.

"Roosevelt, a Poor Man's Friend," parts 1 and 2. Unissued.

Ghent, Aubrey V. *I've Got a Feeling.* On-Pitch Productions cassette 101. Distributed by D. R. Brundidge, 800–324–3333, ext. 92844.

As Aubrey Ghent & Friends. *Can't Nobody Do Me Like Jesus.* Arhoolie CD 463, 1997.

———. As Aubrey & Lori Ghent and Friends. *Everything Will Be Alright.* Self-produced CD, 2004. Distributed by www.aubreyghent.com.

———. *What a Time!* Aulo Records CD (no number), 2006. Distributed by www.aubreyghent.com.

Golden, James "Tubby." *Reverend Mackalee Washburn: Spreading the Gospel.* TSRC LP 2062, circa 1980s. Golden plays country-style pedal steel with the New Revelation Gospel Band, which includes Robert Golden and Andrew "Sonny" Gaines, guitars.

Harrison, Lorenzo. *A Musical Tribute to the Legacy of Bishop Lorenzo L. Harrison.* CD (no number) produced by Del Ray Grace Sr., 2006. Distributed by www.sacredstrings.com. Live recordings made during church services from 1969 through1986.

Jewell Gospel Singers. Naomi Harrison, Nettie Mae Harrison, Canzetta Staton, and Maggie Staton, vocals; Lorenzo Harrison, steel guitar and electric bass; Nettie Mae Harrison, piano; Harvey Jones, rhythm guitar; and Corroneva Burns, drums. Radio Recorders, Los Angeles, Calif., August 25, 1953. 78 rpm:

"At the Cross"/"Rest, Rest, Rest," Aladdin 2039, Score 5053.

"I Shall Know Him"/"Over There," Aladdin 2040, Score 5054.

The Jewell Gospel singers also recorded ten sides for Nashboro, on which Lorenzo Harrison plays only electric bass, not steel guitar.

Lang, Lisa. *Lady of Steel.* Distributed by L&L Productions, 4069 Lakeside Drive, Tamarac, Fla., 33319. Telephone 954–484–9531.

Lee, Glenn R. *Always By My Side.* Cassette album. Blessed Records 9991. Distributed by Young Lord Music Company, P.O. Box 11247, Baltimore, Md. 21239
———. *I Feel Like Praising Him.* Lee Boy Records CD, LBR 1001, 1999. Distributed by www.leeboys.com.
Lee Boys. *It Is No Secret.* Lee Boys Entertainment, Inc., CD, 2002. Distributed by www.leeboys.com.
———. *Say Yes!* Arhoolie Records CD 516, 2005.
Lockley Family Spiritual Music Ensemble. *Glorifying Jesus.* HMR LP 1036, circa 1960s. Features J.R. Lockley Jr. on steel guitar and vibraphone with members of his family.
Nelson, Henry. Accompaniment on Mahalia Jackson's *To Me It's So Wonderful.* Columbia CS 8153, 1959. Reissued on *Mahalia Jackson, Volume 2.* Columbia Legacy C2T 48924.
Randall, Elder Joe. *Jesus Will Fix It.* Self-produced CD containing thirteen pedal-steel instrumentals. Distributed by Elder Joe Randall, 954-562-8195.
Randolph, Robert, with John Medeski and the Mississippi Allstars. *The Word.* Ropeadope CD 93046–2, 2001.
———. *Unclassified.* Warner Bros. CD 48472-2, 2003.
———. *Colorblind.* Warner Bros. CD 44393-2, 2006.
Randolph, Robert, with John Medeski and the Mississippi Allstars, and the Family Band. *Live at the Wetlands.* Family Band Records CD FB001, 2001.
Randolph, Robert, with various artists. *Oh Happy Day,* EMI CD 5099951282622, 2009.
Treadway, Sonny. *Jesus Will Fix It.* Arhoolie Records CD 462, 1997.

VARIOUS ARTISTS

Sacred Steel. Florida Folklife Program (cassette/booklet album) FFP 107,1995. Digital field recordings from church services and concerts. Includes Willie Eason, Aubrey Ghent, Henry Nelson, Glenn Lee, and Sonny Treadway.
Sacred Steel: Traditional Sacred African-American Steel Guitar Music in Florida. Arhoolie CD450, 1997. Recordings above licensed from the Florida Department of State, with slightly different edit and mix.
Fifteen Down Home Gospel Classics. Arhoolie CD 111, 1997. Includes "Just a Closer Walk With Thee" and "Praise Music," Aubrey Ghent and Friends; "Jesus Will Fix It," Sonny Treadway, and "I Feel Good," Campbell Brothers.
Sacred Steel Live! Arhoolie CD 472, 1999. Includes Ted Beard, the Campbell Brothers, Calvin Cooke, Willie Eason, and Robert Randolph.
The Millennium Celebration Choir. House of God CD (no number), 2000. Live recordings of the Keith Dominion millennium celebration, December 30, 1999.

Includes steel guitarists Maurice "Ted" Beard Jr., Darryl Blue, Chuck Campbell, Darick Campbell, Calvin

Cooke, Aubrey Ghent, Dante Harmon, Glenn Lee, and Robert Randolph. Distributed by the House of God, Keith Dominion, 2714 Scovil Street, Nashville, Tenn. 37208. Telephone 615-329-1625.

Train Don't Leave Me. Recorded Live at the First Annual Sacred Steel Convention. Arhoolie CD 489, 2001. Includes Maurice "Ted" Beard Jr., Lonnie "Big Ben" Bennett, the Campbell Brothers, Roosevelt Collier, Calvin Cooke, Aubrey Ghent, Dante Harmon, Glenn Lee, Elton Noble, Robert Randolph, and Bryan "Josh" Taylor.

Recorded Live at the Second Sacred Steel Convention. Arhoolie CD 502, 2002. Includes Lonnie "Big Ben" Bennett, Darryl Blue, Chuck Campbell, Calvin Cooke, Reggie "Footie" Covington, Dante Harmon, Rayfield "Ray Ray" Holloman, Lisa Lang, Lamar Nelson, Elton Noble, Marcus Randolph, Robert Randolph, and Bryan "Josh" Taylor.

None But the Righteous. Ropeadope CD 0-7567-93123-2-7, 2002. Seventeen selections previously issued by Arhoolie. Includes Ted Beard, the Campbell Brothers, Calvin Cooke, Willie Eason, Aubrey Ghent, Glenn Lee, and Sonny Treadway.

Sacred Steel Guitar Masters. Cracker Barrel CD 766436, 2002. Nine selections taken from previous Arhoolie releases. Includes the Campbell Brothers, Aubrey Ghent, and Sonny Treadway.

Sacred Steel Instrumentals. Arhoolie CD 515, 2004. From previously issued material. Includes Lonnie "Big Ben" Bennett, the Campbell Brothers, Willie Eason, Aubrey Ghent, Dante Harmon, Rayfield "Ray Ray" Holloman, Glenn Lee, Lamar Nelson, Sonny Treadway, and Robert Randolph.

OTHER

Armstrong, Louis. *Louis Armstrong's All-Time Greatest Hits.* MCA CD MCAD-11032, 1994. Includes "The Dummy Song," which has the same basic melody as the "House of God March."

De Droit, Johnnie, and the Arcadian Serenaders. *The Complete Sets.* Challenge B00005O4VJ.

Pierce, Webb. "Slowly." Decca single 28991, 1953. Also available on MCA CD 088 112 442-2, *The Best of Webb Pierce.* Includes landmark pedal-steel guitar playing by Bud Isaacs acknowledged as the first recording to feature the twangy sound created by using the pedals to change the pitch of one or more strings while the strings are sounding.

Various Artists. *God's Mighty Hand.* Gospel Heritage CD 09, 1992. Includes two selections by Willie Eason. See Eason, above.

Various Artists. *Slide Guitar Gospel, 1944–64,* by Rev. Utah Smith and Rev. Lonnie Farris. Document Records DoCD-5222, 1993. Reissue of sixteen tracks originally issued on the Farris, Northern Sound, and Proverb labels. Farris was not affiliated with the House of God or the Church of the Living God.

Various Artists. *Musica Tambora*. Arhoolie CD 7048, 2001. Early Mexican tambora music by various *bandas Sinaloenses*. Includes "*Marcha Zacatecas,*" which contains the basic melody of the "House of God March."

Various Artists. *The African American Steel Guitar Tradition*. Sacred Strings Records CD (no number), 2007. Recordings of live Jewell Dominion services featuring James "Tubby" Golden, Lorenzo Harrison, and Wayne White. Distributed by www.sacredstrings.com.

Williams, Connie. *Philadelphia Street Singer Blind Connie Williams: Traditional Blues, Spirituals, and Folksongs*. Testament CD 5024, 1995. Williams played standard guitar and accordion. He is included because he appeared with Walter Johnson, one of Willie Eason's early influences, and because this recording includes "Tell Me Why You Like Roosevelt" and "Oh Lord What a Time," both of which were recorded in the 1940s by Eason.

Videography

Lee Boys: Live on Stage. Self-produced DVD, includes sixty-eight minutes of live performance, a four-minute documentary produced by WMFE Public Television, and a six-minute promotional video. Leeboys, Inc., 2004. Distributed by www.leeboys.com

On My Way to Heaven. French documentary on African American gospel music. Includes the Campbell Brothers and Aubrey Ghent and Friends, DVD, 95 minutes. Frémeaux & Associés, 1998. Available from www.amazon.com and other U.S. distributors.

Press On. Documentary about Robert Randolph, DVD, 77 minutes. Anointed Films, 2005. Not released as of April 2010.

Sacred Steel. Documentary on the Keith Dominion steel guitar tradition, DVD, 55 minutes. Arhoolie Foundation, 2000. Distributed by Arhoolie Records, www.arhoolie.com.

Index

Robert L. Stone is a folklorist, musician, and producer living in Florida. He has produced eight sacred steel albums for Arhoolie Records and directed the documentary video *Sacred Steel* for the Arhoolie Foundation.

Music in American Life

Music of the First Nations: Tradition and Innovation in Native North America *Edited by Tara Browner*

Cafe Society: The Wrong Place for the Right People   *Barney Josephson, with Terry Trilling-Josephson*

George Gershwin: An Intimate Portrait   *Walter Rimler*

Life Flows On in Endless Song: Folk Songs and American History *Robert V. Wells*

I Feel a Song Coming On: The Life of Jimmy McHugh   *Alyn Shipton*

King of the Queen City: The Story of King Records   *Jon Hartley Fox*

Long Lost Blues: Popular Blues in America, 1850–1920   *Peter C. Muir*

Hard Luck Blues: Roots Music Photographs from the Great Depression *Rich Remsberg*

Restless Giant: The Life and Times of Jean Aberbach and Hill and Range Songs *Bar Biszick-Lockwood*

Champagne Charlie and Pretty Jemima: Variety Theater in the Nineteenth Century   *Gillian M. Rodger*

Sacred Steel: Inside an African American Steel Guitar Tradition   *Robert L. Stone*

Gone to the Country: The New Lost City Ramblers and the Folk Music Revival *Ray Allen*

The Makers of the Sacred Harp   *David Warren Steel with Richard H. Hulan*

The University of Illinois Press
is a founding member of the
Association of American University Presses.

Designed by Erin Kirk New
Composed in 10/13 Sabon
with Franklin Gothic and Rhode display
by Barbara Evans
at the University of Illinois Press
Manufactured by Sheridan Books, Inc.

University of Illinois Press
1325 South Oak Street
Champaign, IL 61820-6903
www.press.uillinois.edu